MW00529077

THE MASTER OF GAME

BY EDWARD, SECOND DUKE OF YORK : THE OLDEST ENGLISH BOOK ON HUNTING : EDITED BY WM. A. AND F. BAILLIE-GROHMAN WITH A FOREWORD BY THEODORE ROOSEVELT

NEW YORK
DUFFIELD & COMPANY
MCMIX

CONTENTS

CHAP.   PAGE

INTRODUCTION xi

FOREWORD TO THE FIRST EDITION . . xix

I. THE PROLOGUE 1

II. OF THE HARE AND OF HER NATURE . . 14

III. OF THE HART AND HIS NATURE . . 23

IV. OF THE BUCK AND OF HIS NATURE . . 38

V. OF THE ROE AND OF HIS NATURE . . 41

VI. OF THE WILD BOAR AND OF HIS NATURE 46

VII. OF THE WOLF AND OF HIS NATURE . 54

VIII. OF THE FOX AND OF HIS NATURE . . 64

IX. OF THE GREY (BADGER) AND OF HIS NATURE 68

X. OF THE (WILD) CAT AND ITS NATURE . 70

XI. THE OTTER AND HIS NATURE . . 72

XII. OF THE MANNER AND HABITS AND CONDITIONS OF HOUNDS 75

XIII. OF SICKNESSES OF HOUNDS AND OF THEIR CORRUPTIONS 85

v

CHAP.   PAGE

XIV. Of Running Hounds and of their Nature 105

XV. Of Greyhounds and of their Nature 113

XVI. Of Alauntes and of their Nature . 116

XVII. Of Spaniels and of their Nature . 119

XVIII. Of the Mastiff and of his Nature . 122

XIX. What Manner and Condition a Good Hunter should have . . 123

XX. How the Kennel for the Hounds and the Couples for the Raches and the Ropes for the Lymer should be made 125

XXI. How the Hounds should be led out to Scombre 127

XXII. How a Hunter's Horn should be Driven 128

XXIII. How a Man should lead his Groom in Quest for to know a Hart by his Trace 130

XXIV. How a Man should know a Great Hart by the Fumes . . . 133

XXV. How a Man should know a Great Hart by the Place where he hath Frayed his Head . . 135

CONTENTS

CHAP.   PAGE

XXVI. How the Ordinance should be made for the Hart Hunting by Strength and how the Hart should be Harboured 148

XXVII. How a Hunter should go in Quest by the Sight 152

XXVIII. How an Hunter should go in Quest between the Plains and the Wood 154

XXIX. How a Hunter should go in Quest in the Coppice and the Young Wood 155

XXX. How an Hunter should go in Quest in Great Coverts and Strengths 156

XXXI. How a Hunter should Quest in Clear Spires and High Wood . 157

XXXII. How a Good Hunter shall go in Quest to hear the Harts Bellow 161

XXXIII. How the Assembly that Men call Gathering should be made both Winter and Summer after the guise of beyond the Sea . . 163

XXXIV. How the Hart should be moved with the Lymer and Run to and Slain with Strength . . . 165

CONTENTS

CHAP.   PAGE

XXXV. How an Hunter should Seek and Find the Hare with Running Hounds and Slay her with Strength 181

XXXVI. Of the Ordinance and the Manner of Hunting when the King will Hunt in Forests or in Parks for the Hart with Bows and Greyhounds and Stable . . 188

Appendix 201

List of some Books Consulted and Abbreviations used in Text . 268

Glossary 282

Index 299

ILLUSTRATIONS

FOX HUNTING "ABOVE GROUND"   *Frontispiece*

GASTON   PHŒBUS . SURROUNDED   BY
    HUNTSMEN AND HOUNDS .   . *To face page*   1

THE HARE AND HER LEVERETS .   .   „   14

HOW TO QUEST FOR THE HART IN
    WOODS   .   .   .   .   .   „   22

BUCK-HUNTING WITH RUNNING HOUNDS   „   38

ROEBUCK-HUNTING WITH GREYHOUNDS
    AND RUNNING HOUNDS   .   .   „   44

BADGER-DRAWING   .   .   .   .   „   68

OTTER-HUNTING .   .   .   .   .   „   72

HOW THE HOUNDS WERE LED OUT .   „   86

RACHES OR RUNNING HOUNDS IN THE
    FIFTEENTH CENTURY .   .   .   „   106

THE SMOOTH AND THE ROUGH-COATED
    GREYHOUNDS   .   .   .   .   „   114

THE FIVE BREEDS OF HOUNDS DE-
    SCRIBED IN THE TEXT .   .   „   122

THE KENNEL AND KENNELMEN .   .   „   126

The Master Teaching his Huntsman how to Quest for the Hart with the Limer or Trackhound *To face page* 130

How a great Hart is to be known by his "Fumes" (Excrements) . ,, 134

How the Hunter should view the Hart . . . . . . ,, 152

How to Quest for the Hart in Coverts . . . . . ,, 164

Hare-hunting with Greyhounds and Running Hounds . . ,, 182

Hare-driving with Low Bells . ,, 184

Netting Hares in their "Muses" . ,, 186

The "Undoing" or Gralloching of the Hart: the Master Instructing his Hunters how it is Done ,, 192

Hart-hunting with Greyhounds and Raches . . . . . ,, 196

The "Curée" or Rewarding of the Hounds . . . . . ,, 198

Shooting Hares with Blunt Bolts . ,, 220

INTRODUCTION

THE "Master of Game" is the oldest as well as the most important work on the chase in the English language that has come down to us from the Middle Ages.

Written between the years 1406 and 1413 by Edward III.'s grandson Edward, second Duke of York, our author will be known to every reader of Shakespeare's "Richard II.," for he is no other than the arch traitor Duke of Aumarle, previously Earl of Rutland, who, according to some historians, after having been an accomplice in the murder of his uncle Gloucester, carried in his own hand on a pole the head of his brother-in-law. The student of history, on the other hand, cannot forget that this turbulent Plantagenet was the gallant leader of England's vanguard at Agincourt, where he was one of the great nobles who purchased with their lives what was probably the most glorious victory ever vouchsafed to English arms.

He tells us in his Prologue, in which he dedicates his "litel symple book" to Henry, eldest son of his cousin Henry IV., "Kyng of Jngelond and of Fraunce," that he is the Master of Game at the latter's court.

Let it at once be said that the greater part of the book before us is not the original work of Edward of York, but a careful and almost literal translation from what is indisputably the most famous hunting book of all times, *i.e.* Count Gaston de Foix's *Livre de Chasse*, or, as author and book are often called, *Gaston Phœbus*, so named because the author, who was a kinsman of the Plantagenets, and who reigned over two principalities in southern France and northern Spain, was renowned for his manly beauty and golden hair. It is he of whom Froissart has to tell us so much that is quaint and interesting in his inimitable chronicle. *La Chasse*, as Gaston de Foix tells us in his preface, was commenced on May 1, 1387, and as he came to his end on a bear hunt not much more than four years later, it is very likely that his youthful Plantagenet kinsman, our author, often met him during his prolonged residence in Aquitaine, of which, later on, he became the Governor.

Fortunately for us, the enforced leisure which the Duke of York enjoyed while imprisoned in Pevensey Castle for his traitorous connection with the plots of his sister to assassinate the King and to carry off their two young kinsmen, the Mortimers, the elder of whom was the heir presumptive to the throne, was of sufficient length to permit him not only to translate *La Chasse* but to add five original chapters dealing with English hunting.

These chapters, as well as the numerous interpolations made by the translator, are all of the first importance to the student of venery, for they emphasise the changes—as yet but very trifling ones—that had been introduced into Britain in the three hundred and two score years that had intervened since the Conquest, when the French language and French hunting customs became established on English soil. To enable the reader to see at a glance which parts of the "Master of Game" are original, these are printed in italics.

The text, of which a modern rendering is here given, is taken from the best of the existing nineteen MSS. of the "Master of Game," viz. the Cottonian MS. Vespasian B. XII., in the British Museum, dating from about 1420. The quaint English of Chaucer's day, with its archaic contractions, puzzling orthography, and long, obsolete technical terms in this MS. are not always as easy to read as those who only wish to get a general insight into the contents of the "Master of Game" might wish. It was a difficult question to decide to what extent this text should be modernised. If translated completely into twentieth century English a great part of the charm and interest of the original would be lost. For this reason many of the old terms of venery and the construction of sentences have been retained where possible, so that the general reader will be able to appreciate the "feeling" of the old work without being unduly puzzled. In a few cases where, through the omission of words, the sense was left undetermined, it has been made clear after carefully consulting other English MSS. and the French parent work.

It seemed very desirable to elucidate the textual description of hunting by the reproduction of good contemporary illuminations, but unfortunately English art had not at that period reached the high state of perfection which French art had attained. As a matter of fact, only two of the nineteen English MSS. contain these pictorial aids, and they are of very inferior artistic merit. The French MSS. of *La Chasse*, on the other hand, are in several cases exquisitely illuminated, and MS. f. fr. 616, which is the copy from which our reproductions—much reduced in size, alas!—are made, is not only the best of them, but is one of the most precious treasures of the *Bibliothèque Nationale* in Paris. These superb miniatures are unquestionably some of the finest handiwork of French miniaturists at a period when they occupied the first rank in the world of art.

The editors have added a short Appendix, eluci-

dating ancient hunting customs and terms of the
chase.   Ancient terms of venery often baffle every
attempt of the student who is not intimately acquainted with the French and German literature of
hunting. On one occasion I appealed in vain to Professor Max Müller and to the learned Editor of the
Oxford Dictionary.   " I regret to say that I know
nothing about these words," wrote Dr. Murray;
" terms of the chase are among the most difficult
of words, and their investigation demands a great
deal of philological and antiquarian research."
There is little doubt that but for this difficulty
the " Master of Game " would long ago have
emerged from its seclusion of almost five hundred
years.   It is hoped that our notes will assist the
reader to enjoy this hitherto neglected classic of
English sport.   Singularly enough, as one is
almost ashamed to have to acknowledge, foreign
students, particularly Germans, have paid far
more attention to the " Master of Game " than
English students have, and there are few manuscripts of any importance about which English
writers have made so many mistakes.   This is all
the more curious considering the precise information to the contrary so easily accessible on the
shelves of the British Museum.   All English
writers with a single exception (Thomas Wright)
who have dealt with our book have attributed it
persistently to a wrong man and a wrong period.

b

This has been going on for more than a century; for it was the learned, but by no means always accurate, Joseph Strutt who first thrust upon the world, in his often quoted "Sports and Pastimes of the English People," certain misleading blunders concerning our work and its author. Blaine, coming next, adding thereto, was followed little more than a decade later by "Cecil," author of an equally much quoted book, "Records of the Chase." In it, when speaking of the "Master of Game," he says that he has "no doubt that it is the production of Edmund de Langley," thus ascribing it to the father instead of to the son. Following "Cecil's" untrustworthy lead, Jesse, Lord Wilton, Vero Shaw, Dalziel, Wynn, the author of the chapter on old hunting in the Badminton Library volume on Hunting, and many other writers copied blindly these mistakes.

Five years ago the present editors published in a large folio volume the first edition of the "Master of Game" in a limited and expensive form. It contained side by side with the ancient text a modernised version, extended biographical accounts of Edward of York and of Gaston de Foix (both personalities of singular historical and human interest), a detailed bibliography of the existing mediæval hunting literature up to the end of the sixteenth century, a glossary, and a very much longer appendix than it was possible to insert

in the present volume, which, in order to make it
conform to the series of which it forms part, had
to be cut down to about one-sixth of the first
edition. A similar fate had to befall the illustrations, which had to be reduced materially both in
number and size. We would therefore invite the
reader whose interest in the subject may possibly
be aroused by the present pages, to glance at the
perhaps formidable-looking pages of the first
edition, with its facsimile photogravure reproductions of the best French and English illuminations
to be found in fifteenth century hunting literature.

In conclusion, I desire to repeat also in this place
the expression of my thanks to the authorities of
the British Museum—to Dr. G. F. Warner and
Mr. I. H. Jeayes in particular—to the heads of
the Bodleian Library, the *Bibliothèque Nationale*,
the Mazarin and the Arsenal Libraries in Paris,
the Duc d'Aumale's Library at Chantilly, the
Bibliothèque Royale at Brussels, the *Königliche
Bibliotheken* in Munich and Dresden, the *Kaiser-
liche und Königliche Haus, Hof and Staats Archiv*,
and the *K. and K. Hof Bibliothek* in Vienna, to
Dr. F. J. Furnivall, Mr. J. E. Harting, Mr. T.
Fitzroy Fenwick of Cheltenham, and to express
my indebtedness to the late Sir Henry Dryden, Bt.,
of Canons Ashby, for his kind assistance in my
research work.

To one person more than to any other my

grateful acknowledgment is due, namely to Mr. Theodore Roosevelt, President of the United States, who, notwithstanding the press of official duties, has found time to write the interesting *Foreword*. A conscientious historian of his own great country, as well as one of its keenest sportsmen, President Roosevelt's qualifications for this kindly office may be described as those of a modern Master of Game. No more competent writer could have been selected to introduce to his countrymen a work that illustrates the spirit which animated our common forbears five centuries ago, their characteristic devotion to the chase, no less than their intimate acquaintance with the habits and "nature" of the wild game they pursued : all attributes worthy of some study by the reading sportsmen of the twentieth century, who, as I show, have hitherto neglected the study of English Venery. It was at first intended to print this *Foreword* only in the American Edition, but it soon became evident that this would give to it an advantage which readers in this country would have some reason to complain of, so it was inserted also in the English Edition, and from it taken over into the present one.

William A. Baillie-Grohman

LONDON, *March* 3, 1909.

FOREWORD

TO THE FIRST EDITION

DURING the century that has just closed English-
men have stood foremost in all branches of sport,
at least so far as the chase has been carried on by
those who have not followed it as a profession.
Here and there in the world whole populations have
remained hunters, to whom the chase was part of
their regular work—delightful and adventurous,
but still work. Such were the American back-
woodsmen and their successors of the great plains
and the Rocky Mountains; such were the South
African Boers; and the mountaineers of Tyrol, if
not coming exactly within this class, yet treated
the chase both as a sport and a profession. But
disregarding these wild and virile populations, and
considering only the hunter who hunts for the
sake of the hunting, it must be said of the
Englishman that he stood pre-eminent throughout
the nineteenth century as a sportsman for sport's
sake. Not only was fox-hunting a national pastime, but in every quarter of the globe English-
men predominated among the adventurous spirits
who combined the chase of big game with bold

exploration of the unknown. The icy polar seas, the steaming equatorial forests, the waterless tropical deserts, the vast plains of wind-rippled grass, the wooded northern wilderness, the stupendous mountain masses of the Andes and the Himalayas—in short, all regions, however frowning and desolate, were penetrated by the restless English in their eager quest for big game. Not content with the sport afforded by the rifle, whether ahorse or afoot, the English in India developed the use of the spear and in Ceylon the use of the knife as the legitimate weapons with which to assail the dangerous quarry of the jungle and the plain. There were hunters of other nationalities, of course—Americans, Germans, Frenchmen; but the English were the most numerous of those whose exploits were best worth recounting, and there was among them a larger proportion of men gifted with the power of narration. Naturally under such circumstances a library of nineteenth century hunting must be mainly one of English authors.

All this was widely different in the preceding centuries. From the Middle Ages to the period of the French Revolution hunting was carried on with keener zest in continental Europe than in England; and the literature of the chase was far richer in the French, and even in the German, tongues than in the English.

The Romans, unlike the Greeks, and still more
unlike those mighty hunters of old, the Assyrians,
cared little for the chase; but the white-skinned,
fair-haired, blue-eyed barbarians, who, out of the
wreck of the Roman Empire, carved the States
from which sprang modern Europe, were passionately devoted to hunting. Game of many kinds
then swarmed in the cold, wet forests which
covered so large a portion of Europe. The kings
and nobles, and the freemen generally, of the
regions which now make France and Germany,
followed not only the wolf, boar, and stag—the
last named the favourite quarry of the hunter of
the Middle Ages—but the bear, the bison—which
still lingers in the Caucasus and in one Lithuanian
preserve of the Czar—and the aurochs, the huge
wild ox—the *Urus* of Cæsar—which has now
vanished from the world. In the Nibelungen
Lied, when Siegfried's feats of hunting are described, it is specified that he slew both the bear
and the elk, the bison and the aurochs. One of
the early Burgundian kings was killed while
hunting the bison; and Charlemagne was not
only passionately devoted to the chase of these
huge wild cattle, but it is said prized the prowess
shown therein by one of his stalwart daughters.

By the fourteenth century, when the Count of
Foix wrote, the aurochs was practically or entirely
extinct, and the bison had retreated eastwards,

where for more than three centuries it held its
own in the gloomy morasses of the plain south-
east of the Baltic. In western Europe the game
was then the same in kind that it is now, although
all the larger species were very much more plentiful, the roebuck being perhaps the only one of
the wild animals that has since increased in
numbers. With a few exceptions, such as the
Emperor Maximilian, the kings and great lords
of the Middle Ages were not particularly fond of
chamois and ibex hunting; it was reserved for
Victor Emmanuel to be the first sovereign with
whom shooting the now almost vanished ibex was
a favourite pastime.

Eager though the early Norman and Plantagenet kings and nobles of England were in the
chase, especially of the red deer, in France and
Germany the passion for the sport was still
greater. In the end, on the Continent the chase
became for the upper classes less a pleasure than
an obsession, and it was carried to a fantastic
degree. Many of them followed it with brutal
indifference to the rights of the peasantry and to
the utter neglect of all the serious affairs of life.
During the disastrous period of the Thirty Years
War, the Elector of Saxony spent most of his
time in slaughtering unheard-of numbers of red
deer; if he had devoted his days and his treasure
to the urgent contemporary problems of statecraft

and warcraft he would have ranked more nearly
with Gustavus Adolphus and Wallenstein, and
would have stood better at the bar of history.
Louis XVI. was also devoted to the chase in its
tamer forms, and was shooting at driven game
when the Paris mob swarmed out to take possession of his person. The great lords, with whom
love of hunting had become a disease, not merely
made of game-preserving a grievous burden for
the people, but also followed the chase in ways
which made scant demands upon the hardier qualities either of mind or of body. Such debased
sport was contemptible then ; and it is contemptible now. Luxurious and effeminate arti-
ficiality, and the absence of all demands for the
hardy virtues, rob any pastime of all title to
regard. Shooting at driven game on occasions
when the day's sport includes elaborate feasts in
tents on a store of good things brought in waggons
or on the backs of sumpter mules, while the sport
itself makes no demand upon the prowess of the
so-called sportsman, is but a dismal parody upon
the stern hunting life in which the man trusts to
his own keen eye, stout thews, and heart of steel
for success and safety in the wild warfare waged
against wild nature.

Neither of the two authors now under consideration comes in this undesirable class. Both
were mighty men with their hands, terrible in

battle, of imposing presence and turbulent spirit. Both were the patrons of art and letters, and both were cultivated in the learning of the day. For each of them the chase stood as a hardy and vigorous pastime of the kind which makes a people' great. The one was Count Gaston de Foix, author of the most famous of mediæval hunting-books, a mighty lord and mighty hunter, as well as statesman and warrior. The other was Edward, second Duke of York, who at Agincourt "died victorious." He translated into English a large portion of Gaston de Foix's *La Chasse*, adding to it five original chapters. He called his book "The Master of Game."

Gaston's book is better known as *Gaston Phœbus*, the nickname of the author which Froissart has handed down. He treats not only of the animals of France, but of the ibex, the chamois, and the reindeer, which he hunted in foreign lands. "The Master of Game" is the oldest book on hunting in the English language. The original chapters are particularly interesting because of the light they throw upon English hunting customs in the time of the Plantagenets. The book has never hitherto been published. Nineteen ancient manuscript copies are known; of the three best extant two are on the shelves of the Bloomsbury treasure house, the other in the Bodleian Library. Like others of the famous old authors on venery, both the Count of Foix and the Duke of York show an astonishing familiarity with the habits, nature, and chase of their quarry. Both men, like others of their kind among their contemporaries, made of the chase not only an absorbing sport but almost the sole occupation of their leisure hours. They passed their days in the forest and were masters of woodcraft. Game abounded, and not only the chase but the killing of the quarry was a matter of intense excitement and an exacting test of personal prowess, for the boar, or the bear, or hart at bay was slain at close quarters with the spear or long knife.

"The Master of Game" is not only of interest to the sportsman, but also to the naturalist, because of its quaint accounts of the "nature" of the various animals ; to the philologist because of the old English hunting terms and the excellent translations of the chapters taken from the French; and to the lover of art because of the beautiful illustrations, with all their detail of costume, of hunting accoutrements, and of ceremonies of "la grande venerie" —which are here reproduced in facsimile from one of the best extant French manuscripts of the early fifteenth century. The translator has left out the chapters on trapping and snaring of wild beasts which were contained in the original, the hunting with running hounds being the typical and most esteemed form of the sport.

Gaston Phœbus's *La Chasse* was written just over a century before the discovery of America; "The Master of Game" some fifteen or twenty years later. The former has been reprinted many times. Mr. Baillie-Grohman in reproducing (for the first time) the latter in such beautiful form has rendered a real service to all lovers of sport, of nature, and of books—and no one can get the highest enjoyment out of sport unless he can live over again in the library the keen pleasure he experienced in the wilderness.

In modern life big-game hunting has assumed many widely varied forms. There are still remote regions of the earth in which the traveller must depend upon his prowess as a hunter for his subsistence, and here and there the foremost settlers of new country still war against the game as it has been warred against by their like since time primeval. But over most of the earth such conditions have passed away for ever. Even in Africa game preserving on a gigantic scale has begun. Such game preserving may be of two kinds. In one the individual landed proprietor, or a group of such individuals, erect and maintain a private game preserve, the game being their property just as much as domestic animals. Such preserves ,often fill a useful purpose, and if managed intelligently and with a sense of public spirit and due regard for the interests and feelings of others, may do much good, even in the most democratic community. But wherever the population is sufficiently advanced in intelligence and character, a far preferable and more democratic way of preserving the game is by a system of public preserves, of protected nurseries and breeding-grounds, while the laws define the conditions under which all alike may shoot the game and the restrictions under which all alike must enjoy the privilege. It is in this way that the wild creatures of the forest and the mountain can best and most permanently be preserved. Even in the United States the enactment and observance of such laws has brought about a marked increase in the game of certain localities, as, for instance, New England, during the past thirty years; while in the Yellowstone Park the elk, deer, antelope, and mountain sheep, and, strangest of all, the bear, are not merely preserved in all their wild freedom, but, by living unmolested, have grown to show a confidence in man and a tameness in his presence such as elsewhere can be found only in regions where he has been hitherto unknown.

The chase is the best of all national pastimes, and this none the less because, like every other pastime, it is a mere source of weakness if carried on in an unhealthy manner, or to an excessive degree, or under over-artificial conditions. Every

vigorous game, from football to polo, if allowed
to become more than a game, and if serious work
is sacrificed to its enjoyment, is of course noxious.
From the days when Trajan in his letters to Pliny
spoke with such hearty contempt of the Greek
over-devotion to athletics, every keen thinker has
realised that vigorous sports are only good in their
proper place.   But in their proper place they are
very good indeed.   The conditions of modern life
are highly artificial, and too often tend to a soften-
ing of fibre, physical and moral.   It is a good
thing for a man to be forced to show self-reliance,
resourcefulness in emergency, willingness to endure fatigue and hunger, and at need to face risk.
Hunting is praiseworthy very much in proportion
as it tends to develop these qualities. Mr. Baillie-
Grohman, to whom most English-speaking lovers
of sport owe their chief knowledge of the feats in
bygone time of the great hunters of continental
Europe, has himself followed in its most manly
forms this, the manliest of sports. He has hunted
the bear, the wapiti, and the mountain ram in the
wildest regions of the Rockies, and, also by fair
stalking, the chamois and the red deer in the Alps.
Whoever habitually follows mountain game in
such fashion must necessarily develop qualities
which it is a good thing for any nation to see
brought out in its sons.   Such sport is as far removed as possible from that in which the main

object is to make huge bags at small cost of effort, and with the maximum of ease, no good quality save marksmanship being required. Laying stress upon the mere quantity of game killed, and the publication of the record of slaughter, are sure signs of unhealthy decadence in sportsmanship. As far as possible the true hunter, the true lover of big game and of life in the wilderness, must be ever ready to show his own power to shift for himself. The greater his dependence upon others for his sport the less he deserves to take high rank in the brotherhood of rifle, horse, and hound. There was a very attractive side to the hunting of the great mediæval lords, carried on with an elaborate equipment and stately ceremonial, especially as there was an element of danger in coming to close quarters with the quarry at bay ; but after all, no form of hunting has ever surpassed in attractiveness the life of the wilderness wanderer of our own time—the man who with simple equipment, and trusting to his own qualities of head, heart, and hand, has penetrated to the uttermost regions of the earth, and single-handed slain alike the wariest and the grimmest of the creatures of the waste.

THEODORE ROOSEVELT.

THE WHITE HOUSE,
February 15, 1904.

GASTON PHŒBUS SURROUNDED BY HUNTSMEN
AND HOUNDS

(From MS. f. fr. 616, *Bib. Nat.*, Paris)

THE MASTER OF GAME

CHAPTER I

THE PROLOGUE

To the honour and reverence of you my right worshipful and dread Lord Henry by the grace of God eldest son and heir unto the high excellent and Christian Prince Henry IV. by the aforesaid grace King of England and of France, Prince of Wales, Duke of Guienne of Lancaster and of Cornwall, and Earl of Chester.

I your own in every humble wise have me ventured to make this little simple book which I recommend and submit to your noble and wise correction, which book if it pleaseth your aforesaid Lordship shall be named and called MASTER OF GAME. And for this cause: for the matter that this book treateth of what in every season of the year is most durable, and to my thinking to every gentle heart most disportful of all games, that is to say hunting. For though it be that hawking with gentle hounds and hawks for the heron and the river be noble and com-

A

mendable, it lasteth seldom at the most more than half a year. For though men find from May unto Lammas (August 1st) *game enough to hawk at, no one will find hawks to hawk with.*[1] *But as of hunting there is no season of all the year, that game may not be found in every good country, also hounds ready to chase it. And since this book shall be all of hunting, which is so noble a game, and lasting through all the year of divers beasts that grow according to the season for the gladdening of man, I think I may well call it MASTER OF GAME.*

And though it be so my dear Lord, that many could better have meddled with this matter and also more ably than I, yet there be two things that have principally emboldened and caused me to take this work in hand. The first is trust of your noble correction, to which as before is said, I submit this little and simple book. The second is that though I be unworthy, I am Master of this Game with that noble prince your Father our all dear sovereign and liege Lord aforesaid. And as I would not that his hunters nor yours that now be or that should come hereafter did not know the perfection of this art, I shall leave for these this simple memorial, for as Chaucer saith in his prologue of "The 25[2] *Good Women": "By writing have men mind of things*

---

[1] As the hawks would be mewing and unfit to fly.
[2] The Shirley MS. in the British Museum has "XV."

passed, for writing is the key of all good remem-
brance."

And first I will begin by describing the nature
of the hare,[1] secondly of the nature of the hart,
thirdly of the buck and of his nature, fourthly of
the roe and of his nature, fifthly of the wild boar
and of his nature, sixthly of the wolf and of his
nature, seventhly of the fox and of his nature,
eighthly of the badger and of his nature, ninthly
of the cat and of his nature, tenthly of the marten
and his nature, eleventhly of the otter and of his
nature. Now have I rehearsed how I will in this
little book describe the nature of these aforesaid
beasts of venery and of chace, and therefore will
I name the hounds the which I will describe hereafter, both of their nature and conditions. And
first I will begin with raches (running hounds)[2]
and their nature, and then greyhounds and their
nature, and then alaunts and their nature, and
then spaniels and their nature, and then mastiffs
that men call curs and their nature, and then of

---

[1] Gaston de Foix has a different sequence, putting the hart
first and the hare sixth, and having four animals more, namely,
the reindeer, the chamois (including ibex), the bear and the
rabbit, while the "Master of Game" has one animal, the
Marten, of which Gaston de Foix does not speak.

[2] Gaston de Foix follows a different sequence, commencing
with alaunts, then greyhounds, raches, spaniels, and says
"fifthly I will speak of all kinds of mongrel dogs, such as
come from mastiffs and alaunts, from greyhounds and running
hounds, and other such."

small curs that come to be terriers and their
nature, and then I shall devise and tell the sicknesses of hounds and their diseases. And furthermore I will describe what qualities and manners
a good hunter should have, and of what parts he
should be, and after that I will describe , the
manner and shape of the kennel, and how it
should be environed and arrayed. Also I will
describe of what fashion a hunter's horn should
be driven, and how the couplings should be made
for the raches and of what length. Furthermore
I will prove by sundry reasons in this little prologue, that the life of no man that useth gentle
game and disport be less displeasable unto God
than the life of a perfect and skilful hunter,
or from which more good cometh. The first
reason is that hunting causeth a man to eschew
the seven deadly sins. Secondly men are better
when riding, more just and more understanding,
and more alert and more at ease and more undertaking, and better knowing of all countries and all
passages ; in short and long all good customs and
manners cometh thereof, and the health of man
and of his soul. For he that fleeth the seven
deadly sins as we believe, he shall be saved, therefore a good hunter shall be saved, and in this
world have joy enough and of gladness and of
solace, so that he keep himself from two things.
One is that he leave not the knowledge nor the

service of God, from whom all good cometh, for his hunting. The second that he lose not the service of his master for his hunting, nor his own duties which might profit him most. Now shall I prove how a hunter may not fall into any of the seven deadly sins. When a man is idle and reckless without work, and be not occupied in doing some thing, he abides in his bed or in his chamber, a thing which draweth men to imaginations of fleshly lust and pleasure. For such men have no wish but always to abide in one place, and think in pride, or in avarice, or in wrath, or in sloth, or in gluttony, or in lechery, or in envy. For the imagination of men rather turns to evil than to good, for the three enemies which mankind hath, are the devil, the world and the flesh, and this is proved enough.

Nevertheless there be many other reasons which are too long to tell, and also every man that hath good reason knoweth well that idleness is the foundation of all evil imaginations. Now shall I prove how imagination is lord and master of all works, good or evil, that man's body or his limbs do. You know well, good or evil works small or great never were done but that beforehand they were imagined or thought of. Now shall you prove how imagination is the mistress of all deeds, for imagination biddeth a man do good or evil works, whichever it be, as before is said. And if a man notwithstanding that he were wise should imagine always that he were a fool, or that he hath other sickness, it would be so, for since he would think steadfastly that he were a fool, he would do foolish deeds as his imagination would command, and he would believe it steadfastly. Wherefore methinks I have proved enough of imagination, notwithstanding that there be many other reasons the which I leave to avoid long writing. Every man that hath good sense knoweth well that this is the truth.

Now I will prove how a good hunter may not be idle, and in dreaming may not have any evil imaginations nor afterwards any evil works. For the day before he goes out to his office, the night before he shall lay him down in his bed, and shall not think but for to sleep, and do his office well and busily, as a good hunter should. And he shall have nothing to do, but think about all that which he has been ordered to do. And he is not idle, for he has enough to do to think about rising early and to do his office without thinking of sins or of evil deeds. And early in the dawning of the day he must be up for to go unto his quest, *that in English is called searching*, well and busily, for as I shall say more explicitly hereafter, when I shall speak of how men shall quest and search to harbour the hart. And in so doing he shall not be idle, for he is always busy. And when he shall come again to the assembly or meet, then he hath most to do, for he must order his finders and relays for to move the hart, and uncouple his hounds. With that he cannot be idle, for he need think of nothing but to do his office, and when he hath uncoupled, yet is he less idle, and he should think less of any sins, for he hath enough to do to ride *or to foot it well* with his hounds and to be always near them and to hue or rout well, and blow well, and to look whereafter he hunteth, and which hounds are *vanchasers and parfiters*,[1] and redress and bring his hounds on the right line again when they are at fault[2] or hunting rascal.[3] And when the hart is dead or what other chase he was hunting, then is he less idle, for he hath enough to do to think how to undo the hart in his manner and to raise that which appertaineth[4] to him, and well to do his curée.[5] And he should look how many of his hounds are missing of those that he brought to the wood in the morning, and he should search for them, and couple them up. And when he has come home,

[1] The hounds that came in the first relay (van) and those in the subsequent relays. See Appendix: Relays.

[2] Diverted or off the line.

[3] Chasing small or lean deer. See Appendix: Hart.

[4] To take those parts of the deer which fell to him by custom.

[5] Curée : The ceremony of giving the hounds their reward on the skin of the animal they have chased. See Appendix: Curée.

should he less think to do evil, for he hath enough
to do to think of his supper, and to ease himself
and his horse, and to sleep, and to take his rest,
for he is weary, and to dry himself of the dew or
peradventure of the rain.   And therefore I say
that all the time of the hunter is without idleness
and without evil thoughts, and without evil works
of sin, for as I have said idleness is the foundation
of all vices and sins.   And the hunter may not be
idle if he would fill his office aright, and also he
can have no other thoughts, for he has enough to
do to think and imagine of his office, the which
is no little charge, for whoso will do it well and
busily, especially if they love hounds and their
office.

Wherefore I say that such an hunter is not idle,
he can have no evil thoughts, nor can he do
evil works, wherefore he must go into paradise.[1]
For by many other reasons which are too long to
write can I prove these things, but it sufficeth
that every man that hath good sense knoweth well
that I speak the real truth.

Now shall I prove how hunters live in this world
more joyfully than any other men.   For when the
hunter riseth in the morning, and he sees a sweet
and fair morn and clear weather and bright, and he

---

[1] Gaston de Foix in the French parent work puts it even
more forcefully; he says: "tout droit en paradis."   See
Lavallée's ed. 1854.

heareth the song of the small birds, the which
sing so sweetly with great melody and full of love,
each in it's own language in the best wise that
it can according that it learneth of it's own kind.
And when the sun is arisen, he shall see fresh dew
upon the small twigs and grasses, and the sun by
his virtue shall make them shine.   And that is
great joy and liking to the hunter's heart.   After
when he shall go to his quest or searching, he shall
see or meet anon with the hart without great seeking, and shall harbour [1] him well and readily within
a little compass.   It is great joy and liking to the
hunter.   And after when he shall come to the
assembly or gathering, and he shall report before
the Lord and his company that which he hath seen
with his eyes, or by scantilon (measure) of the
trace (slot) which he ought always of right to
take, or by the fumes [2] (excrements) that he shall
put in his horn or in his lap.   And every man shall
say : Lo, here is a great hart and a deer of high
meating or pasturing ; go we and move him ; the
which things I shall declare hereafter, then can
one say that the hunter has great joy.   When he
beginneth to hunt and he hath hunted but a little
and he shall hear or see the hart start before
him and shall well know that it is the right one,
and his hounds that shall this day be finders, shall

[1] Trace the deer to its lair.
[2] See Appendix : Excrements.

come to the lair (bed), or to the fues (track), and
shall there be uncoupled without any be left
coupled, and they shall all run well and hunt,
then hath the hunter great joy and great pleasure.
Afterwards he leapeth on horseback, *if he be of
that estate, and else on foot* with great haste to
follow his hounds. And in case peradventure
the hounds shall have gone far from where he
uncoupled, he seeketh some advantage to get
in front of his hounds. And then shall he see
the hart pass before him, and shall holloa and
rout mightily, and he shall see which hound come
in the van-chase, and in the middle, and which
are parfitours,[1] according to the order in which
they shall come. And when all the hounds have
passed before him then shall he ride after them
and shall rout and blow as loud as he may with
great joy and great pleasure, and I assure you
he thinketh of no other sin or of no other evil.
And when the hart be overcome and shall be
at bay he shall have pleasure. And after, when
the hart is spayed[2] and dead, he undoeth him
and maketh his curée and enquireth or rewardeth
his hounds, and so he shall have great pleasure,
and when he cometh home he cometh joyfully,
for his lord hath given him to drink of his good
wine at the curée, and when he has come home

[1] See Appendix: Relays.
[2] Despatched with a sword or knife. See Appendix: Spay.

he shall doff his clothes and his shoes and his hose, and he shall wash his thighs and his legs, and peradventure all his body. And in the meanwhile he shall order well his supper, with *wortes* (roots) *and of the neck* of the hart and of other good meats, and good wine *or ale*. And when he hath well eaten and drunk he shall be glad and well, and well at his ease. And then shall he take the air in the evening of the night, for the great heat that he hath had. And then he shall go and drink and lie in his bed in fair fresh clothes, and shall sleep well and steadfastly all the night without any evil thoughts of any sins, wherefore I say that hunters go into Paradise when they die, and live in this world more joyfully than any other men. Yet I will prove to you how hunters live longer than any other men, for as Hippocras the doctor telleth : " full repletion of meat slayeth more men than any sword or knife." They eat and drink less than any other men of this world, for in the morning at the assembly they eat a little, and if they eat well at supper, they will by the morning have corrected their nature, for then they have eaten but little, and their nature will not be prevented from doing her digestion, whereby no wicked humours or superfluities may be engendered. And always, when a man is sick, men diet him and give him to drink water made of sugar and tysane and of such things for two or three days to put down evil humours and his superfluities, and also make him void (purge). But for a hunter one need not do so, for he may have no repletion on account of the little meat, and by the travail that he hath. And, supposing that which can not be, and that he were full of wicked humours, yet men know well that the best way to terminate sickness that can be is to sweat. And when the hunters do their office on horseback or on foot they sweat often, then if they have any evil in them, it must (come) away in the sweating ; so that he keep from cold after the heat. Therefore it seemeth to me I have proved enough. Leeches ordain for a sick man little meat and sweating for the terminating and healing of all things. And since hunters eat little and sweat always, they should live long and in health. Men desire in this world to live long in health and in joy, and after death the health of the soul. And hunters have all these things. Therefore be ye all hunters and ye shall do as wise men. Wherefore I counsel to all manner of folk of what estate or condition that they be, that they love hounds and hunting and the pleasure of hunting beasts of one kind or another, or hawking. For to be idle and to have no pleasure in either hounds or hawks is no good token. *For as saith in his book Phœbus the Earl of Foix that noble hunter*, he saw never a good man that had not pleasure in some of these things, were he ever so great and rich. For if he had need to go to war he would not know what war is, for he would not be accustomed to travail, and so another man would have to do that which he should. For men say in old saws: " The lord is worth what his lands are worth." [1] *And also he saith in the aforesaid book,* that he never saw a man that loved the work and pleasure of hounds and hawks, that had not many good qualities in him ; for that comes to him of great nobleness and gentleness of heart of whatever estate the man may be, whether he be a great lord, or a little one, or a poor man or a rich one.

[1] Gaston de Foix says: "Tant vaut seigneur tant vaut sa gent et sa terre," p. 9.

CHAPTER II

THE hare is a common beast enough, and therefore I need not tell of her making, for there be
few men that have not seen some of them. They
live on corn, and on weeds growing on waste land,
on leaves, on herbs, on the bark of trees, on
grapes and on many other fruits. The hare is a
good little beast, and much good sport and liking
is the hunting of her, more than that of any other
beast that *any man knoweth*, if he [1] were not so
little. And that for five reasons: the one is, for
her hunting lasteth all the year as with running
hounds without any sparing, and this is not with
all the other beasts. And also men may hunt at
her both in the morning and in the evening. In
the eventide, when they be relieved,[2] and in the
morning, when they sit in form. And of all

[1] The hare was frequently spoken of in two genders in the
same sentence, for it was an old belief that the hare was at
one time male, and at another female. See Appendix: Hare.

[2] Means here: when the hare has arisen from her form to
go to her feeding. Fr. *relever*. G. de F. explains, p. 42:
un lievre se relève pour aler à son vianders. Relief, which
denoted the act of arising and going to feed, became afterwards
the term for the feeding itself. "A hare hath greater scent

THE HARE AND HER LEVERETS

(From MS. f. fr. 616, *Bib. Nat.*, Paris)

other beasts it is not so, for if it rain in the morning your journey is lost, and of the hare it is not so. That other [reason] is to seek the hare; it is a well fair thing, especially who so hunteth her rightfully, for hounds must need find her by mastery and quest point by point, and undo all that she hath done all the night of her walking, and of her pasture unto the time that they start her. And it is a fair thing when the hounds are good and can well find her. And the hare shall go sometimes from her sitting to her pasture half a mile or more, specially in open country. And when she is started it is a fair thing. And then it is a fair thing to slay her with strength of hounds, for she runneth long and gynnously (cunningly). A hare shall last well four miles or more or less, if she be an old male hare. And therefore the hunting of the hare is good, for it lasteth all the year, as I have said. And the seeking is a well fair thing, and the chasing of the hare is a well fair thing, and the slaying of him with strength (of hounds) is a fair thing, for it requireth great mastery on account of her cunning. When a hare ariseth out of her form to go to her pasture or return again to her

and is more eagerly hunted when she relieves on green corn" (*Comp. Sportsman*, p. 86). It possibly was used later to denote the excrements of a hare; thus Blome (1686) p. 92, says: "A huntsman may judge by the relief and feed of the hare what she is."

seat, she commonly goes by one way, and as she goes she will not suffer any twig or grass to touch her, for she will sooner break it with her teeth and make her way. Sometime she sitteth a mile or more from her pasturing, and sometimes near her pasture. But when she sitteth near it, yet she may have been the amount of half a mile or more from there where she hath pastured, and then she ruseth again from her pasture. And whether she go to sit near or far from her pasture she goes so gynnously (cunningly) and wilily that there is no man in this world that would say that any hound could unravel that which she has done, or that could find her. For she will go a bow shot or more by one way, and ruse again by another, and then she shall take her way by another side, and the same she shall do ten, twelve, or twenty times, from thence she will come into some hedge or strength (thicket), and shall make semblance to abide there, and then will make cross roads ten or twelve times, and will make her ruses, and thence she will take some false path, and shall go thence a great way, and such semblance she will make many times before she goeth to her seat.

The hare cannot be judged, either by the foot or by her fumes (excrements), for she always crotieth [1] in one manner, except when she goeth

---

[1] Casting her excrements.

in her love that hunters call ryding time, for then she crotieth her fumes more burnt (drier) and smaller, especially the male. The hare liveth no long time, for with great pain may she pass the second [1] year, though she be not hunted or slain. She hath bad sight [2] and great fear to run [3] on account of the great dryness of her sinews. She windeth far men when they seek her. When hounds grede of her (seek) and quest her she flieth away for the fear that she hath of the hounds. Sometimes men find her sitting in her form, and sometimes she is bitten (taken) by hounds in her form before she starts. They that abide in the form till they be found are commonly stout hares, and well running. The hare that runneth with right standing ears is but little afraid, and is strong, and yet when she holdeth one ear upright and the other laid low on her ryge (back), she feareth but little the hounds. An hare that crumps her tail upon her rump when she starteth out of her form as a

[1] A mistake of the old scribes which occurs also in other MSS.; it should, of course, read "seventh" year. G. de F. has the correct version.

[2] G. de F. says : "She hears well but has bad sight," p. 43.

[3] "Fear to run" is a mistake occasioned by the similarity of the two old French words "pouair," power, and "paour" or fear. In those of the original French MS. of G. de F. examined by us it is certainly "power" and not "fear." Lavallée in his introduction says the same thing. See Appendix : Hare.

B

coney (does) it is a token that she is strong and well running. The hare runneth in many diverse manners, for some run all they are able a whole two miles or three, and after run and ruse again and then stop still when they can no more, and let themselves be bitten (by the hounds), although she may not have been seen all the day. And sometimes she letteth herself be bitten the first time that she starteth, for she has no more might (strength). And some run a little while and then abide and squat, and that they do oft. And then they take their flight as long as they can run ere they are dead. And some be that abide till they are bitten in their form, especially when they be young that have not passed half a year. Men know by the outer side of the hare's leg if she has not passed a year.[1] And so men should know of a hound, of a fox, and of a wolf, by a little bone that they have in a bone which is next the sinews, where there is a little pit (cavity).

Sometimes when they are hunted with hounds they run into a hole as a coney, or into hollow trees, or else they pass a great river. Hounds do not follow some hares as well as others, for four reasons. Those hares who be begotten of the kind of a coney, as some be in warrens, the hounds lust not, nor scenteth them not so well. The other (is) that the fues (footing) of some

[1] See Appendix :2Hare.

hares carry hotter scent than some, and therefore
the hounds scenteth of one more than of the
other, as of roses, some smell better than others,
and yet they be all roses. The other reason is
that they steal away ere they be found, and the
hounds follow always forth right. The others
run going about and then abide,[1] wherefore the
hounds be often on stynt (at fault). The other
(reason) is according to the country they run in,
for if they run in covert, hounds will scent them
better than if they run in plain (open) country,
or in the ways (paths), for in the covert their
bodies touch against the twigs and leaves, because
it is a strong (thick) country. And when they
run in plain country or in the fields they touch
nothing, but with the foot, and therefore the
hound can not so well scent the fues of them.
And also I say that some country is more sweet
and more loving (to scent) than another. The
hare abideth commonly in one country, and if
she hath the fellowship of another or of her
kyndels or leverettes, they be five or six, for
no strange hare will they suffer to dwell in their
marches (district), though they be of their nature
(kind),[2] and therefore men say in old saws : " Who

---

[1] G. de F. has: "vonts riotans tournions et demourant,"
i.e. run rioting, turning and stopping, p. 44.

[2] Both the Vespasian and the Shirley MS. in the British
Museum have the same, but G. de F., p. 45, has, "except those
of their nature" (*fors que celle de leur nature*).

so hunteth the most hares shall find the most."
*For Phebus the Earl of Foix, that good hunter,
saith that* when there be few hares in a country
they should be hunted and slain, so that the
hares of other countries about should come into
that march.

Of hares, some go faster and be stronger than
others, as it is of men and other beasts. Also the
pasture and the country where they abide helpeth
much thereto. For when the hare abideth and
formeth in a plain country where there are no
bushes, such hares are commonly strongest and
well running. Also when they pasture on two
herbs—that one is called Soepol (wild thyme) and
that other be Pulegium (pennyroyal) they are
strong and fast running.

The hares have no season of their love for, as I
said, it is called ryding time, for in every month
of the year that it shall not be that some be not
with kindles (young). Nevertheless, commonly
their love is most in the month of January, and
in that month they run most fast of any time of
the year, both male and female. And from May
unto September they be most slow, for then they
be full of herbs and of fruits, or they be great
and full of kindles, and commonly in that time
they have their kindles. Hares remain in sundry
(parts of the) country, according to the season of
the year ; sometimes they sit in the fern, sometimes

in the heath, sometimes in the corn, and in growing weeds, and sometimes in the woods.   In April
and in May when the corn is so long that they
can hide themselves therein, gladly will they sit
therein.   And when men begin to reap the corn
they will sit in the vines and in other strong (thick)
heaths, in bushes and in hedges, and commonly in
cover under the wind and in cover from the rain,
and if there be any sun shining they will gladly
sit against the beams of the sun.   For a hare of
its own kind knoweth the night before what
weather it will be on the next morrow, and therefore she keepeth herself the best way she may from
the evil weather.   The hare beareth her kindles
two months,[1] and when they are kindled she
licketh her kindles as a bitch doeth her whelps.
Then she runneth a great way thence, and goeth
to seek the male, for if she should abide with her
kindles she would gladly eat them.   And if she
findeth not the male, she cometh again to her
kindles a great while after and giveth them to suck,
and nourisheth them for the maintainance of 20
days or thereabouts.   A hare beareth commonly
2 kindles, but I have seen some which have kindled
at once sometime 6, sometime 5 or 4 or 2 ;[2] and
but she find the male within three days from the

---

[1] This is incorrect : the hare carries her young thirty days
(Brehm, vol. ii. p. 626; Harting, *Ency. of Sport*, vol. i.
p. 504).
[2] Should read "three" (G. de F., p. 47).

time she hath kindled, she will eat her kindles. And when they be in their love they go together as hounds, save they hold not together as hounds. They kindle often in small bushes or in little hedges, or they hide in heath or in briars or in corn or in vines. If you find a hare which has kindled the same day, and the hounds hunt after her, and if you come thither the next morrow ye shall find how she has removed her kindles, and has borne them elsewhere with her teeth, as a bitch doth her whelps. Men slay hares with greyhounds, and with running hounds by strength, *as in England, but elsewhere they slay them also* with small pockets, and with purse nets, and with small nets, *with hare pipes*, and with long nets, and with small cords that men cast where they make their breaking of the small twigs when they go to their pastures, as I have before said.[1] But, *truly, I trow no good hunter would slay them so for any good*. When they be in their heat of love and pass any place where conies be, the most part of them will follow after her as the hounds follow after a bitch or a brache.

[1] See Appendix : Snares.

HOW TO QUEST FOR THE HART IN WOODS

(From MS. f. fr. 616, *Bib. Nat.*, Paris)

CHAPTER III

OF THE HART AND HIS NATURE

THE hart is a common beast enough and therefore me needeth not to tell of his making, for there be few folk that have not seen some. The harts be the lightest (swiftest) beasts and strongest, and of marvellous great cunning. They are in their love, which men call rut, about the time of the Holy Rood[1] in September and remain in their hot love a whole month and ere they be fully out thereof they abide (in rut) nigh two months. And then they are bold, and run upon men as a wild boar would do if he were hunted. And they be wonderfully perilous beasts, for with great pain shall a man recover that is hurt by a hart, and therefore men say in old saws: "after the boar the leech and after the hart the bier." For he smiteth as the stroke of the springole,[2] for he has great strength in the head and the body. They slay, fight and hurt each other, when they be in rut, that is to say in their love, and they sing in

[1] September 14. See Appendix: Hart, Seasons.
[2] An engine of war used for throwing stones.

their language *that in England hunters call bellowing* as man that loveth paramour.[1]   They slay
hounds and horses and men at that time and
turn to the abbay (be at bay) as a boar does
especially when they be weary.   And yet have
men seen at the parting of their ligging (as they
start from the lair)[2] that he hath hurt him that
followeth after, and also the greyhounds[3] and
furthermore a courser.   And yet when they are
in rut, which is to say their love, in a forest
where there be few hinds and many harts or male
deer, they slay, hurt and fight with each other,
for each would be master of the hinds.   And
commonly the greatest hart and the most strong
holdeth the rut and is master thereof.   And when
he is well pured and hath been long at rut all
the other harts that he hath chased and flemed
away (put to flight) from the rut then run upon
him and slay him, and that is sooth.   And in
parks this may be proved, for there is never a
season but the greatest hart will be slain by the
others not while he is at the rut, but when he
has withdrawn and is poor of love.   In the woods
they do not so often slay each other as they do in

---

[1] G. de F., p. 12.   "Ainsi que fet un homme bien amoureus"
("As does a man much in love)."

[2] This word ligging is still in use in Yorkshire, meaning lair,
or bed, or resting-place.   In Devonshire it is spelt "layer."
Fortescue, p. 132.

[3] G. de F., p. 12, has "limer" instead of "greyhound."

the plain country. And also there are divers ruts in the forest, but in the parks there are none but that are within the park.[1] After that they be withdrawn from the hinds they go in herds and in soppes (troops) with the rascal (young lean deer) and abide in (waste) lands and in heathes more than they do in woods, for to enjoy the heat of the sun, they be poor and lean for the travail they have had with the hinds, and for the winter, and the little meat that they find. After that they leave the rascal and gather together with two or three or four harts in soppes till the month of March when they mew (shed) their horns, and commonly some sooner than others, if they be old deer, and some later if they be young deer, or that they have had a hard winter, or that they have been hunted, or that they have been sick, for then they mew their heads and later come to good points. And when they have mewed their heads they take to the strong (thick) bushes as privily as they may, till their heads be grown again, and they come into grease; after that they seek good country for meating (feeding)

[1] This passage is confused. In G. de F., p. 12, we find that the passage runs : "Et aussi il y a ruyt en divers lieux de la forest et on paix ne peut estre en nul lieu, fors que dedans le part." Lavallée translates these last five words, "C'est à dire qu'il n'y a de paix que lorsque les biches sont pleines." In the exceedingly faulty first edition by Verard, the word "part" is printed "*parc*," as it is in our MS.

of corn, of apples, of vines, of tender growing
trees, of peas, of beans, and other fruits and
grasses whereby they live.   And sometimes a
great hart hath another fellow that is called his
squire, for he is with him and doth as he will.
And so they will abide all that season if they be
not hindered until the last end of August. And
then they begin to look, and to think and to bolne
and to bellow and to stir from the haunt in which
they have (been) all the season, for to go seek
the hinds.   They recover their horns and are
summed of their tines as many as they shall have
all the year between March when they mewed
them to the middle of June ; and then be they
recovered of their new hair that *men call polished*
and their horns be recovered with a soft hair *that
hunters call velvet* at the beginning, and under
that skin and that hair the horn waxes hard and
sharp, and about Mary Magdalene day (July 22)
they fray their horns against the trees, and have
(rubbed) away that skin from their horns and then
wax they hard and strong, and then they go to
burnish and make them sharp in the colliers
places (charcoal pits) that men make sometimes
in the great groves.   And if they can find none
they go against the corners of rocks *or to crabbe
tree or to hawthorn or other trees.*[1]

[1] G. de F., p. 14, says the harts go to gravel-pits and bogs
to fray.

They be half in grease or thereabouts by the middle of June when their head is summed, and they be highest in grease during all August. Commonly they be calved in May, and the hind beareth her calf nine months or thereabout as a sow,[1] and sometimes she has three[2] calves at a calving time. And I say not that they do not calve sometime sooner and sometime later, much according to causes and reasons. The calves are calved with hair red and white, which lasteth them that colour into the end of August, and then they turn red of hair, as the hart and the hind. And at that time they run so fast that a hare[3] should have enough to do to overtake him within the shot of an haronblast (cross-bow). Many men judge the deer of many colours of hair and especially of three colours. Some be called brown, some dun and some yellow haired. And also their heads be of divers manners, the one is called a head well-grown, and the other is called well affeted,[4] and well affeted is when the head has waxed by ordinance according to the neck and

---

[1] The MS. transcriber's mistake. It should be "cow."

[2] G. de F. has "2 calves" as it should be.

[3] G. de F. has "greyhound," as it should be (p. 15): "Et dès lors vont ils jà si tost que un levrier a assés à fere de l'ateindre, ainsi comme un trait d'arcbaleste" ("And from that time they go so quickly that a greyhound has as much to do to catch him as he would the bolt from a crossbow)."

[4] Well proportioned. See Appendix: Antler.

shape, when the tines be well grown in the beam
by good measure, one near the other, then it is
called well affeted. Well grown is when the
head is of great beam and is well affeted and
thick tined, well high and well opened (spread).
That other head is called counterfeit (abnormal)
when it is different and is otherwise turned behind
or wayward in other manner than other common
deer be accustomed to bear. That other high
head is open, evil affeted with long tines and
few. That other is low and great and well
affeted with small tines. And the first tine that
is next the head is called antler, and the second
Royal and the third above, the Sur-royal, and the
tines[1] which be called fourth if they be two, and
if they be three or four or more be called troching.
And when their heads be burnished at the colliers'
pits commonly they be always black, and also
commonly when they be burnished at the colliers'
pits they be black on account of the earth which
is black of its kind. And when they are burnished
against *rock* they abide all white, but some have
their heads naturally white and some black. And
when they be about to burnish they smite the
ground with their feet and welter like a horse.
And then they burnish their heads, and when
they be burnished which they do all the month
of July they abide in that manner till the feast of

[1] Shirley MS. has the addition here : "Which be on top."

the Holy (Cross) in September 14th and then they go to rut as I have said.

And the first year that they be calved they be called a Calf, the second year a bullock ; and that year they go forth to rut ; the third year a brocket ; the fourth year a staggard, the fifth a stag ; the sixth year a hart of ten[1] *and then first is he chase-able, for always before shall he be called but rascal or folly.* Then it is fair to hunt the hart, for it is a fair thing to seek well a hart, and a fair thing well to harbour him, and a fair thing to move him, and a fair thing to hunt him, and a fair thing to retrieve him, and a fair thing to be at the abbay, whether it be on water or on land. A fair thing is the curée,[2] and a fair thing to undo him well, and for to raise the rights. And a well fair thing and good is the devision[3] and it be a good deer. In so much that considering all things I hold that it is the fairest hunting, that any man may hunt after. They crotey their fumes (cast their excrements) in divers manners according to the time and season and according to the pasture that they find, now black or dry either in flat forms or engleymed (glutinous) or pressed, and in many other divers manners the which I shall more plainly devise when I shall declare how the hunter shall judge, for sometimes they misjudge

[1] In modern sporting terms, a warrantable deer.
[2] See Appendix : Curée.   [3] Should be : venison.

by the fumes and so they do by the foot.   When
they crotey their fumes flat and not thick, it is in
April or in May, into the middle of June, when they
have fed on tender corn, for yet their fumes be
not formed, and also they have not recovered their
grease.   But yet have men seen sometimes a great
deer and an old and high in grease, which about
mid-season crotey their fumes black and dry.   And
therefore by this and many other things many
men may be beguiled by deer, for some goeth
better and are better running and fly better than
some, as other beasts do, and some be more cunning and more wily than others, as it is with men,
for some be wiser than others.   And it cometh to
them of the good kind of their father and mother,
and of good getting (breeding) and of good nurture and from being born in good constellations,
and in good signs of heaven, and that (is the
case) with men and all other beasts.   Men take
them with hounds, with greyhounds and with
nets and with cords, and with other harness,[1]
with pits and with shot[2] and with other gins
(traps) and with strength, as I shall say hereafter.   *But in England they are not slain except
with hounds or with shot or with strength of
running hounds.*

An old deer is wonder wise and felle (cunning)

---

[1] Harness, appurtenances. See Appendix : Harness.
[2] Means from a cross-bow or long-bow.

for to save his life, and to keep his advantage
when he is hunted and is uncoupled to, as the
lymer moveth him or other hounds findeth him
without lymers, and if he have a deer (with him)
that be his fellow he leaveth him to the hounds,
so that he may warrant (save) himself, and let the
hounds enchase after that other deer. And he
will abide still, and if he be alone and the hounds
find him, he shall go about his haunt wilily and
wisely and seek the change of other deer, for
to make the hounds envoise,[1] and to look where
he may abide. And if he cannot abide he taketh
leave of his haunt and beginneth to fly there where
he wots of other change and then when he has
come thither he herdeth among them and sometimes he goeth away with them. And then he
maketh a ruse on some side, and there he stalleth
or squatteth until the hounds be forth after the
other (deer) the which be fresh, and thus he
changeth so that he may abide. And if there be
any wise hounds, the which can bodily enchase
him from the change, and he seeth that all can
not avail, then he beginneth to show his wiles and
ruseth to and fro. And all this he doth so that
the hounds should not find his fues (tracks) in
intent that he may be freed from them and that
he may save himself.

Sometimes he fleeth forth with the wind and

[1] Go off the scent.

that for three causes, for when he fleeth against
the wind it runneth into his mouth and dryeth him
and doth him great harm. Therefore he fleeth
oft forth with the wind so that he may always
hear the hounds come after him. And also that
the hounds should not scent nor find him, for his
tail is in the wind and not his nose.[1] Also, that
when the hounds be nigh him he may wind them
and hye him well from them. *But nevertheless
his nature is for the most part to flee ever on the
wind till he be nigh overcome, or at the last side-
ways to the wind so that it be aye* (ever) *in his
nostrils.* And when he shall hear that they be far
from him, he hieth him not too fast. And when
he is weary and hot, then he goeth to yield, and
soileth to some great river. And some time he
foils down in the water half a mile or more ere
he comes to land on any side. And that he doeth
for two reasons, the one is to make himself cold,
and for to refresh himself of the great heat that
he hath, the other is that the hounds and the
hunter may not come after him nor see his fues
in the water, as they do on the land. And if in
the country (there) is no great river he goeth then
to the little (one) and shall beat up the water or

[1] This should read as G. de F. has it (p. 20): "Et aussi affin
que les chiens ne puissent bien assentir de luy, quar ilz auront
la Cueue au vent et non pas le nez" ("And also that the
hounds shall not be able to wind him, as they will have their
tails in the wind and not their noses ").

foil down the water as he liketh best for the main-
tenance (extent) of a mile or more ere he come
to land, and he shall keep himself from touching
any of the brinks or branches but always (keep)
in the middle of the water, so that the hounds
should not scent of him.   And all that doth he
for two reasons before said.

And when he can find no rivers then he draweth
to great stanks[1] and meres or to great marshes.
And he fleeth then mightily and far from the
hounds, that is to say that he hath gone a great way
from them,[2] then he will go into the stank, and
will soil therein once or twice in all the stank
and then he will come out again by the same
way that he went in, and then he shall ruse again
the same way that he came (the length of) a
bow shot or more, and then he shall ruse out
of the way, for to stall or squatt to rest him,
and that he doeth for he knoweth well that the
hounds shall come by the fues into the stank
where he was.   And when they should find that
he has gone no further they will seek him no
further, for they will well know that they have
been there at other times.

An hart liveth longest of any beast for he may

[1] Ponds, pools. See Appendix: Stankes.
[2] G. de F., p. 21 : "Et s'il fuit de fort longe aux chiens,
c'est à dire que il les ait bien esloinhés." See Appendix:
"Forlonge."

c

well live an hundred years[1] and the older he is
the fairer he is of body and of head, and more
lecherous, but he is not so swift, nor so light,
nor so mighty. And many men say, but I make
no affirmation upon that, when he is right old he
beateth a serpent with his foot till she be wrath,
and then he eateth her and then goeth to drink,
and then runneth hither and thither to the water
till the venom be mingled together and make him
cast all his evil humours that he had in his body,
and maketh his flesh come all new.[2] The head of
the hart beareth medicine against the hardness of
the sinews and is good to take away all aches, especially when these come from cold : and so is the
marrow. They have a bone within the heart
which hath great medicine, for it comforteth the
heart, *and helpeth for the cardiac,* and many other
things which were too long to write, the which
bear medicine and be profitable in many diverse
manners. The hart is more wise in two things
than is any man or other beast, the one is in
tasting of herbs, for he hath better taste and better
savour and smelleth the good herbs and leaves
and other pastures and meating the which be
profitable to him, better than any man or beast.
The other is that he hath more wit and malice

---

[1] Most old writers on the natural history of deer repeat this
fable. See Appendix : Hart.

[2] See Appendix : Hart.

(cunning) to save himself than any other beast or man, for there is not such a good hunter in the world that can think of the great malice and gynnes (tricks or ruses) that a hart can do, and there is no such good hunter nor such good hounds, but that many times fail to slay the hart, and that is by his wit and his malice and by his gins.

As of the hinds some be barren and some bear calves, of those that be barren their season beginneth when the season of the hart faileth and lasteth till Lent. And they which bear calves, in the morning when she shall go to her lair she will not remain with her calf, but she will hold (keep) him and leave him a great way from her, and smiteth him with the foot and maketh him to lie down, and there the calf shall remain always while the hind goeth to feed. And then she shall call her calf in her language and he shall come to her. And that she doeth so that if she were hunted her calf might be saved and that he should not be found near her. The harts have more power to run well from the entry of May into St. John's tide [1] than any other time, for then they have put on new flesh and new hair and new heads, for the new herbs and the new coming out (shoots) of trees and of fruits and be not too heavy, for as yet they have not recovered their

[1] Nativity of St. John the Baptist, June 24.

grease,[1] neither within nor without, nor their
heads, wherefore they be much lighter and swifter.
But from St. John's into the month of August
they wax always more heavy. Their skin is right
good for to do many things with when it is well
tawed and taken in good season. Harts that
be in great hills, when it cometh to rut, sometimes they come down into the great forests and
heaths and to the launds (uncultivated country)
and there they abide all the winter until the
entering of April, and then they take to their
haunts for to let their heads wax, near the towns
and villages in the plains there where they find
good feeding in the new growing lands. And
when the grass is high and well waxen they withdraw into the greatest hills that they can find for
the fair pastures and feeding and fair herbs that
be thereupon. And also because there be no flies
nor any other vermin, as there be in the plain
country. And also so doth the cattle which
come down from the hills in winter time, and
in the summer time draw to the hills. And all
the time from rutting time into Whitsunday
great deer and old will be found in the plains,
but from Whitsunday[2] to rutting time men shall
find but few great deer save upon the hills, if there

[1] See Appendix: Grease.
[2] This sentence reads somewhat confusedly in our MS., so
I have taken this rendering straight from G. de F., p. 23.

are any (hills) near or within four or five miles, and this is truth unless it be some young deer calved in the plains, but of those that come from the hills there will be none. *And every day in the heat of the day, and he be not hindered, from May to September, he goes to soil though he be not hunted.*

CHAPTER IV

OF THE BUCK AND OF HIS NATURE

A BUCK is a diverse beast, he hath not his hair
as a hart, for he is more white, and also he hath
not such a head. He is less than a hart and
is larger than a roe. A buck's head is palmed
with a long palming, and he beareth more tines
than doth a hart. His head cannot be well described without painting. They have a longer
tail than the hart, and more grease on their
haunches than a hart. They are fawned in the
month of June and shortly to say they have the
nature of the hart, save only that the hart goeth
sooner to rut and is sooner in his season again,
also in all things of their kind the hart goeth
before the buck. For when the hart hath been
fifteen days at rut the buck scarcely beginneth to
be in heat and bellow.

And also men go not to sue him with a lymer,
nor do men go to harbour him as men do to the
hart. Nor are his fumes put in judgment as
those of the hart, but men judge him by the foot
other head as I shall say more plainly hereafter.

BUCK-HUNTING WITH RUNNING HOUNDS

(From MS. f. fr. 616, *Bib. Nat.*, Paris)

UofM

They crotey their fumes in diverse manners according to the time and pasture, as doth the hart, but oftener black and dry than otherwise. When they are hunted they bound again into their coverts and fly not so long as doth the hart, for sometimes they run upon the hounds.[1] And they run long and fly ever if they can by the high ways and always with the change. They let themselves be taken at the water and beat the brooks as a hart, but not with such great malice as the hart, nor so gynnously (cunningly) and also they go not to such great rivers as the hart. They run faster at the beginning than doth the hart. They bolk (bellow) about when they go to rut, not as a hart doth, but much lower than the hart, and rattling in the throat. Their nature and that of the hart do not love (to be) together, for gladly would they not dwell there where many harts be, nor the harts there where the bucks be namely together in herds. The buck's flesh is more savoury[2] than is that of the hart or of the roebuck. The venison of them is right good if kept and salted as that of the hart. They abide

---

[1] They do not make such a long flight as the red deer but by ringing return to the hounds.

[2] G. de F., p. 29, completes the sense of this sentence by saying that "the flesh of the buck is more savoury to all hounds than that of the stag or of the roe, and for this reason it is a bad change to hunt the stag with hounds which at some other time have eaten buck."

oft in a dry country and always commonly in herd with other bucks. Their season lasteth from the month of May into the middle of September. And commonly they dwell in a high country where there be valleys and small hills. He is undone as the hart.

CHAPTER V

OF THE ROE AND OF HIS NATURE

THE roebuck is a common beast enough, and therefore I need not to tell of his making, for there be few men that have not seen some of them. It is a good little beast and goodly for to hunt to whoso can do it as I shall devise hereafter, for there be few hunters that can well devise his nature. They go in their love that is called bokeyng in October,[1] and the bucking of them lasteth but fifteen days or there about. At the bucking of the roebuck he hath to do but with one female for all the season, and a male and a female abide together as the hinds[2] till the time that the female shall have her kids; and then the female parteth from the male and goeth to kid her kids far from thence, for the male would slay the young if he could find them. And when they be big that they can eat by themselves of the herbs and of the leaves and can run away, then

---

[1] This is wrong; they rut in the beginning of August. See Appendix: Roe.
[2] A clerical error. G. de F. (p. 36) says, "as do birds," which makes good sense.

41

the female cometh again to the male, and they
shall ever be together unless they be slain, and if
one hunt them and part them asunder one from
another, they will come together again as soon as
they can and will seek each other until the time
that one of them have found the other. And the
cause why the male and the female be evermore
together as no other beast in this world, is that
commonly the female hath two kids at once,
one male and the other female, and because they
are kidded together they hold evermore together.
And yet if they were not kidded together of one
female, yet is the nature of them such that they
will always hold together as I have said before.
When they withdraw from the bucking, they mew
their heads, for men will find but few roebucks
that have passed two years that have not mewed
their heads by All Hallowtide. And after the
heads come again rough as a hart's head, and
commonly they burnish their horns in March.
The roebuck hath no season to be hunted, for
they bear no venison [1] but men should leave them
the females for their kids that would be lost unto
the time that they have kidded, and that the kids
can feed themselves and live by themselves without their dame. It is good hunting for it lasteth
all the year and they run well, and longer than
does a great hart in high season time. Roebucks

[1] See Appendix: Grease.

cannot be judged by their fumes, and but little by their track as one can of harts, for a man cannot know the male from the female by her feet or by her fumes.

They have not a great tail and do not gather venison as I have said, the greatest grease that they may have within is when the kidneys be covered all white. When the hounds hunt after the roebuck they turn again into their haunts and sometimes turn again to the hounds.[1] When they see that they cannot dure [2] (last) they leave the country and run right long ere they be dead. And they run in and out a long time and beat the brooks in the same way a hart doth. And if the roebuck were as fair a beast as the hart, I hold that it were a fairer hunting than that of the hart, for it lasteth all the year and is good hunting and requires great mastery, for they run right long and gynnously (cunningly). Although they mew their heads they do not reburnish them, nor repair their hair till new grass time. It is a diverse (peculiar) beast, for it doth nothing after the nature of any other beast, and he followeth men into their houses, for when he is hunted and overcome he knoweth never where he goeth. The flesh of the roebuck is the most wholesome to eat

---

[1] "They ring about in their own country, and often bound back to the hounds" would be a better translation..

[2] From the French *durer*, to last.

of any other wild beast's flesh, they live on good
herbs and other woods and vines and on briars
and hawthorns [1] with leaves and on all growth of
young trees.   When the female has her kids she
does all in the manner as I have said of a hind.
When they be in bucking they sing a right foul
song, for it seemeth as if they were bitten by
hounds.   When they run at their ease they run
ever with leaps, but when they be weary or followed
by hounds they run naturally and sometimes they
trot or go apace, and sometimes they hasten and
do not leap, and then men say that the roebuck
hath lost his leaps, and they say amiss, for he ever
leaves off leaping when he is well hasted and also
when he is weary.

When he runneth at the beginning, as I have
said, he runneth with leaps and with rugged
standing hair and the eres [2] (target) and the tail
cropping up all white.

And when he hath run long his hair lyeth sleek
down, not standing nor rugged and his eres
(target) does not show so white.

And when he can run no longer he cometh and
yieldeth himself to some small brook, and when
he hath long beaten the brook upward or down-
ward he remaineth in the water under some roots
so that there is nothing out of water save his head.

[1] G. de F. says "acorns."
[2] Middle English *ars*, hinder parts called target of roebuck.

ROEBUCK-HUNTING WITH GREYHOUNDS AND RUNNING
HOUNDS

(From MS. f. fr. 616, *Bib. Nat.*, Paris)

And sometimes the hounds and the hunters shall pass above him and beside him and he will not stir. For although he be a foolish beast he has many ruses and treasons to help himself. He runneth wondrous fast, for when he starts from his lair he will go faster than a brace of good greyhounds. They haunt thick coverts of wood, or thick heathes, and sometimes in carres (marshes) and commonly in high countries or in hills and valleys and sometimes in the plains.

The kids are kidded with pomeled [1] (spotted) hair as are the hind calves. And as a hind's calf of the first year beginneth to put out his head, in the same wise does he put out his small brokes [2] (spikes) ere he be a twelvemonth old. He is hardeled [3] but not undone as a hart, for he has no venison that men should lay in salt. And sometimes he is given all to the hounds, and sometimes only a part. They go to their feeding as other beasts do, in the morning and in the evening, and then they go to their lair. The roebuck remains commonly in the same country both winter and summer if he be not grieved or hunted out thereof.

[1] From the old French *pomelé*.
[2] See Appendix : Roe.
[3] See Appendix : Hardel.

CHAPTER VI

A WILD boar is a common beast enough and therefore it needeth not to tell of his making, for there be few gentlemen that have not seen some of them. It is the beast of this world that is strongest armed, and can sooner slay a man than any other. Neither is there any beast that he could not slay if they were alone sooner than that other beast could slay him,[1] be they lion or leopard, unless they should leap upon his back, so that he could not turn on them with his teeth. And there is neither lion nor leopard that slayeth a man at one stroke as a boar doth, for they mostly kill with the raising of their claws and through biting, but the wild boar slayeth a man with one stroke as with a knife, and therefore he can slay any other beast sooner than they could slay him. It is a proud[2] beast

---

[1] In spite of the boar being such a dangerous animal a wound from his tusk was not considered so fatal as one from the antlers of a stag. An old fourteenth-century saying was: "Pour le sanglier faut le mire, mais pour le cerf convient la bière."

[2] Proud. G. de F., p. 56, *orguilleuse*. G. de F., p. 57, says after this that he has often himself been thrown to the ground,

and fierce and perilous, for many times have men
seen much harm that he hath done. For some
men have seen him slit a man from knee up to the
breast and slay him all stark dead at one stroke
so that he never spake thereafter.

They go in their love to the brimming [1] as sows
do about the feast of St. Andrew,[2] and are in
their brimming love three weeks, and when the
sows are cool the boar does not leave them.[3]

He stays with them till the twelfth day after
Christmas, and then the boar leaves the sows and
goeth to take his covert, and to seek his livelihood alone, and thus he stays until the next year
when he goeth again to the sows. They abide
not in one place one night as they do in another,
but they find their pasture for (till) all pastures
fail them as hawthorns [4] and other things. Sometimes a great boar has another with him but this
happens but seldom. They farrow [5] in March,
and once in the year they go in their love. And

---

he with his courser, by a wild boar and the courser killed ("et
moy meismes a il porté moult de fois à terre moy et mon
coursier, et mort le coursier").

[1] Brimming. From Middle English *brime*, burning heat.
It was also used in the sense of valiant-spirited (Stratmann).

[2] November 30.

[3] G. de F., p. 57, adds : " comme fait l'ours."

[4] A badly worded phrase, the meaning of which is not quite
clear. G. de F. has "acorns and beachmast" instead of
hawthorns.

[5] Farrow. See Appendix : Wild Boar.

there are few wild sows that farrow more than once in the year, nevertheless men have seen them farrow twice in the year.

Sometimes they go far to their feeding between night and day, and return to their covert and den ere it be day. But if the day overtakes them on the way ere they can get to their covert they will abide in some little thicket all that day until it be night. They wind a man[1] as far as any other beast or farther. They live on herbs and flowers especially in May, which maketh them renew[2] their hair and their flesh. And some good hunters *of beyond the sea* say that in that time they bear medicine on account of the good herbs and the good flowers that they eat, but thereupon I make no affirmation. They eat all manner of fruits and all manner of corn, and when these fail them they root[3] in the ground with the rowel of their snouts which is right hard ; they root deep in the ground till they find the roots of the ferns and of the spurge and other roots of which they have the savour (scent) in the earth. And therefore have I said they wind wonderfully far and marvellously well. And also they eat all the vermin and carrion and other foul things. They

---

[1] G. de F., p. 58, says they wind acorns as well or better than a bear, but nothing about winding a man. See Appendix : Wild Boar.

[2] From F. *renouveler*.   [3] See Appendix : Wild Boar.

have a hard skin and strong flesh, especially upon their shoulders which is called the shield. Their season begins from the Holy Cross day in September [1] to the feast of St. Andrew [2] for then they go to the brimming of the sows. For they are in grease when they be withdrawn from the sows. The sows are in season from the brimming time *which is to say the twelfth day after Christmas* till the time when they have farrowed. The boars turn commonly to bay on leaving their dens for the pride that is in them, and they run upon some hounds and at men also. But when the boar is heated, or wrathful, or hurt, then he runneth upon all things that he sees before him. He dwelleth in the strong wood and the thickest that he can find and generally runneth in the most covered and thickest way so that he may not be seen as he trusteth not much in his running, but only in his defence and in his desperate deeds.[3] He often stops and turns to bay, and *especially when he is at the brimming* and hath a little advantage before the hounds of the first running, and these will never overtake him unless other new hounds be uncoupled to him.

He will well run and fly from the sun rising to the going down of the sun, if he be a young boar

---

[1] September 14.　　　　[2] November 30.

[3] Despiteful or furious deeds. G. de F., p. 60, says that he only trusts in his defences and his weapons ("en sa défense et en ses armes").

D

of three years old. In the third March counting
that in which he was farrowed, he parteth from his
mother and may well engender at the year's end.[1]

They have four tusks, two in the jaw above and
two in the nether jaw; of small teeth speak not
I, the which are like other boar's teeth. The two
tusks above serve for nothing except to sharpen
his two nether tusks and make them cut well *and
men beyond the sea call* the nether tusks of the
boar his arms or his files, with these they do great
harm, and also they call the tusks above gres[2]
(grinders) for they only serve to make the others
sharp as I have said, and when they are at bay they
keep smiting their tusks together to make them
sharp and cut better. When men hunt the boar
they commonly go to soil and soil in the dirt and if
they be hurt the soil is their medicine. The boar
that is in his third year or a little more is more
perilous and more swift and doth more harm than
an old boar, as a young man more than an old
man. An old boar will be sooner dead than a
young one for he is proud and heavier and deigneth
not to fly, and sooner he will run upon a man than
fly, and smiteth great strokes but not so perilously
as a young boar.

A boar heareth wonderfully well and clearly,

---

[1] As this is somewhat confused we have followed G. de F.'s
text in the modern rendering.

[2] From the French *grès*, grinding-stone or grinders.

and when he is hunted and cometh out of the forest or bush or when he is so hunted that he is compelled to leave the country, he sorely dreads to take to the open country and to leave the forest,[1] and therefore he puts his head out of the wood before he puts out his body, then he abideth there and harkeneth and looketh about and taketh the wind on every side. And if that time he seeth anything that he thinks might hinder him in the way he would go, then he turneth again into the wood. Then will he never more come out though all the horns and all the holloaing of the world were there. But when he has undertaken the way to go out he will spare for nothing but will hold his way throughout. When he fleeth he maketh but few turnings, but when he turneth to bay, and then he runneth upon the hounds and upon the man. And for no stroke or wound that men do him will he complain or cry, but when he runneth upon the men he menaceth, strongly groaning. But while he can defend himself he defendeth himself without complaint, and when he can no longer defend himself there be few boars that will not complain or cry out when they are overcome to the death.[2]

---

[1] G. de F., p. 60, has "fortress," instead of "forest."

[2] After the word "death" a full stop should occur, for in this MS. and, singularly enough, also in the Shirley MS. the following words have been omitted: "They drop their lesses," continuing "as other swine do."

They drop their lesses (excrements) as other swine do, according to their pasture being hard or soft.

But men do not take them to the curée nor are they judged as of the hart or other beasts of venery.

A boar can with great pain live twenty years; he never casts his teeth nor his tusks nor loses them unless by a stroke.[1] The boar's grease is good as that of other tame swine, and their flesh also. Some men say that by the foreleg of a boar one can know how old he is, for he will have as many small pits in the forelegs as he has years, but of this I make no affirmation. The sows lead about their pigs with them till they have farrowed twice and no longer, and then they chase their first pigs away from them for by that time they be two years old and three Marches counting the March in which they were farrowed.[2] In short they are like tame sows, excepting that they farrow but once in a year and the tame sows farrow twice. When they be wroth they run at both men and hounds and other beasts as (does) the wild boar and if they cast down a man they abide longer upon him than doeth a boar, but she cannot slay

[1] At this point G. de F., p. 61, adds : "One says of all biting beasts the trace, and of red beasts foot or view, and one can call both one or the other the paths or the fues."

[2] See Appendix : Wild Boar.

a man as soon as a boar for she has not such tusks as the boar, but sometimes they do much harm by biting. Boars and sows go to soil gladly when they go to their pasture, all day and when they return they sharpen their tusks and cut against trees when they rub themselves on coming from the soil. *What men call a trip of tame swine is called of wild swine a sounder, that is to say if there be passed a five or six together.*

CHAPTER VII

OF THE WOLF AND OF HIS NATURE

A WOLF is a common beast enough and therefore I need not tell of his make, for there are few men *beyond the sea*, that have not seen some of them. They are in their love in February with the females and then be jolly and do in the manner as hounds do, and be in their great heat of love ten or twelve days, and when the bitch is in greatest heat then if there are any wolves in the country they all go after her as hounds do after a bitch when she is jolly. But she will not be lined by any of the wolves save by one. She doth in such a wise that she will lead the wolves for about six or eight days without meat or drink and without sleep for they have so great courage towards her, that they have no wish to eat nor to drink, and when they be full weary she lets them rest until the time that they sleep, and then she claweth him with her foot and waketh him that seemeth to have loved her most, and who hath most laboured for her love, and then they go a great way thence and there he lines her. And therefore men say *beyond the seas in some countries* when any woman doth amiss, that she is like to the wolf bitch for she taketh to her the worst and the foulest and the most wretched and it is truth that the bitch of the wolf taketh to her the foulest and most wretched, for he hath most laboured and fasted [1] for her and is most poor, most lean and most wretched. And this is the cause why men say that the wolf saw never his father and it is truth sometimes but not always, for it happeneth that when she has brought the wolf that she loveth most as I have said, and when the other wolves awaken they follow anon in her track, and if they can find the wolf and the bitch holding together then will all the other wolves run upon him and slay him, and all this is truth in this case. But when in all the country there is but one wolf and one bitch of his kind then this rule cannot be truth.

And sometimes peradventure the other wolves may be awake so late that if the wolf is not fast with the bitch or peradventure he hath left her then he fleeth away from the other wolves, so they slay him not so in this case the first opinion is not true.

They may get young whelps at the year's end, and then they leave their father and their mother. And sometimes before they are twelve months

[1] G. de F., p. 63, has: "Pource qu'il a plus travaillé et plus jeuné que n'ont les autres."

old if so be that their teeth are fully grown after
their other small teeth which they had first, for
they teethe twice in the year when they are whelps.
The first teeth they cast when they are half a
year old *and also their hooks.* Then other teeth
come to them which they bear all their life-time
and never cast.   When these are full grown again
then they leave their father and mother and go on
their adventures, but notwithstanding that they
go far they do not bide long away from each
other and if it happens that they meet with their
father and with their mother the which hath
nourished them they will make them joy and
great reverence alway.   And also I would have
you know that when a bitch and a wolf of her
kind hath fellowship together they generally stay
evermore together, and though they sometimes
go to seek their feeding the one far from the
other they will be together at night if they can
or at the farthest at the end of three days.   And
such wolves in fellowship together get meat for
their whelps the father as well as the mother,
save only that the wolf eateth first his fill and
then bears the remnant to his whelps.   The bitch
does not do so for she beareth all her meat to her
whelps and eateth with them.   And if the wolf
is with the whelps when the mother cometh and
she bringeth anything and the wolf has not
enough he taketh the feeding from her and her

whelps, and eateth his fill first, and then he leaveth them the remnant, if there be any, and if there be not any left they die of hunger, if they will, for he recketh but little so that his belly be full. And when the mother seeth that, and has been far to seek her meat she leaveth her meat a great way thence for her whelps, and then she cometh to see if the wolf is with them, and if he be there she stayeth till he be gone and then she bringeth them her meat. But also the wolf is so malicious that when he seeth her come without food he goeth and windeth her muzzle and if he windeth she hath brought anything he taketh her by the teeth and biteth her so that she must show him where she hath left her food. And when the bitch perceiveth that the wolf doth this when she returneth to her whelps she keepeth in the covert and doth not show herself if she perceiveth that the wolf is with them, and if he be there she hideth herself until the time he hath gone to his prey on account of his great hunger, and when he is gone she brings her whelps her food for to eat. And this is truth.

Some men say that she bathes her body and her head so that the wolf should wind nothing of her feeding when she cometh to them, but of this I make no affirmation.

There be other heavy wolves of this nature, the which be not so in fellowship, they do not help

the bitch to nourish the whelps but when a wolf
and a bitch are in fellowship and there are no
wolves in that country by very natural smelling he
knoweth well that the whelps are his and therefore he helpeth to nourish them but not well.   At
the time that she hath whelps the wolf is fattest
in all the year, for he eateth and taketh all that
the bitch and whelps should eat.   The bitch
beareth her whelps nine weeks and sometimes
three or four days more.   Once in the year they
are in their love and are jolly.   Some men say
that the bitches bear no whelps while their
mother liveth, but thereof I make no affirmation.
The bitches of them have their whelps as other
tame bitches, sometimes more, sometimes less.
They have great strength especially before (fore-
quarters), and evil[1] they be and strong, for sometimes a wolf will slay a cow or a mare and he
hath great strength in his mouth.   Sometime he
will bear in his mouth a goat or a sheep or a
young hog and not touch the ground (with it),
and shall run so fast with it that unless mastiffs
or men on horseback happen to run before him
neither the shepherds nor no other man on foot
will ever overtake him.   They live on all manner
of flesh and on all carrion and all kinds of vermin.
And they live not long for they live not more
than thirteen or fourteen years.   Their biting is

---

[1] G. de F., p. 66, has "evil biting."

evil and venomous on account of the toads and other vermin that they eat. They go so fast when they be void (are empty) that men have let run four leashes of greyhounds, one after the other and they could not overtake him, for he runs as fast as any beast in the world, and he lasts long running, for he has a long breath. When he is long hunted with running hounds he fleeth but little from them, but if the greyhounds or other hounds press him, he fleeth all the covert [1] as a boar does and commonly he runs by the high ways. And commonly he goeth to get his livelihood by night, but sometimes by day, when he is sore ahungered. And there be some (wolves) that hunt at the hart, at the wild boar and at the roebuck, and windeth as far as a mastiff, and taketh hounds when they can. There are some that eat children and men and eat no other flesh from the time that they be acherned [2] (blooded) by men's flesh, for they would rather be dead. They are called wer-wolves, for men should beware of them, and they be so cautious that when they assail a man they have a holding upon him before the man can see them, and yet if men see them they will come upon them so gynnously (cunningly) that with great difficulty a man will escape being taken and slain, for they can wonder

[1] He keeps to the coverts.
[2] Acherned, from O. Fr. *acharné*, to blood, from *chair*, flesh.

well keep from any harness (arms) that a man
beareth.   There are two principal causes why
they attack men; one is when they are old and
lose their teeth and their strength, and cannot
carry their prey as they were wont to do, then
they mostly go for children, which are not difficult to take for they need not carry them about
but only eat them.   And the child's flesh is more
tender than is the skin or flesh of a beast.   The
other reason is that when they have been acharned
(blooded) in a country of war, where battles have
been, they eat dead men.   Or if men have been
hanged or have been hanged so low that they
may reach thereto, or when they fall from the
gallows.   And man's flesh is so savoury and so
pleasant that when they have taken to man's flesh
they will never eat the flesh of other beasts,
though they should die of hunger.   For many
men have seen them leave the sheep they have
taken and eat the shepherd.   It is a wonderfully
wily and gynnous (cunning) beast, and more false
than any other beast to take all advantage, for
he will never fly but a little save when he has
need, for he will always abide in his strength
(stronghold), and he hath good breath, for every
day it is needful to him, for every man that seeth
him chaseth him away and crieth after him.
When he is hunted he will fly all day unless he is
overset by greyhounds.   He will gladly go to

some village or in a brook, he will be little at bay
except when he can go no further. Sometimes
wolves go mad and when they bite a man he will
scarcely get well, for their biting is wonderfully
venomous on account of the toads they have
eaten as I have said before, and also on account of
their madness. And when they are full or sick
they feed on grasses as a hound does in order to
purge themselves. They stay long without meat
for a wolf can well remain without meat six days
or more. And when the wolf's bitch has her
whelps commonly she will do no harm near
where she has them, for fear she hath to lose
them. And if a wolf come to a fold of sheep
if he may abide any while he will slay them all
before he begins to eat any of them. Men take
them *beyond the sea* with hounds and greyhounds
with nets and with cords, but when he is taken
in nets or cords he cutteth them wonderfully fast
with his teeth unless men get quickly to him to
slay him. Also men take them within pits and
with needles [1] and with haussepieds [2] or with venomous powders that men give them in flesh, and
in many other manners. When the cattle come
down from the hills the wolves come down also
to get their livelihood. They follow commonly

[1] Needles. See Appendix : Snares.
[2] *Aucepis* (Shirley MS.). G. de F., p. 69: *haussepiez*, a
snare by which they were jerked from the ground by a noose.

after men of arms for the carrion of the beasts
or dead horses or other things. They howl like
hounds and if there be but two they will make
such a noise as if there were a route of seven or
eight if it is by night, when the weather is clear
and bright, or when there are young wolves that
have not yet passed their first year. When men
lay trains to acharne (with flesh) so as to take
them, they will rarely come again to the place
where men have put the flesh, especially old
wolves, leastways not the first time that they
should eat. But if they have eaten two or three
times, and they are assured that no one will do
them harm, then sometimes they will abide. But
some wolves be so malicious that they will eat in
the night and in the day they will go a great way
thence, two miles or more, especially if they have
been aggrieved in that place, or if they feel that
men have made any train with flesh for to hunt
at them. They do not complain (cry out) when
men slay them as hounds do, otherwise they be
most like them. When men let run greyhounds
at a wolf he turns to look at them, and when he
seeth them he knoweth which will take him, and
then he hasteneth to go while he can, and if they
be greyhounds which dare not take him, the wolf
knows at once, and then he will not hasten at his
first going. And if men let run at him from the
side, or before more greyhounds which will seize

him, when the wolf seeth them, and he be full, he voideth both before and behind all in his running so as to be more light and more swift. Men cannot nurture a wolf, though he be taken ever so young and chastised and beaten and held under discipline, for he will always do harm, if he hath time and place for to do it, he will never be so tame, but that when men leave him out he will look hither and thither to see if he may do any harm, or he looks to see if any man will do him any harm. For he knoweth well and woteth well that he doth evil, and therefore men ascrieth (cry at) and hunteth and slayeth him. And yet for all that he may not leave his evil nature.

Men say that the right fore foot of the wolf is good for medicine for the evil of the breast and for the botches (sores) which come to swine under the shoulder.[1] And also the liver of the wolf dried is good for a man's liver, but thereof I make no affirmation, for I would put in my book nothing but very truth. The wolf's skin is warm to make cuffs or pilches (pelisses), but the fur thereof is not fair, and also it stinketh ever unless it be well tawed.[2]

[1] This should be "jaw." G. de F., p. 70, has *maisselles*, *i.e.* Mâchoires.

[2] Prepared. Tawing is a process of making hides into leather —somewhat different from tanning. There were tawers and tanners.

CHAPTER VIII

OF THE FOX AND OF HIS NATURE

THE fox is a common beast and therefore I need
not tell of his making and there be but few gentlemen that have not seen some. He hath many
such conditions as the wolf, for the vixen of the
fox bears as long as the bitch of the wolf bears
her whelps, sometimes more sometimes less, save
that the vixen fox whelpeth under the earth
deeper than doth the bitch of the wolf. The
vixen of the fox is a saute[1] (in heat) once in the
year. She has a venomous biting like a wolf and
their life is no longer than a wolf's life. With
great trouble men can take a fox, especially the
vixen when she is with whelps, for when she is
with whelps and is heavy, she always keeps near
her hole, *for sometimes she whelpeth in a false hole
and sometimes in great burrows and sometimes in
hollow trees, and therefore she draweth always near
her burrow*, and if she hears anything anon she
goeth therein before the hounds can get to her.
She is a false beast and as malicious as a wolf.

[1] The term used by Turbervile (p. 188) is "goeth a
clicqueting."

The hunting for a fox is fair for the *good cry of* the hounds[1] that follow him so nigh and with so good a will. Always they scent of him, for he flies through the thick wood and also he stinketh evermore. And he will scarcely leave a covert when he is therein, he taketh not to the plain (open) country for he trusteth not in his running neither in his defence, for he is too feeble, and if he does, it is because he is (forced to) by the strength of men and hounds. And he will always hold to covert, and if he can only find a briar to cover himself with, he will cover himself with that. When he sees that he cannot last, then he goeth to earth the nearest he can find which he knoweth well and then men may dig him out and take him, if it is easy digging, but not among the rocks.[2] If greyhounds *give him many touches and*

---

[1] G. de F., p. 72, says, "because the hounds hunt him closely."

[2] Our MS. only gives this one chapter on the fox, while Gaston Phœbus has another: *Comment on doit chassier et prendre le renard.* In this he gives directions as to earth-stopping, and taking him in pursenets, and smoking him out with "orpiment and sulphur and nitre or saltpetre." He says January, February, and March are the best months for hunting, as the leaf is off the trees and the coverts are clearer, so that the hounds have more chance of seeing the fox and hunt him closer. He says that one-third of the hounds should be put in to draw the covert, and the others in relays should guard the boundaries and paths, to be slipped as required. Although this is a Frenchman's account of fox-hunting, we have no reason to believe that the fox was treated at that period better by English sportsmen, for until comparatively recent times the fox was accounted vermin, and any means by which his death

E

overset him, his last remedy, if he is in an open
country, will be that he vishiteth gladly (the act
of voiding excrements) so that the greyhounds
should leave him for the stink of the dirt, and
also for the fear that he hath.

A little greyhound is very hardy when (if) he
takes a fox by himself, for men have seen great
greyhounds which might well take a hart and a
wild boar and a wolf and would let the fox go.
And when the vixen is assaute, and goeth in her
love to seek the dog fox she crieth with a hoarse
voice as a mad hound doth, and also when she
calleth her whelps when she misses any of them,
she calleth in the same way. The fox does not
complain (cry) when men slay him, but he defendeth himself with all his power while he is alive.
He liveth on all vermin and all carrion and on
foul worms. His best meat that he most loveth
are hens, capons, duck and young geese and other
wild fowls when he can get them, also butterflies
and grasshoppers, milk and butter. They do
great harm in warrens of coneys and of hares which

could be encompassed were considered legitimate, his exter-
mination being the chief object in hunting him, and not the
sport. Even as late as the seventeenth century we find that
such treatment was considered justifiable towards a fox, for,
as Macaulay tells us, Oliver St. John told the Long Parliament
that Strafford was to be regarded, not as a stag or a hare, to
whom some law was to be given, but as a fox, who was to be
snared by any means, and knocked on the head without pity
(vol. i. p. 149).

they eat, and take them so gynnously (cunningly) and with great malice and not by running.   There be some that hunt as a wolf[1] and some that go nowhere but to villages to seek the prey for their feeding.   As I have said they are so cunning and subtle that neither men nor hounds can find a remedy to keep themselves from their false turns. Also foxes commonly dwell in great hedges or in great coverts or in burrows near some towns or villages for to evermore harm hens and other things as I have said.   The foxes' skins be wonderfully warm to make cuffs and furs, but they stink evermore if they are not well tawed.   The grease of the fox and the marrow are good for the hardening of sinews.   Of the other manners of the fox and of his cunning I will speak more openly hereafter.   Men take them with hounds, with greyhounds, with hayes and with purse-nets, but he cutteth them with his teeth, as the male of the wolf doth but not so soon (quickly).

[1] According to G. de F., p. 74, it should not read that some are hunted like wolves, but that they themselves hunt like wolves.

CHAPTER IX

OF THE GREY (BADGER) AND OF HIS NATURE

THE grey (badger) is a common beast enough and therefore I need not tell you of his making, for there be few men that have not seen some of them, and also I shall take no heed to speak much of him, for it is not a beast that needeth any great mastery to devise of how to hunt him, or to hunt him with strength, for a grey can fly but a little way before he is overcome with hounds, or else he goes to bay and then he is slain anon. His usual dwelling is in the earth in great burrows and if he comes out he will not walk far thence. He liveth on all vermin and carrion and all fruits and on all things such as the fox. But he dare not venture so far by day as the fox, for he cannot flee. He liveth more by sleeping than by any other thing. Once in the year they farrow as the fox.[1] When they be hunted they defend themselves long and mightily and have evil biting and venomous as the fox, and yet they defend themselves better than the fox. It is the beast of the

[1] G. de F., p. 76, adds : "And they farrow their pigs in their burrows as does the fox."

BADGER-DRAWING

(From MS. f. fr. 616, *Bib. Nat.*, Paris)

world that gathereth most grease within and that
is because of the long sleeping that he sleepeth.
And his grease bears medicine as does that of the
fox, *and yet more*, and men say that if a child
that hath never worn shoes is first shod with those
made of the skin of the grey that child will heal
a horse of farcy if he should ride upon him, but
thereof I make no affirmation. His flesh is not
to eat, neither is that of the fox nor of the wolf.

CHAPTER X

OF THE (WILD) CAT AND ITS NATURE

THE cat is a common beast enough therefore I
need not tell of his making, for there be few men
that have not seen some of them.   Nevertheless
there be many and diverse kind of cats, after
some masters' opinions, and namely of wild (cats).
Especially there be some cats as big as leopards
and some men call them *Guyenne* loup cerviers [1]
and other cat-wolves, and this is evil said for they
are neither wolves nor cerviers nor cat-wolves.
Men might (better) call them cat-leopards than
otherwise, for they draw more to a leopard kind
than to any other beast.   They live on such meat
as other cats do, save that they take hens in hedges [2]
and goats and sheep, if they find them alone, for
they be as big as a wolf, and almost formed and
made as a leopard, but their tail is not so long.
A greyhound alone could not take one of them

---

[1] According to the Shirley MS. this passage runs, "Men
calleth him in Guyene loupeceruyers." See Appendix: Wild
Cat.

[2] Shirley MS. has "and egges," instead of "in hedges," which
is the rendering G. de F. gives.

to make him abide, for a greyhound could sooner take and hold fast and more steadfastly a wolf than he could one of them. For he claws as a leopard and furthermore bites right (hard). Men hunt them but seldom, but if the hounds find peradventure such a cat, he would not be long hunted for soon he putteth him to his defence or he runneth up a tree. And because he flieth not long therefore shall I speak but little of his hunting, for in hunting him there is no need of great mastery. They bear their kittens and are in their love as other cats, save that they have but two kittens at once. They dwell in hollow trees and there they make their ligging[1] and their beds of ferns and of grass. The cat helpeth as badly to nourish his kittens as the wolf doth his whelps. *Of common wild cats I need not to speak much, for every hunter in England knoweth them, and their falseness and malice are well known. But one thing I dare well say that if any beast hath the devil's spirit in him, without doubt it is the cat, both the wild and the tame.*

[1] Bed or resting-place. See Appendix.

CHAPTER XI

An otter is a common beast enough and therefore I need not tell of his making. She liveth with (on?) fish and dwelleth by rivers and by ponds and *stanks* (pools). And sometimes she feedeth on grass of the meadows and bideth gladly under the roots of trees near the rivers, and goeth to her feeding as doth other beasts to grass, but only in the new grass time, and to fish as I have said. They swimmeth in waters and rivers and sometimes diveth under the water when they will, and therefore no fish can escape them unless it be too great a one. They doth great harm specially in ponds and in stanks, for a couple of otters without more shall well destroy the fish of a great pond or great stank, and therefore men hunt them. They go in their love at the time that ferrets do, so they that hold (keep) ferrets in their houses may well know the time thereof. They bear their whelps as long as the ferrets and sometimes more and sometimes less. They whelp in holes under the trees near the rivers. Men hunt at them with

OTTER-HUNTING

(From MS. f. fr. 616, *Bib. Nat.*, Paris)

hounds by great mastery, as I say hereafter.[1] And also men take them at other times in rivers with small cords as men do the fox with nets and with other gins. She hath an evil biting and venomous and with her strength defendeth herself mightily from the hounds. And when she is taken with nets unless men get to her at once she rendeth them with her teeth and delivereth herself out of them. Longer will I not make mention of her, nor of her nature, for the hunting at her is the best that men may see of her, save only that she has the foot of a goose, for she hath a little skin from one claw to another, and she hath no heel save that she hath a little lump under the foot, and men speak of the steps or the marches of the otter as men speak of the trace of the hart, and his fumes (excrements) tredeles or spraints. The otter dwelleth but little in one place, for where she goeth the fish be sore afraid. Sometimes she will swim upwards and downwards seeking the fish a mile or two unless it be in a stank.

Of the remnant of his nature I refer to Milbourne [2] *the king's otter hunter. As of all other vermin I speak not, that is to say of martens and pole cats, for no good hunter goeth to the wood with his hounds*

[1] The author of "Master of Game" does not say anything more about the otter.

[2] In Priv. Seal 674/6456, Feb. 18, 1410, William Melbourne is valet of our otterhounds. See Appendix: Otter.

*intending to hunt for them, nor for the wild cat
either.   Nevertheless when men seek in covert for
the fox and can find none, and the hounds happen
to find them and then the hunter rejoiceth his
hounds for the exploit of his hounds, and also because
it is vermin that they run to.   Of conies I do not
speak, for no man hunteth them unless it be bish-
hunters* (fur hunters), *and they hunt them with
ferrets and with long small hayes.   Those raches
that run to a coney at any time ought to be rated
saying to them loud, "Ware riot, ware," for no
other wild beast in England is called riot save the
coney only.*

CHAPTER XII

OF THE MANNER AND HABITS AND
CONDITIONS OF HOUNDS

AFTER that I have spoken of the nature of beasts
of venery and of chase which men should hunt,
now I will tell you of the nature of the hounds
which hunt and take them. And first of their
noble conditions that be so great and marvellous
in some hounds that there is no man can believe
it, unless he were a good skilful hunter, and well
knowing, and that he haunted them long, for a
hound is a most reasonable beast, and best knowing of any beast that ever God made. And yet
in some case I neither except man nor other thing,
for men find it in so many stories and (see) so
much nobleness in hounds, always from day to
day, that as I have said there is no man that liveth,
but must think it. Nevertheless natures of men
and all beasts go ever more descending and de-
creasing both of life and of goodness and of
strength and of all other things so wonderfully,
as the Earl of Foix Phebus sayeth in his book, that
when he seeth the hounds that be now hunting
and thinketh of the hounds that he hath seen in

75

the time that is passed, and also of the goodness
and the truth, which was sometimes in the lords
of this world, and other common men, and seeth
what now is in them at this time, truly he saith
that there is no comparison, and this knoweth well
every man that hath any good reason.   But now
let God ordain thereof whatever His good will
is.   But to draw again to my matter, and tell the
nobleness of the hounds, the which have been, some
good tales I shall tell you the which I find in true
writings.   First of King Claudoneus [1] of France,
the which sent once after his great court whereof
were other kings which held of him land, among
the which was the King Appollo of Lyonnys that
brought with him to the court his wife and a greyhound that he had, that was both good and fair.
The King Claudoneus of France had a seemly
young man for his son, of twenty years of age, and
as soon as he saw the Queen of Lyonnys he loved
her and prayed her of (for her) love.   The Queen
was a good lady and loved well her lord, forsook
him and would him not, and said (to) him that if
he spake to her any more thereof that she would
tell it to the King of France, and to her Lord.
And after that the feast was passed, King Appollo
of Lyonnys turned again, he and his wife to their
country.   And when they were so turned again,
he and his wife, the King Claudoneus son of

[1] In G. de F. "Clodoveus," p. 82.

France was before him with a great fellowship of
men of arms for to ravish his wife from him.   The
King Appollo of Lyonnys that was a wonderful
good knight of his hounds (hands?) notwithstanding that he was unarmed, defended himself and
his wife in the best wise that he could unto the
time that he was wounded to the death, then he
withdrew himself and his wife into a tower.   And
the King Claudoneus son, the which would not
leave the lady, went in and took the lady, and
would have defiled her, and then she said to him
" Ye have slain my lord, and (now) ye would dis-
honour me, certes I would sooner be dead," then
she drew herself to (from) a window and leapt into
the river of Loire that ran under the tower and
anon she was drowned.   And after that within a
little while, the King Appollo of Lyonnys died
of his wounds that he had received, and on the
same day he was cast into the river.   The greyhound that I have spoke of, the which was always
with the king his master, when his lord was cast
in the river leapt after him into the river, insomuch
that with his teeth he drew his lord out of the
river, and made a great pit with his claws in the
best wise that he could, and with his muzzle.
And so the greyhound always kept his lord about
half a year in the pit, and kept his lord from all
manner of beasts and fowls.   And if any man ask
whereof he lived I say that he lived on carrion

and of other feeding such as he might come to. So it befell that the King Claudoneus of France rode to see the estate of his realm, and (it) befell that the king passed there where the greyhound was that kept his lord and master, and the greyhound arose against him, and began to yelp at him. The King Claudoneus of France the which was a good man and of good perception, anon when he saw the greyhound, knew that it was the greyhound that King Appollo of Lyonnys had brought to his court, whereof he had great wonder, and he went himself there where the greyhound was and saw the pit, and then he made some of his men alight from their horses for to look what was therein, and therein they found the King Appollo's body all whole. And anon as the King Claudoneus of France saw him, he knew it was the King Appollo of Lyonnys, whereof he was right sorry and sore aggrieved, and ordained a cry throughout all his realm, that whoso would tell him the truth of the deed he would give him whatsoever that he would ask. Then came a damsel that was in the tower when the King Appollo of Lyonnys was dead, and thus she said to the King Claudoneus of France, "Sir," quoth she, "if you will grant me a boon that I shall ask and assure me to have it, before all your men, I shall show you him that hath done the deed," and the King swore to her before his men, and it

so befell that the King Claudoneus son of France
was beside his father. "Sir," she said, "here is
your son the which hath done this deed. Now
require I you as ye have sworn to me that ye give
him to me, I will no other gift of you." The
King Claudoneus of France turned him then
towards his son and said thus : "Thou cursed
harlot, thou hast shamed and shent (disgraced)
me and truly I shall shend (disgrace) you. And
though I have no more children yet shall I not
spare." Then he commanded to his men to
make a great fire, and cast his son therein, and he
turned him toward the damsel when the fire was
great alight, and thus to her he said : "Damsel,
now take ye him for I deliver him to you, as I
promised and assured you." The damsel durst
not come nigh, for by that time he was all burnt.
This ensample have I brought forth for the nobleness of hounds and also of lords that have been
in olden times. But I trow that few lords be
now that would do so even and so open justice.
A hound is true to his lord and his master, and
of good love and true.

A hound is of great understanding and of great
knowledge, a hound hath great strength and great
goodness, a hound is a wise beast and a kind (one).
A hound has a great memory and great smelling,[1]

----

[1] G. de F., p. 84, says "*sentement*," good sense, feeling, or
sympathy.

a hound has great diligence and great might, a
hound is of great worthiness and of great subtlety,
a hound is of great lightness and of great perseverance (?), a hound is of good obedience, for he
will learn as a man all that a man will teach him.
A hound is full of good sport; hounds are so
good that there is scarcely a man that would not
have of them, some for one craft, and some for
another.   Hounds are hardy, for a hound dare
well keep his master's house, and his beasts, and
also he will keep all his master's goods, and he
would sooner die than anything be lost in his
keeping.   And yet to affirm the nobleness of
hounds, I shall tell you a tale of a greyhound
that was Auberie's of Moundydier, of which men
may see the painting in the realm of France in
many places.   Aubery was a squire of the king's
house of France, and upon a day that he was
going from the court to his own house, and as he
passed by the woods of Bondis, the which is nigh
Paris, and led with him a well good and a fair
greyhound that he had brought up.   A man that
hated him for great envy without any other
reason, who was called Makarie, ran upon him
within the wood and slew him without warning,
for Auberie was not aware of him.   And when
the greyhound sought his master and found him
he covered him with earth and with leaves with
his claws and his muzzle in the best way that he

could. And when he had been there three days
and could no longer abide for hunger, he turned
again to the king's court. There he found
Makarie, who was a great gentleman, who had
slain his master, and as soon as the greyhound
perceived Makarie, he ran upon him, and would
have maimed him, unless men had hindered him.
The King of France, who was wise and a man of
perception, asked what it was, and men told him
the truth. The greyhound took from the boards
what he could, and brought to his master and put
meat in his mouth, and the same wise the greyhound did three days or four. And then the
King made men follow the greyhound, for to see
where he bare the meat that he took in the court.
And then they found Auberie dead and buried.
And then the King, as I have said, made come
many of the men of his court, and made them
stroke the greyhound's side, and cherish him and
made his men lead him by the collar towards the
house, but he never stirred. And then the King
commanded Makarie to take a small piece of flesh
and give it to the greyhound. And as soon as
the greyhound saw Makarie, he left the flesh, and
would have run upon him. And when the King
saw that, he had great suspicions about Makarie,
and said (to) him that he must needs fight against
the greyhound. And Makarie began to laugh,
but anon the King made him do the deed, and one

F

of the kinsmen of Auberie saw the great marvel
of the greyhound and said that he would swear
upon the sacrament as is the custom in such a case
for the greyhound, and Makarie swore on the
other side, and then they were led into our Lady's
Isle at Paris and there fought the greyhound and
Makarie. For which Makarie had a great two-
handed staff, and they fought so that Makarie
was discomfitted, and then the king commanded
that the greyhound the which had Makarie under
him should be taken up, and then the King made
enquiry of the truth of Makarie, the which
acknowledged he had slain Aubrey in treason, and
therefore he was hanged and drawn.

The bitches be jolly in their love commonly
twice in a year, but they have no term of their heat,
for every time of the year some be jolly. When
they be a twelvemonth old, they become jolly,
and be jolly while they await the hounds without
any defence, twelve days or less,[1] and sometimes
fifteen days, according as to whether they be of
hot nature or of cold, the one more than another,
or whether some be in better condition than others.
And also men may well help them thereto, for if
they give them much meat they abide longer in
their heat than if they had but little. And also
if they were cast in a river twice in a day they
should be sooner out of their jollity. They bear

[1] G. de F., p. 85, "Au moins," at least.

their whelps nine weeks or more; the whelps be blind when they be whelped till they be nine days old and then they may well see and lap well when they be a month old, but they have great need of their dam to the time that they be two months old, and then they should be well fed with goat's milk or with cow's milk and crumbs of bread made small and put therein, especially in the morn and at night. Because that the night is more cold than the day. And also men should give them crumbs in flesh-broth, and in this wise men may nourish them till they be half a year old, and by that time they shall have cast their hooks, and when they have cast their hooks, they should teach them to eat dry bread and lap water little by little, for a hound that is nourished with grease and fat broth when he casts his hooks, and if he hath always sops or tit-bits, he is a chis [1] (dainty) hound and of evil ward. And also they be not so well breathed than if they have eaten always bread and water. When the bitches be lined they lose their time, and also while they be great with whelps, and also while their whelps suck. If they are not lined, soon they will lose their time, for their teats remain great and grow full of wind until the time that they should have had their

---

[1] "Chis," or "cheese," hound, probably dainty hound, a chooser, from "cheosan," Mid. Eng. "choose," to distinguish: also written "ches," "chees." (Stratmann.)

whelps. And so that they should not lose their time men spaye them, save these that men will keep open to bear whelps. And also a spayed bitch lasteth longer in her goodness than other two that be not spayed.[1] And if a bitch be with whelps the which be not of ward let the bitch fast all the whole day, and give her then with a little grease the juice of a herb men calleth titimal, the which the apothecaries knoweth well, and she shall cast her whelps. Nevertheless it is a great peril namely if the whelps be great and formed within the bitch. The greatest fault of hounds is that they live not long enough, most commonly they live but twelve years. And also men should let run no hounds of what condition that they be nor hunt them until the time that they were a twelve month old and past. And also they can hunt but nine years at the most.

[1] Lasts longer good, *i.e.* lasts as long as two hounds that have not been spayed. G. de F. (p. 86) adds : "or at least one and a half."

CHAPTER XIII

OF SICKNESSES OF HOUNDS AND OF THEIR CORRUPTIONS

THE hounds have many divers sicknesses and their greatest sickness is the rage whereof there be nine manners, of the which I shall tell you a part. The first is called furious madness. The hounds that be mad of that madness cry and howl with a loud voice, and not in the way that they were wont to when they were in health. When they escape they go everywhere biting both men and women and all that they find before them. And they have a wonderful perilous biting, for if they bite anything, with great pain it shall escape thereof if they draw blood, that it shall go mad whatever thing it be. A token for to know at the beginning, is this, that they eat not so well as they were wont to, and they bite the other hounds, making them cheer with the tail[1] first, smelleth[2] upon them and licketh[3] them

[1] Cherish, "wagging their tayles and seeming to cherish them," Turbervile, p. 223. See Appendix: Madness.

[2] It should read "smelleth," as it is in Shirley MS. and in G. de F., p. 87.

[3] The friendly licking of other dogs has often been noticed as an early symptom of rabies in a pack of hounds.

and then he bloweth a great blast with his nose,
and then he looketh fiercely, and beholdeth his
own sides and maketh semblant that he had flies
about him, and then he crieth.   And when men
know such tokens men should take him from
the others until the fourth day, for then men
may see the sickness all clearly, or else that he is
not mad for some time.   Many men be beguiled
in that way.   And if any hound be mad of any
of the nine madnesses he shall never be whole.
And their madness cannot last but nine days [1]
but they shall never be whole but dead.   That
other manner of madness is known by these signs :
In the beginning he doth as I said before, save
that they neither bite man nor beast save only the
hounds, as perilous is his biting.as the first, and
ever more they go up and down without any
abiding.   And this madness is called running
madness.   And these two madnesses beforesaid
taketh the other hounds that they be with, though
they bite them not.   That other madness is called
ragemuet (dumb madness) for they neither bite
nor run not, eke they will not eat for their mouth

---

[1] Du Fouilloux in his *La Venerie* (published 1561) copied
much from Gaston de Foix's book, but either he or his editors
made the ridiculous mistake of saying nine *months* instead
of *days*. Turbervile, who translated, or rather cribbed, Du
Fouilloux's book, has copied this absurd mistake, and says
a hound may continue thus nine months, but not past (p.
222).

HOW THE HOUNDS WERE LED OUT

(From MS. f. fr. 616, *Bib. Nat.*, Paris)

132

is somewhat gaping as if they were enosed [1] in their throat, and so they die, within the term beforesaid without doing any harm. Some men say that it cometh to them from a worm [2] that they have under the tongue, and ye should find but few hounds that hath not a worm under the tongue. And many men say that if that worm was taken from them they would never go mad, but thereof I make no affirmation. Nevertheless it is good to take it from them, and men should take it away in this manner. Men should take the hound when he is past half a year old and hold fast his fore-feet, and put a staff athwart his mouth so that he should not bite. And after take the tongue and ye should find the worm under the tongue, then ye should slit the tongue underneath and put a needle with a thread betwixt the worm and tongue and cut and draw the worm out with the thread *or else with a small pin of wood.* And notwithstanding that men call it a worm it is but a great vein that hounds have under their tongue. This madness diseaseth not other hounds, neither man nor other beast. That other madness is called falling, for when they want to walk straight they fall now on one side and now on the other side, and so die within the

[1] Means "a bone in their throat." G. de F. (p. 88): "comme si ils avoient un os en la gueule." In the Shirley MS. "enosed," *i.e. "un os."* See Appendix: Madness.

[2] See Appendix: Worming.

aforesaid term. This madness stretcheth to no
other hound nor man or beast. That other
madness is called flank madness,[1] for they be so
sore and tucked up by the middle of the flanks
as though they never ate meat, and pant in their
flanks with much pain, and will not eat, but stoop
low with the head and always look downwards,
and when they go they take up their feet high
and go rolling *as a drunken man*. This madness
stretcheth to no other hound nor to any other
things, and they die as it is said before. The other
madness is called sleeping madness, for they lie
always and make semblant as if they were asleep,
and so they die without meat. This sickness
stretcheth to no other thing. That other madness
is called madness of head. Nevertheless all madnesses are of foolishness of the head and of the
heat of the heart, for their head becometh great
and swelleth fast. They eat no meat and so they
die in that madness. This madness stretcheth to
no other thing. And certainly I never saw a
hound that had any of all these madnesses that
ever might be healed. Nevertheless many men
think sometime that a hound be mad when it
is not so, and therefore the best proof that any
man may do, is to draw him from the other hounds
and assaye him three whole days each one after

---

[1] "Lank madness" in Turbervile, p. 223. Tucked up. G. de
F. (p. 88) : "cousus parmi les flans" ("the flanks drawn in").

the other following, if he will eat flesh or any other
thing.   And if he will not eat within three days
slay him as a mad hound.   The remedies for men
or for beasts that be bitten by mad hounds must
need be done a short time after the biting, for if
it were past a whole day it were hard to undertake
to heal him of the two first madnesses whereof
I spake at the beginning, for all the others can
do no harm, and the remedy may be of divers
manners.   Some goeth to the sea, and that is but
a little help, and maketh nine waves of the sea
pass over him that is so bitten.   Some take an old
cock and pull all the feathers from above his vent
and hangeth him by the legs and by the wings, and
setteth the cock's vent upon the hole of the biting,
and stroketh along the cock by the neck and by
the shoulders because that the cock's vent should
suck all the venom of the biting.   And so men do
long upon each of the wounds, and if the wounds
be too little they must be made wider with a barber's
lancet.   And many men say, but thereof I make
no affirmation, that if the hound were mad, that
the cock shall swell and die, and he that was bitten
by the hound shall be healed.   If the cock does
not die it is a token that the hound is not mad.
There is another help, for men may make sauce
of salt, vinegar and strong garlic pulled and
stamped, and nettles together and as hot as it may
be suffered to lay upon the bite.   And this is

a good medicine and a true, for it hath been proved, and every day should it be laid upon the biting twice, as hot as it can be suffered, until the time when it be whole, or else by nine days. And yet there is another medicine better than all the other. Take leeks and strong garlic and chives and rue and nettles and hack them small with a knife, and then mingle them with olive oil and vinegar, and boil them together, and then take all the herbs, also as hot as they may be suffered, and lay them on the wound every day twice, till the wound be healed, or at least for nine days. But at the beginning that the wound be closed or garsed [1] (cupped) for to draw out the venom out of the wound because that it goeth not to the heart. And if a hound is bit by another mad hound it is a good thing for to hollow it all about the biting with a hot iron. The hounds have also another sickness that is called the mange, that cometh to them because that they be melancholy. There are four manners of mange, that one is called the quick mange the which pulleth [2] the hounds and breaketh their skins in many places, and the skin waxeth great and thick, and

[1] In Shirley MS. "ventoused upon or gersed." G. de F.: "ventouses, que on appelle coupes," hence "cupped and lanced" would be the proper meaning.

[2] Makes them lose their hair. G. de F. (p. 90), "et si *poile* le chien."

this is wonderfully evil to heal, for though the hounds may be whole it cometh to them again. Commonly to this mange, this is the best ointment that men may make thereto. Nevertheless many men would put many others thereto, first take ye six pounds of honey and a quart of verdigris, and that the honey be first melted and stirred in the bottom with a ladle, and then let it cool, and let it boil often with as much of oil of nuts as of the honey and of water, wherein an herb has been boiled that men call in Latin Cleoborum, and in other language Valerian, the which make men sneeze, and put all these things together and mingle them upon the fire, stir them well and let it be cold, and anoint the hound by the fire or in the sun.   And look that he lick not himself, for it should do him harm.   And unless he be whole at the first time anoint him from eight days (to eight days)[1] until the time that he be whole, for certainly he shall be whole.   And if he will make any more of that ointment, take of the things aforesaid in the same wise or more or less as seemeth to you that need is.   That other manner (of) mange is called flying mange,[2] for it is not in all the body but it cometh more commonly about the hounds' ears, and in their legs than in any

---

[1] "To viii. days" has been omitted.

[2] Some confusion, which is still common, between eczema from various causes, and true parasitic mange or scabies.

other place of the body,[1] as the farcy, and this is
the worst to heal, and the best ointment that any
man can make for this manner of mange is this :
take quicksilver for as much as ye will make
ointment, as ye have need, and put it in a dish
with spittle of three or four fasting men, and stir
it altogether against the bottom of the dish with
a pot-stick, until the time that the quicksilver be
quenched with the water, and then take ye as much
verdigris as of the quicksilver and mingle it with
spittle, always stirring with a pot-stick, as I have
said before, until the time that they can be all
mingled together.   And after take old swine's
grease without salt, a great piece, and take away
the skin above, and put it in the dish that I spake
of, with the things before said, and mingle and
stamp it altogether a long while, then keep it to
anoint the hound there where he hath the mange
and in no other place, and certainly he shall be
whole.   This ointment is marvellous and good and
true not only for this thing, but also against the
canker and fistula and farcy and other quick evils,
the which have been hard to heal in other beasts.
That other is a common mange when the hounds
claw themselves with their feet and snap with
their teeth, and it is on all the body of the hound.
And all manners of mange come to hounds from

[1] G. de F. (p. 91) adds : " et est vermeille et saute d'un lieu
en autre."

great travel and from long hunting, as when they be hot they drink of foul water and unclean, which corrupteth their bodys, and also when they hunt in evil places of pricklings of thorns, of briers, or per-adventure it raineth upon them, and they be not well tended afterwards. Then cometh the scab, and also the scab cometh upon them when they abide in their kennel too long[1] and goeth not hunt-ing. Or else their litter and couch is uncleanly kept, or else the straw is not removed and their water not freshened, and shortly the hounds un-clean, I hold, and evil kept *or long waterless*, have commonly this mange. For the cure of which take ye the root of an herb that groweth upon houses and walls, the which is called in Latin iroos[2] (iris) and chop it small and boil it well in water, and then put thereto as much of oil made of nuts as of water, and when it is well boiled cast out the herb, and then take of black pitch and of rosin as much of the one as of the other, well stamped, and cast it in the water and the oil before said, and stir it well about on the fire with a pot-stick : and then let it well grow cold, and anoint the hound as before

---

[1] In the Shirley MS. the words are added : "to(o) hye plyte," *i.e.* too high condition. G. de F. (p. 91) adds "gresse."

[2] *Ireos*, Eng. Iris. This word is also constantly recurring in old household books. Aniseed and orris powder were placed among linen to preserve it from insects. In Edward IV.'s Wardrobe Accounts we read of bags of fustian stuffed with anneys and ireos.

is said.   Sometime cometh to the hounds sickness
in their eyes, for there cometh a web upon them,
and growing flesh which cometh into that one side
of the eye, and is called a nail,[1] and so they grow
blind unless a man take care thereof.   Some men
put about their necks a collar of an elm tree both
of leaves and of bark, and seeth that when that
shall be dry the nail shall fall away, but that is
but a little help.   But the true help that may be
thereto is this, take ye the juice of a herb that men
call Selidoyn (Celandine)[2] powder of ginger and
of pepper, and put all together thrice in the day
within the eye, and let him not claw nor rub it
a long while, and that customarily by nine days

[1] *Pterygium*, name for the "sickness" in the eyes of hounds
which our MS. describes as a "web coming upon them." It
is called *pterygium* from its resemblance to an insect's wing ;
is an hypertrophy of the conjunctiva or lining membrane of the
eye, due to irritation ; it extends from the inner angle to the
cornea, which it may cover : the treatment is excision.   The
cure for "the nail" mentioned in our MS. of hanging a collar
of elm leaves round the dog is taken by G. de F. (p. 92) from
Roy Modus xliv., where it is given without the saving clause
"Mès cela est bien petit remède."

[2] *Celandine, Chalidonium Majus*, from χελιδων, a swallow.
The name was derived from the tradition that swallows used
it to open the eyes of their young or to restore their sight.   Has
a yellow flower and an acrid, bitter, orange juice.   Internally
an irritant poison.   Infusions in wine used by Galen and
Bioscorides for jaundice, probably from the colour of the juice
and flowers.   Externally the juice was much used for wounds,
ulcers, ophthalmic cases, and for the removal of warts.   The
Old French name for this plant was *herbe d'arondelles* (*kiron-
delles*).

until the time that the hound's eyes be whole, and
also it is good to put therein of the Sousse [1] of the
which men find enough at the apothecary's for the
same sickness, and if the nail were so hard grown
and so strong that he might not be healed therewith, take a needle and bow it in the middle that
it be crooked, and take well and subtly the flesh
that is upon the eye with the needle and draw it
up on high, and then cut it with a razor, but
take good care that the needle touch not the eye.
These things the smiths can do well,[2] for as the
nail is drawn out of a horse's eye, right so it must
be drawn out of the hound's eye, *and without fault
he shall be whole.*   And also another sickness
cometh into the hound's ears the which cometh
out of the rewme (cold) of the head of the hound,
for they claw themselves so much with the hinder
feet that they make much foul things come out
thereof, and so out of her ears cometh much foul
things, and some time thereof they become deaf.
Therefore they should take wine luke-warm and
with a cloth wash it well, and clean three or four
times in the day, and when it is washed ye should
cast therein oil and camomile milk, warm, three
drops, and suffer him not to claw it nor rub it a
great while, and do so continually until the time

[1] Shirley MS. has "foussye," G. de F. (p. 92) "de la poudre
de la tutie," oxide of zinc.
[2] Shirley MS. adds : "that be marshals for horses."

that he be whole.   Also hounds have another
sickness that cometh to them of the rewme, that
is to say, they have the malemort (glanders) in their
nostrils as horses have, wherefore they can smell
nothing nor wind, and at the last some die thereof,
and they take it most when they hunt in snow. For
this sickness boil mastic and incense in small powder
in fair water, and of a thing that men call Ostoraces
calamynt,[1] brygella[2] of rue[3] and mint and of sage,
and hold the hound's nose upon the pot's mouth
wherein these things should boil so that he may
retain within his nostrils the smoke that cometh
thereof out of the pot.   And in this wise serve
him a long while, three or four times every day,
until the time that he be whole, and this is good
also for a horse when he hath the glanders strongly

[1] *Estoracis calamita,* G. de F., p. 93. Lavallée appends the
note: "*Storax et Styrax calamita.*" Storax, a resin resembling
benzoin, was in high esteem from the time of Pliny to the
eighteenth century. It was obtained from the stem of *Styrax
officinalis,* a native of Greece and the Levant. In our MS. four
other ingredients mentioned by G. de F. have been left out,
but the Shirley MS. gives them : "and oyle of Kamamyle and
of Mallyor of aushes and of calamynt," *i.e.* oil of camomile,
melilot (Meliters), rosemary, thymus calamita, a species of
balm. Possibly this is a mint called *Calaminta nepeta,* a plant
formerly much used in medicine as a gentle stimulant and tonic.
Melilot, a genus of clover-like plants of the natural order of
Leguminose.
[2] Mildew. G. de F. (p. 93), Nigella, Nielle.
[3] *Rewe,* Mod. Eng. *rue,* Lat. *ruta.* This herb was in great
repute among the ancients, and is still employed in medicine
as a powerful stimulant.

coming out of the nose.   Also there is another
sickness of hounds, the which cometh to them in
their throats and sometime cometh so to men in
such wise that they may not keep down their meat,
and so they must cast it out again.   In some time
the sickness is so strong on them, that they can
keep nothing down in their bodies and so die.
The best medicine is to let them go wherever they
will, and let them eat all that ever they will.   For
sometime the contrary things turneth them to
good.   And give them to eat flesh right small
cut, and put in broth or in goat's milk a little,
and a little because that they may swallow it
down without labour, and give him not too much
at once, that they may digest better.   And also
buttered eggs doeth them much good.   And
sometimes the hounds hurt themselves in their
feet, and in their legs, and in their breast.   And
when it is in the joints of their feet that be run
out of their places, the best help that there is is
to bring them again into joint, by such men as
can well do it, and then lay upon that place flax
wetted in white of egg, and let them rest until
the time that they be whole.   And if there be any
broken bones men should knit it again in the best
wise, the one bone against that other and bind it
with flax above as I have said, and with four
splints well bound thereto that one against that
other, because that the bone should not unjoin,

G

and men should remove the bands from four days
to four days all whole.   And give them to drink
the juice of herbs that are called consolida major [1]
and minor,[2] and mix it in broth or in her meat,
and that shall make the bones join together.   Also
many hounds be lost by the feet, and if some time
they be heated take vinegar and soot that is
within the chimney, and wash his feet therewith
until the time that they be whole, and if the soles
of the feet be bruised because, peradventure, they
have run in hard country or among stones, take
water, and small salt therein, and therewith wash
their feet, the same day that they have hunted,
and if they have hunted in evil country among
thorns and briars that they be hurt in their legs
or in their feet, wash their legs in sheep's tallow
well boiled in wine when it is cold, and rub them
well upward against the hair.   The best that men
may do to hounds that they lose not their claws
is that they sojourn not too long, for in long
sojourning they lose their claws, and their feet, and
therefore they should be led three times in the
week a-hunting, and at the least twice.   If they
have sojourned too much, cut ye a little off the
end of their claws with pincers ere they go hunt-

[1] *Consolida major.* Lavallée in his note (p. 94) translates
this *consoude*, which in English is comfrey, Latin *Symphytum.*
[2] *Consolida minor* (Lavallée : note, *petit consoude*), Mod. Fr.
Brunelle. G. de F. p. 94. Eng. Selfheal. Lat. *Prunella
vulgaris.* It was at one time in repute as a febrifuge.

ing, so that they may not break their claws in running. Also when they be at sojourn, men should lead them out every day a mile or two upon gravel or upon a right hard path by a river side, so that their feet may be hard. Hounds also sometimes be chilled as horses when they have run too long, and come hot in some water, or else when they come to rest in some cold place, then they go all forenoon and cannot eat, nor cannot walk well, then should men let blood on the four legs. From the forelegs in the joints within the leg, from the hinder legs men should let blood in the veins that goeth overthwart above the hocks on the other side, and in the hinder legs men may well see clearly the veins that I speak of, and also in the forelegs, thus he shall be whole. And give him one day sops or some other thing comfortable till the morrow or other day. The hounds also have a sickness in the yerde that men calleth the canker, and many be lost thereby. Men should take such a hound and hold him fast and upright and bind his mouth and his four legs also, and then men should take his yerde backward by the ballocks and put him upward, and another man shall draw the skin well in manner that the yerde may all come out, and then a man may take away the canker with his fingers, for if it were taken away with a knife men might cut him. And then men should wash it with wine, milk warm, and then put therein honey and salt, so that the sickness shall not come again, and then put again the yerde within the skin as it was before, and look every week that the sickness come not again, and take it always out if aught come thereto until the time that it be whole.   And in the same wise a man should do to a bitch, if such a sickness were taken in her nature.   In this sickness many hounds and bitches die for default of these cures, whereof all hunters have not full knowledge. Sometimes the hounds have a great sickness that they may not piss, and be lost thereby and also when they may not scombre (dung).   Then take ye the root of a cabbage and put it in olive oil, and put it in his fundament so that ye leave some of the end without, so much that it may be drawn out when it is needful.   And if he may not be whole thereby make him a clyster as men do to a man, of mallows, of beets, and of mercury, a handful of each, and of rue and of incense, and that all these things be boiled in water and put bran within, and let pass all that water through a strainer, and thereto put two drachms of agarite [1] and of honey and of olive oil, and all this together put into his anus and he shall scombre.

[1] *Agarys.* G. de F. *d'agret,* probably *agrimony*, Lat. *agrimonia.* It is bitter and styptic, and was much valued in domestic medicine ; a decoction of it being used as a gargle and the dried leaves as a kind of tea, and the root as a vermifuge.

And then take five corns of spurge[1] and stamp them and temper them with goat's milk or with broth, and put it in the hound's throat to the amount of a glassful. And if he may not piss take the leaves of leeks and of a herb that is called marrubium album[2] and of modirwort[3] and of peritorie[4] and morsus galline[5] and of nettles and parsley leaves as much of the one as of the other, and stamp them with swine's grease therewith, and make a plaster thereof, and make it a little hot, and lay it upon the hound's yerde and along his belly, and that which is hard to understand ye shall find at the apothecary's, the which know well all these things. Also to the hounds cometh sores, that cometh to them under the throat or in other parts of the body. Then take ye of the

[1] *Euphorbia resinifera*, common spurge, exudes a very acrid milky juice which dries into a gum resin. Still used for some plasters.

[2] *Marrubium vulgare.* G. de F. *marrabre blanc*, Eng. white horehound. It enjoyed a great reputation as a stimulating expectorant employed in asthma, consumption, and other pulmonary affections.

[3] *Leonurus cardiaca.* G. de F. *Artemise*, Eng. Motherwort, Mod. Fr. *armoise.* A plant allied to the horehound as a vascular stimulant and diuretic and a general tonic, employed in dropsy, gout, rheumatism, and uterine disorders.

[4] *Parietaria.* Eng. Wall pellitory. An old domestic remedy. It was supposed to be astringent and cooling, and used locally for inflammation, burns, erysipelas, and internally as a diuretic. It grows on old walls and heaps of rubbish.

[5] *Morsus gallinus.*

mallows and of the onions and of white lilies,[1]
and cut them small with a knife, and put them in
a ladle of iron and mingle these herbs whereof I
speak, and lay them upon the sores, and that shall
make them rise, and when they be risen, slit them
with a sharp knife.   And when they be so broken,
lay upon them some good drawing salve, and he
be whole.   Sometimes the hounds fight and bite
each other, and then they shall take sheep's wool
unwashed, and a little olive oil, and wet the wool
in the oil, and lay it upon the hound's wound, and
bind it thereupon, and do so three days, and then
after twice each day anoint it with olive oil, and
lay nothing upon it.   And he shall lick it with his
tongue and heal himself.[2]   If peradventure in the
wound come worms as I have seen some time,
every day ye shall pick them out with a stick, and
ye shall put in the wound the juice of leaves of a
peach tree mingled with quicklime until the time
that they be whole.   Also it happeneth to many
hounds that they smite the forelegs against the
hinder wherefore their thighs dry[3] and be lost

[1] *Lilies.*   The white lilies here mentioned are probably
Lilium connalium (lilies of the valley).   In an old book of
recipes I find them mentioned as an antidote to poison.   (*Haus
und Land Bib.* 1700.)   They have medicinal qualities, purgative
and diuretic in effect.   Dried and powdered they become a
sternutatory.
[2] In the Shirley MS. there is added: "the hound tongue
beareth medicine and especially to himself."   G. de F. has the
same (p. 97).   [3] Wither or dry up.

thereby, and then if ye see that it last them longer than three days that they set not their foot to the earth, then slit ye the thigh along and athwart within the thigh, crosswise upon the bone, that is upon the turn bone of the knee behind, and then put thereupon wool wet in olive oil as before is said, for three whole days. And then after anoint the wound with oil without binding as I have said, and he shall heal himself with his tongue. Sometimes a hound is evil astyfled,[1] so that he shall sometime abide half a year or more ere he be well, *and if he be not so tended he will never recover.* Then it needeth that ye let him long sojourn until the time that he be whole, until he is no longer halting, that is that one thigh be no greater than the other. And if he may not be all whole, do to him as men do to a horse that is spauled in the shoulder in front, draw throughout a cord of horsehair[2] and he shall be whole. Sometimes an evil befalls in the ballock purse,[3] sometimes from too long hunting or from long journeys, or from rupture,[4] or sometimes when bitches be jolly, and

[1] Inflammation of the stifle joint.
[2] *Seton.* G. de F. (p. 98) says: "une ortie et un sedel de corde." His word *sedel* came from the Spanish *sedal.* The English "seton" comes from *seta,* a hair, because hair was originally employed as the inserted material.
[3] Testicles.
[4] The following words, which are in Shirley MS. and in G. de F., are left out: "some tyme for they more foundeth as an hors."

they may not come to them at their ease as they would, and that the humours runneth into the ballocks, and sometimes when they be smitten upon in hunting or in other places. To this sickness and to all others in that manner, the best help is for to make a purse of cloth three or four times double, and take linseed and put it within, and put it in a pot, and let it mingle with wien, and let them well boil together, and mix it always with a stick, and when it is well boiled put it within the purse that I spoke of, as hot as the hound may suffer it, and put his ballocks in that purse, and bind it with a band betwixt the thighs above the back, make well fast the ballocks upwards, and leave a hole in the cloth for to put out the tail and his anus, and another hole before for the yerde so that he may scombre and piss and renew that thing once or twice until the time that he be whole. Also it is a well good thing for a man or for a horse that hath this sickness.[1]

[1] The Shirley MS. has the following ending to this chapter: "And God forbid that for (a) little labour or cost of this medicine, man should see his good kind hound perish, that before hath made him so many comfortable disports at divers times in hunting," which is not taken from G. de F.

CHAPTER XIV

OF RUNNING HOUNDS AND OF THEIR NATURE

A RUNNING hound is a kind of hound there be few men that have not seen some of them. Nevertheless I shall devise how a running hound shall be held for good and fair, and also shall I devise of their manners. Of all hues of running hounds, there are some which be good, and some which be bad or evil as of greyhounds. But the best hue of running hounds and most common for to be good, is called brown tan. Also the goodness of running hounds, and of all other kinds of good hounds, cometh of true courage and of the good nature of their good father and of their good mother. And also as touching greyhounds, men may well help to make them good by teaching as by leading them to the wood and to fields, and to be always near them, in making of many good curées when they have done well, and of rating at and beating them when they have done amiss, for they are beasts, and therefore have they need to learn that which men will they should do. A running hound should be well born, and well grown of body, and should have great nostrils and open, and a long snout, but not small, and great lips and well hanging down, and great eyes red or black, and a great forehead and great head, and large ears, well long and well hanging down, broad and near the head, a great neck, and a great breast and great shoulders, and great legs and strong, and not too long, and great feet, round and great claws, and the 'foot a little low, small flanks and long sides, a little pintel not long, small hanging ballocks and well trussed together, a good chine bone and great back, good thighs, and great hind legs and the hocks straight and not bowed, the tail great and high, and not cromping up on the back, but straight and a little cromping upward. Nevertheless I have seen some running hounds with great hairy tails the which were very good. Running hounds hunt in divers manners, for some followeth the hart fast at the first, for they go lightly and fast and when they have run so awhile, they have hied them so fast that they be relaxed and all breathless, and stop still and leave the hart when they should chase him. This kind of running hounds men should find usually in the land of Basco and Spain. They are right good for the wild boar, but are not good for the hart, for they be not good to enchase at a long flight, but only for to press him, for they seek not well, and they run not well nor they hunt not (well) from a distance, for they be accustomed to hunt close.

RACHES OR RUNNING HOUNDS IN THE FIFTEENTH CENTURY

(From MS. f. fr. 616, *Bib. Nat.*, Paris)

No 35

And at the beginning they have shown their best.
Other manners of running hounds there are which
hunt a good deal more slowly and heavily, but as
they begin, so they hold on all the day. These
hounds force not so soon a hart as the other, but
they bring him best by mastery and strength to
his end, for they retrieve and scent the line better
and farther, because they are somewhat slow.
They must hunt the hart from farther off, and
therefore they scent the fues better than the other
that goes so hastily without stopping until the
time that they be weary. A bold hound should
never complain or howl, unless if he were out of
the rights. And also he should again seek the
rights, for a hart flieth and ruseth. Commonly
a bold hound hunteth with the wind when he seeth
his time. He dreads his master and understands
him and does as he bids him. A bold hound
should not leave the hart neither for rain, nor for
heat, nor for cold, nor for any evil weather, but
at this time there be few such, and also should
he hunt the hart well by himself without help of
man, as if the man were always with him. *But alas!
I know not now any such hounds.* Hounds there
are which be bold and brave, and be called bold
for they are bold and good for the hart, for when
the hart comes in danger[1] they will chase him,

---

[1] Danger of his being lost to the hounds.

but they will not open[1] nor quest while he is among the change, for dread to envoyse[2] and do amiss, but when they have dissevered[3] him, then they will open and hunt him and should overcome the hart well, and perfectly and masterfully throughout all the change.   These hounds be not so good nor so perfect as be the bold hounds before said *to most men* for two reasons,[4] that one reason is for they hunt not at men's best pleasure for they hunt nought but the hart, and the first bold hound hunts all manner of beasts that his master will uncouple him to.   He opens always through all the changes, and a bold hound for the hart opens not for the hart, as I have said when the hart is amid the changes.   He dreadeth where he goeth that men see him lest he do amiss or envoise, but men cannot always see him.[5]   Of this kind of hound have I seen many a one.   There be other

---

[1] Challenge—*i.e.* the noise the hounds make on finding the scent of an animal.

[2] Get off the line.

[3] Separated him from the other deer.

[4] From here to the middle of the 13th line on the next page the text is copied from the Shirley MS., the scribe who wrote the Vespasian B. XII. MS. having made a mistake in his transcript, copying on folio 65 the folio 64, which therefore appears twice over, to the exclusion of the matter here copied from the Shirley MS.

[5] This sentence is difficult to understand without consulting G. de F. (p. 110), who says: "as the hound does not challenge when the stag is with change, one does not know where he is going unless one sees him, and one cannot always see him."

kinds of hounds which men *beyond the sea call*
hart hounds, good and restrained hart hounds.[1]
They hunt no other beast but the hart, and therefore they are called hart hounds and bold hounds,
for they be bold and good and wise for the hart ;
they be called restrained, because if the hart fall
among the change they should abide still[2] until
the hunter come, and when they see their master
they make him welcome, and wag their tails upon
him, and will by-piss the way and the bushes,
but in England men make them not so. These be
good hounds *of our land*, but not so good as the
bold hounds aforesaid. They be well wise, for they
know well that they should not hunt the change,
and they are not so wise as to dissever the hart
from the change, for they abide still and restive.
These hounds I hold full good, for the hunter
that knows them may well help them to slay the
hart. None of all these three kinds of hounds
hunt at the hart in rutting time, unless it be the
good bold hound,[3] which is the best of all other
hounds. The best sport that men can have is
running with hounds, for if he hunt at hare or
at the roe or at buck or at the hart, or at any other

---

[1] G. de F. : "cerfs baus restifz" is the name which he gives
these hounds.

[2] G. de F. adds : "and remain quite quiet."

[3] "Le chien baud," G. de F., p. 111. See Appendix : Running Hounds.

beast without greyhound [1] it is a fair thing, and
pleasant to him that loveth them; the seeking
and the finding is also a fair thing, and a great
liking to slay them with strength, and for to see
the wit and the knowledge that God hath given
to good hounds, and for to see good recovering
and retrieving, and the mastery and the subtleties
that be in good hounds. For with greyhounds
and with other kinds of hounds whatever they be,
the sport lasteth not, for anon a good greyhound
or a good alaunte taketh or faileth a beast, and so
do all manner of hounds save running hounds,
the which must hunt all the day questeying and
making great melody in their language and saying
great villainy and chiding the beasts that they
chase.   And therefore I prefer them to all other
kinds of hounds, for they have more virtue it
seems to me than any other beast.   Other kind
of hounds there be the which open and jangle
when they are uncoupled, as well when they be
not in her fues (on their line), and when they
be in her fues they questey [2] too much in seeking
their chase whatever it be, and if they learn the
habit when they are young and are not chastised

[1] The text of the MS. differs from G. de F., who says if one
hunts stags "ou autres bestes en traillant sans limier" (drawing
from them without having first harboured them with a lymer),
and does not say "without greyhounds"; p. 111.

[2] G. de F. has here: "Ils crient trop en quérant leur beste
quelle que soit," p. 111.

thereof, they will evermore be noisy and wild, and namely when they seek their chase, for when the chase is found, the hounds cannot questey too much so that they be in the fues.[1] And to rente and make hounds there are many remedies. *There be also many kinds of running hounds, some small and some big, and the small be called kenets, and these hounds run well to all manner of game, and they (that) serve for all game men call them harriers.*[2] *And every hound that hath that courage will come to be a harrier by nature with little making. But they need great nature and making in youth, and great labour to make a hound run boldly to a chase where there is great change, or other chases.* Hounds which are not perfectly wise take the change commonly from May until St. John's tide (June 24th), for then they find the change of hinds. The hinds will not fly far before the hounds, but they turn about and the hound sees them very. often, and therefore they run to them with a better will, because they keep near their calves the which cannot fly, therefore they hunt them gladly ; and commonly when the harts go to rut, hounds hunt the change, for the harts and the hinds be commonly standing in herds together, and so they

---

[1] "The hounds cannot challenge too loudly when they are on the line." G. de F.: "Chien ne peut trop crier," p. 112.

[2] From Mid. Eng. *harien, harren*, to harry or worry game. See Appendix : Harrier.

find them and run to them sooner than at any
other time of the year. Also the hounds scent
worse from May until St. John's time than in
any other time of all the year, for as I shall say
the burnt heath and the burning of fields taketh
away the scent from the hounds of the beasts that
they hunt. Also in that time the herbs be best
and flowers in their smelling, each one in their
kind, and when the hounds hope to scent the beast
that they hunt, the sweet-smelling of the herbs
takes the scent of the beast from them.

CHAPTER XV

THE greyhound is a kind of hound there be few which have not seen some. Nevertheless for to devise how a greyhound should be held for good and fair, I shall devise their manner. Of all manner of greyhounds there be both good and bad, nevertheless the best hue is red fallow with a black muzzle. The goodness of greyhounds comes of right courage, and of the good nature of their father and their mother. And also men may well help to make them good in the encharning [1] of them with other good greyhounds, and feed them well with the best that he taketh. The good greyhound should be of middle size, neither too big nor too little, and then he is good for all beasts. If he were too big he is nought for small beasts, and if he were too little he were nought for the great beasts. Nevertheless whoso can maintain both, it is good that he have both of the great and of the small, and of the middle size. A greyhound should have a long head and some-

---

[1] Encharning, feed with the flesh of game, to blood.

H

what large made, resembling the making of a bace[1] (pike). A good large mouth and good seizers the one against the other, so that the nether jaw pass not the upper, nor that the upper pass not the nether.   Their eyes are red or black as those of a sparrow hawk, the ears small and high in the manner of a serpent, the neck great and long bowed like a swan's neck, his chest great and open, the hair under his chyn hanging down in the manner of a lion.[2]   His shoulders as a roebuck, the forelegs straight and great enough and not too high in the legs, the feet straight and round as a cat, great claws, long head as a cow[3] hanging down.

The bones and the joints of the chine great and hard like the chine of a hart. And if his chine be a little high it is better than if it were flat. A little pintel and little ballocks, and well trussed near the ars, small womb,[4] the hocks straight and not bent as of an ox, a cat's tail

[1] Should be "luce," and G. de F. has "luz," from Lat. *lucius,* pike, p. 103.

[2] G. de F., p. 104, says : "La harpe bien avalée en guise de lion," *harpe* meaning in this instance "flanks."

[3] "Long head as a cow" is evidently a mistake of translator or scribe. G. de F. has : "le costé lonc comme une biche et bien avalé" ("the sides long as a hind, and hanging down well").

[4] The following words should be added here, a line having been omitted by the scribe : "and straight near the back as a lamprey, the thighs great and straight as a hare." They are in Shirley MS. and G. de F., p. 104.

en aide a le trauuter a la ville.
er toir de pou de temps, ou ils
nicuquent les odours a s bou
droit. et auſi gar tour ils losti
et leur maſtir. et ſont tous
pour la chaſe des ours et des
ſangliers. ou ſoit auec leurer
auſ int. ou ſoit auec chiens
courant auec ding tiém les
ſors. car quant vu ſangler
eſt eu vnſort pays, la le tour
le tour par auctrour ne vild
tour pour les chiens courant.

er quant on gert relle maſti
naille. ou ils prcirent en
iui les fort. et le tout auec a
auant louraut. ou ils li ſont
vadier le pays quil ne deuoz
in guirs longuement aur
abau. et auſi ſont ils tous
pour trauurier de nuig. ſi com
ire le duroy quant re pleuim
du teneur.

Cp apres deuiſt du leurter et de tourr ſa nature.

THE SMOOTH AND THE ROUGH-COATED GREYHOUNDS

(From MS. f. fr. 616, *Bib. Nat.*, Paris)

making a ring at the end and not too high, the
two bones of the chine behind broad of a large
palm's breadth or more.   Also there are many
good greyhounds with long tails right swift.   A
good greyhound should go so fast that if he be
well slipped he should overtake any beast, and
there where he overtakes it he should seize it
where he can get at it the soonest, *nevertheless he
shall last longer if he bite in front or by the side.*[1]
He should be courteous and not too fierce,
following well his master and doing whatever he
command him.   He shall be good and kindly
and clean, glad and joyful and playful, well will-
ing and goodly to all manner of folks save to the
wild beasts to whom he should be fierce, spiteful
and eager.

[1] In lieu of this original passage G. de F., p. 105, has : "sans
abayer, et sans marchander" ("without baying or bargaining").

CHAPTER XVI

OF ALAUNTES AND OF THEIR NATURE

AN alaunte is of the manner and nature of hounds.
And the good alauntes be those which men call
alauntes gentle. Others there be that men call
alauntes veutreres, others be alauntes of the
butcheries. They that be gentle should be made
and shaped as a greyhound, even of all things save
of the head, the which should be great and short.
And though there be alauntes of all hues, the true
hue of a good alaunte, and that which is most
common should be white with black spots about
the ears, small eyes and white standing ears and
sharp above. Men should teach[1] alauntes better,
and to be of better custom than any other beasts,
for he is better shaped and stronger for to do
harm than any other beast. And also commonly
alauntes are stordy [1] (giddy) of their own nature
and have not such good sense as many other
hounds have, for if a man prick [2] a horse the

---

[1] G. de F. has "estourdiz," which the "Master of Game"
translates as "stordy" or sturdy, but the modern sense would
be hairbrained, giddy, not sturdy.

[2] Means *chase* a horse. G. de F. says: "Se on court un
cheval, ils le prennent voulentiers," p. 100.

alauntes will run gladly and bite the horse.   Also
they run at oxen and sheep, and swine, and at all
other beasts, or at men or at other hounds.   For
men have seen alauntes slay their masters.   In
all manner of ways alauntes are treacherous and
evil understanding, and more foolish and more
harebrained than any other kind of hound.   And
no one ever saw three well conditioned and good.
For the good alaunte should run as fast as a greyhound, and any beast that he can catch he should
hold with his seizers and not leave it.   For an
alaunte of his nature holds faster of his biting
than can three greyhounds the best any man can
find.   And therefore it is the best hound to hold
and to nyme (seize) all manner of beasts and hold
them fast.   And when he is well conditioned and
perfect, men hold that he is good among all
other hounds.   But men find few that be perfect.
A good alaunte should love his master and follow
him, and help him in all cases, and do what his
master commands him.   A good alaunte should
go fast and be hardy to take all kinds of beasts
without turning, and hold fast and not leave it,
and be well conditioned, and well at his master's
command, and when he is such, men hold, as I have
said, that he is the best hound that can be to take
all manner of beasts.   That other kind of alaunte is
called veutreres.   They are almost shaped as a
greyhound of full shape, they have a great head,

great lips and great ears, and with such men help
themselves at *the baiting of the bull* and at hunting
of a wild boar, for it is their nature to hold fast,
but they be (heavy) and foul (ugly) that if they be
slain by the wild boar or by the bull, it is not very
great loss.   And when they can overtake a beast
they bite it and hold it still, but by themselves
they could never take a beast unless greyhounds
were with them to make the beast tarry.   That
other kind of alauntes of the butcheries is such as
you may always see in good towns, *that are called
great butchers' hounds*, the which the butchers keep
to help them to bring their beasts that they buy in
the country, for if an ox escape from the butchers
that lead him, his hounds would go and take him
and hold him until his master has come, and
should help him to bring him again to the town.
They cost little to keep as they eat the foul things
in the butcher's row.   Also they keep their master's
house, they be good *for bull baiting* and for hunting wild boar, whether it be with greyhounds at
the tryst or with running hounds at bay within the
covert.   For when a wild boar is within a strong
hatte of wood (thicket), perhaps all day the running
hounds will not make him come out.   And when
men let such mastiffs run at the boar they take
him in the thick spires (wood) so that any man
can slay him, or they make him come out of his
strength, so that he shall not remain long at bay.

CHAPTER XVII

OF SPANIELS AND OF THEIR NATURE

ANOTHER kind of hound there is that be called hounds for the hawk and spaniels, for their kind cometh from Spain, notwithstanding that there are many in other countries. And such hounds have many good customs and evil. Also a fair hound for the hawk should have a great head, a great body and be of fair hue, white or tawny, for they be the fairest, and of such hue they be commonly best. A good spaniel should not be too rough, but his tail should be rough. The good qualities that such hounds have are these : they love well their masters and follow them without losing, although they be in a great crowd of men, and commonly they go before their master, running and wagging their tail, and raise or start fowl and wild beasts. But their right craft is of the partridge and of the quail. It is a good thing to a man that hath a noble goshawk or a tiercel or a sparrow hawk for partridge, to have such hounds. And also when they be

taught to be couchers,[1] they be good to take
partridges and quail with a net. And also they
be good when they are taught to swim and to be
good for the river, and for fowls when they have
dived, but on the other hand they have many
bad qualities like the country that they come
from. For a country draweth to two natures of
men, of beasts, and of fowls, and as men call
greyhounds *of Scotland* and of Britain,[2] so the
alauntes and the hounds for the hawk come out
of Spain, and they take after the nature of the
generation of which they come. Hounds for
the hawk are fighters and great barkers if you
lead them a hunting among running hounds,
whatever beasts they hunt to they will make
them lose the line, for they will go before now
hither now thither, as much when they are at
fault as when they go right, and lead the hounds
about and make them overshoot and fail. Also
if you lead greyhounds with you, and there be a
hound for the hawk, that is to say a spaniel, if he
see geese or kine, or horses, or hens, or oxen or
other beasts, he will run anon and begin to bark
at them, and because of him all the greyhounds
will run to take the beast through his egging on,

---

[1] Setters, from *coucher*, to lie down. G. de F.: "chien
couchant" (p. 113).

[2] Brittany. In Shirley MS. "England" precedes "Scotland."
G. de F. says nothing about Scotland. He says "Bretainhe,"
meaning Brittany (p. 113).

for he will make all the riot and all the harm.
The hounds for the hawk have so many other evil
habits that unless I had a goshawk or falcon or
hawks for the river, or sparrow hawk, or the net,
I would never have any, *especially there where I
would hunt.*

CHAPTER XVIII

OF THE MASTIFF AND OF HIS NATURE

A MASTIFF is a manner of hound. The mastiff's nature and his office is to keep his master's beasts and his master's house, and it is a good kind of hound, for they keep and defend with all their power all their master's goods. They be of a churlish nature and ugly shape. Nevertheless there are some *that come to be berslettis,*[1] *and also to bring well and fast and wanlace* (range) *about.*[2] Sometimes there be many good, especially for men who hunt for profit of the household to get flesh. Also of mastiffs and alaunts there be (bred) many good for the wild boar. Also from mastiffs and hounds for the hawk (there be bred) hounds that men should not make much mention of, therefore I will no more speak of them, for there is no great mastery nor great readiness in the hunting that they do, *for their nature is not to be tenderly nosed.*

[1] Bercellettis or bercelettes, hounds, most likely shooting dogs, from *berser,* to shoot, *bercel,* an archer's butt.
[2] *Wanlasour,* one who drives game. Appendix: Wanlace.

THE FIVE BREEDS OF HOUNDS DESCRIBED IN THE TEXT

(From MS. f. fr. 616, *Bib. Nat.*, Paris)

CHAPTER XIX

WHAT MANNER AND CONDITION A GOOD HUNTER SHOULD HAVE.

THOU, Sir, whatever you be, great or little, that would teach a man to be a good hunter, first he must be a child past seven or eight years of age or little older, and if any man would say that I take a child in too tender age for to put him to work, I answer that all nature shortens and descends. For every man knoweth well that a child of seven years of age is more capable in these times of such things that he liketh to learn than was a child of twelve years of age (in times that I have seen). And therefore I put him so young thereto, for a craft requires all a man's life ere he be perfect thereof. And also men say that which a man learns in youth he will hold best in his age. And furthermore from this child many things are required, first that he love his master, and that his heart and his business be with the hounds, and he must take[1] him, and beat him when he will not do what his master commands

---

[1] "Take" is probably the scribe's mistake for "tache," teach.

him, until the time that the child dreads to fail.
And first I shall take and teach him for to take in
writing all the names of the hounds and of the
hues of the hounds, until the time that the child
knoweth them both by the hue and by the name.
After I will teach him to make clean every day
in the morning the hounds' kennel of all foul
things. After I will learn him to put before them
twice a day fresh water and clean, from a well, in
a vessel there where the hound drinks, or fair
running water, in the morning and the evening.
After I will teach him that once in the day he empty
the kennel and make all clean, and renew their
straw, and put again fresh new straw a great deal
and right thick. And there where he layeth it the
hounds should lie, and the place where they should
lie should be made of trees a foot high from the
earth, and then straw should be laid thereupon,
because the moisture of the earth should not make
them morfounder nor engender other sicknesses
by the which they might be worse for hunting.
Also that he be both *at field and at wood delivered*
(active) *and well eyed and well advised of his speech
and of his terms, and ever glad to learn and that he
be no boaster nor jangler.*

CHAPTER XX

HOW THE KENNEL FOR THE HOUNDS AND THE COUPLES FOR THE RACHES AND THE ROPES FOR THE LYMER SHOULD BE MADE

THE hounds' kennel should be ten fathoms in length and five in breadth, if there be many hounds. And there should be one door in front and one behind, and a fair green, where the sun shineth all day from morning till eve, and that green should be closed about with a paling or with a wall of earth or of stone of the same length and breadth as the hounds' kennel is. And the hinder door of the kennel should always be open so that the hounds may go out to play when they like, for it is a great liking to the hounds when they may go in and out at their pleasure, for the mange comes to them later.[1] In the kennel should be pitched small stones wrapped about with straw of the hounds' litter, unto the number of six stones, that the hounds might piss against them. Also a kennel should have a gutter or two whereby all the piss of the hounds and all the other

---

[1] They are not likely to get the mange so soon.

water may run out that none remains in the kennel. The kennel should also be in a low house, and not in a solere (an upper chamber), but there should be a loft above, so that it might be warmer in winter and cooler in summer, and always by night and by day I would that some child lie or be in the kennel with the hounds to keep them from fighting.   Also in the kennel should be a chimney to warm the hounds when they are cold or when they are wet with rain or from passing and swimming over rivers.   And also he should be taught to spin horse hair to make couples for the hounds, which should be made of a horse tail or a mare's tail, for they are best and last longer than if they were of hemp or of wool.   And the length of the hounds' couples between the hounds should be a foot, and the rope of a limer three fathoms and a half, be he ever so wise a limer it sufficeth. *The which rope should be made of leather of a horse skin well tawed.*

Cy deuise du chenil ou les chiens doiuent demourer et comment il doit estre fait.

Le chenil doit estre grant de vingt toises de long. et cinq de large. se il a grant foyson de chiens. et doit auoir vne porte deuant et au ne derrier. Et doit auoir ier deuant vn biau plael. ou quel le chiel se voye tout le iour. les qui le tiend usques a mont quil se couchra. Et cellup plael doit estre cuilloy

ne le palnisse ou la touoier ouuiur. sautant et long et le large comme le chenil. et doit estre la porte deuant toulsiours ouuerte. asin que les chiens puissent aler a tous estenc! trs le plael quant leur plaura. car trop chaut quant bien a chiel quant ils puclient aler detang et tous la ou leur plaist. et plus rart en sont uigneur. et doit auoir ou chenil pres enduns

THE KENNEL AND KENNELMEN

(From MS. f. fr. 616, *Bib. Nat.*, Paris)

CHAPTER XXI

HOW THE HOUNDS SHOULD BE LED OUT TO SCOMBRE

ALSO I will teach [1] the child to lead out the hounds to scombre twice in the day in the morning and in the evening, so that the sun be up, especially in winter. Then should he let them run and play long in a fair meadow in the sun, and then comb every hound after the other, and wipe them with a great wisp of straw, and thus he shall do every morning. And then shall he lead them into some fair place there where tender grass grows as corn and other things, that therewith they may feed them (selves) as it is medicine for them, for sometimes hounds are sick and with the grass that they eat they void and heal themselves.

[1] The first four words are omitted in our MS., but they are in the Shirley MS. and in others, and in G. de F.

CHAPTER XXII

HOW A HUNTER'S HORN SHOULD BE DRIVEN

There are divers kinds of horns, that is to say bugles, great Abbot's, hunter's horns, Ruets (trumpets), small Forester's horns and meaner horns of two kinds. That one kind is waxed with green wax and greater of sound, and they be best for good hunters, therefore will I devise how and in what fashion they should be driven. First a good hunter's horn should be driven of two spans in length, and not much more nor much less, and not too crooked neither too straight, but that the flue be three or four fingers uppermore than the head, that unlearned [1] *hunters call the great end of the horn. And also that it be as great and hollow driven as it can for the length, and that it be shorter on the side of the baldric* [2] *than at the nether end. And that the head be as wide as it can be, and always driven smaller and smaller to the flue, and that it be well waxed thicker or thinner according as the hunter thinks that it will sound best. And that it be the*

---

[1] Shirley MS.: "lewed," *i.e.* laewed or unlearned (Stratmann).

[2] Baldric, the belt on which the horn was carried.

*length of the horn from the flue to the binding, and
also that it be not too small driven from the binding
to the flue, for if it be the horn will be too mean of
sound. As for horns for fewterers[1] and woodmen,
I speak not for every small horn and other mean
horn unwaxed be good enough for them.*

[1] Fewterer, the man who held the greyhounds in slips or
couples.

I

CHAPTER XXIII

HOW A MAN SHOULD LEAD HIS GROOM IN QUEST FOR TO KNOW A HART BY HIS TRACE

THEN should his groom lead his lymer (tracking hound) in quest after him in the morning, and teach him to know what difference is between a hart's trace and a hind's. *As I have said before, this word quest is a term of hart hunters beyond the sea, and is as much for to say as when the hunter goeth to find of a hart and to harbour him.* For to know a great hart's trace from a young, and to know the trace of a young deer of antler from a hind's, and how many judgments and what knowledge there be, and for to make more certain thereof, he should have an old hart's foot and a young hart's and a hind's foot also, and should put it in hard earth and in soft, and once put it fast in the earth as though the hart were hunted and another time soft, as if the hart went a pase (slowly), thereby he may advise him to know the differences of a hart's feet, and he shall find that there is no deer so young if he be from a brocket upwards, that his talon (heel) is not larger and better and hath greater ergots (dew claws) than

THE MASTER TEACHING HIS HUNTSMAN HOW TO QUEST FOR
THE HART WITH THE LIMER OR TRACKHOUND

(From MS. f. fr. 616, *Bib. Nat.*, Paris)

hath a hind, and commonly longer traces. Nevertheless there are some hounds well traced, which
have the sole of the foot as a staggard or a small
stag, but the talon and the ergots are not so great
nor so large. Also a great hart and an old one
has a better sole to his foot, and a better talon
and better bones and greater and larger than has
a young deer or hind. And so in putting in the
earth the hart's foot and the hind's foot as I have
said, he shall know the difference and better than
I can devise. And also the hinds commonly have
their traces more hollow than a staggard or a stag,
and more open the cleeves (toes) in front than
a hart of ten, for of the others reck I never.
The judgment is in the talon (when it is great
and large; and in the sole of the foot)[1] when it
is great and broad, and the point of the foot
broad. And men have seen a great hart and an
old one, the which had hollow traces, and that
cannot matter so that he hath the other signs
before said. For a hollow trace and sharp cleeves
betoken no other thing than that the country the
hart hath haunted is a soft country or hard, and
where there be but few stones, or that he has been
hunted but little. And also if a man find such a
hart, and men ask him what hart it is, he may answer

[1] The words in brackets have been omitted in our MS. but
are in the Shirley MS. and G. de F. p. 129; they have been
thus inserted to complete the sense.

that it is a hart chaceable of ten, that should not
be refused.   And if he sees an hart's foot that
hath these signs aforesaid the which are great and
broad, he may say that it is an hart that some
time had borne ten tines, and if he see that the
aforesaid signs are greater and broader he may
say that it is a great hart and an old (one), and
this is all he may say of the hart.   Also he should
call the foot of the hart the trace, and of the
wild boar also.   *Also the hunters of beyond the sea*
call of an hart and of a boar the routes and
the pace (path) and both is one.   Nevertheless
pace, they call their goings where a beast goes
in the routes, there where he has passed, *nevertheless I would not set this in my book, but for
as much as I would English hunters should know
some of the terms that hunters use beyond the sea,
but not with intent to call them so in England.*

CHAPTER XXIV

HOW A MAN SHOULD KNOW A GREAT HART BY THE FUMES [1]

AFTER I shall teach you to know a great hart by the fumes of the hart, for sometimes they crotey in wreaths, and sometimes flat and sometimes formed, and sometimes sharp at both ends, and sometimes pressed together, and sometime in many other manners as I have said before. When they crotey flat and it be in April or in May or in June if the croteyes be great and thick it is a token that it is a hart chaceable, and if he find the fumes wreathed, and it be from the middle of June to the middle of August in great forms and in great wreaths and well soft, it is a token that it is a hart chaceable, and if he find the fumes that are formed and not holding together as it is from the beginning of July into the end of August, if they are great and black and long and are not sharp at the ends, and are heavy and dry without slime, it is a token that it is a hart chaceable. And if the fumes are faint and light and

---

[1] See Appendix: Excrements.

full of slime, or sharp at both ends, or at one end, these are the tokens that he is no deer chaceable. But if it be when they burnish that they crotey their fumes more burnt and more sharp at the one end, but anon when they have burnished, they crotey their fumes as before, and for that the fumes be good and great; if they be slimy it is a token that he has suffered some disease. From the end of August forward, the fumes are of no judgment for they undo themselves for the rut.

HOW A GREAT HART IS TO BE KNOWN BY HIS "FUMES"

(EXCREMENTS)

(From MS. f. fr. 616, *Bib. Nat.*, Paris)

III.

CHAPTER XXV

HOW A MAN SHOULD KNOW A GREAT HART BY THE PLACE WHERE HE HATH FRAYED HIS HEAD

FURTHERMORE ye should know a great hart by the fraying (for if ye find where the hart hath frayed),[1] and see that the wood is great where he hath frayed, and he hath not bent it, and the tree is frayed well high, and he hath frayed the bark away, and broken the branches and wreathed them a good height, and if the branches are of a good size, it is a sign that he is a great hart and that he should bear a high head and well troched, for by the troching[2] he breaketh such high the boughs that he cannot fold them under him. For if the fraying were bare and he had frayed the boughs under him, it is no token that it be a great hart, and especially if the trees where he had frayed were small. Nevertheless men have seen some great deer fray sometimes to a little tree, but not commonly, but a young deer shall

---

[1] The words in brackets are omitted in our MS. but are in the Shirley MS. and in G. de F. p. 132.
[2] The tines at top. See Appendix: Antler.

ever more [1] fray to a great tree, and therefore
should ye look at several frayings. And if ye
see the aforesaid tokens oftener upon the great
trees than upon the small ye may deem him a
great hart. And if the frayings be continually
in small trees and low, he is not chaceable and
should be refused. Also ye may know a great
hart by his lairs. When a great hart shall come
in the morning from his pasture, he shall go to
his lair and then a great while after he shall rise
and go elsewhere there where he would abide all
the day. Then when ye shall rise and come to
the lair there where the hart hath lain and rested,
if ye see it great and broad and well trodden and
the grass well pressed down, and at the rising
when he passeth out of his lair, if ye see that the
foot and the knees have well thrust down the
earth and pressed the grass down it is a token
that it is a great deer and a heavy (one). And if
at the rising he make no such tokens, because
that he hath been there but a little while, so that
his lair be long and broad ye may deem him a hart
chaceable. Also ye may know a great hart by the
bearing of the wood, for when a great hart hath
a high head and a large (one) and goeth through
a thick wood, he findeth the young wood and

---

[1] Ever more is here a mistake ; it should be never more.
G. de F. says : "Mes jeune cerf ne froyera jà en gros arbre"
(p. 132). Also in the Shirley MS.

tender boughs, his head is harder than the wood, then he breaketh the wood aside and mingleth the boughs one upon the other, for he beareth them and putteth them otherwise than they were wont to be by their own kind. And when the glades of the woods are high and broad then he may deem him a great hart, for if he had not a high head and wide he could not make his ways high and large. If it happen so that ye find such glades and have no lymer with you, if ye will know at what time this glade was made, ye must set your visage in the middle of this glade, and keep your breath, in the best wise that ye may, and if ye find that the spider hath made her web in the middle of them, it is a token that it is of no good time [1] or at the least it is of the middle (of the noon) of the day before. Nevertheless ye should fetch your lymer for so ye should know better. Also ye may know a great hart by the steps *that in England is called trace.* And that is called stepping,[2] when he steppeth in a place where the grass is well thick, so that the man may not see therein the form of the foot, or when he steppeth in other places, where no grass is but dust or sand and hard country, where fallen leaves or other things hinder to see the

---

[1] Not of "good time" means in the old sporting vocabulary an old track, not a recent one.

[2] G. de F. calls the track of deer on grass "*foulées*," from which the modern "foil," "stepping on grass," is derived.

form of the foot.   And when the hart steppeth
upon the grass and ye cannot see the stepping with
your eyes, then ye shall put your hand in the
form of the foot that hunters call the trace, and
if ye see that the form of the foot be of four
fingers of breadth, ye may judge that it is a great
hart by the trace.   And if the sole of the foot be
of three fingers' breadth ye may judge him a hart
of ten, and if ye see that he hath well broken
the earth and trodden well the grass, it is a token
that it is a great hart and a heavy deer.   And if
ye cannot well see it for the hardness of the
earth, or for the dust, then ye must stoop down
for to take away the dust and blow it away from
the form of the foot until the time that ye may
clearly see the form that is called the trace.   And
if ye cannot see it in one place, ye should follow
the trace until the time that ye can well see it at
your ease.   And if ye can see none in any place,
ye should put your hand in the form of the foot,
for then ye shall find how the earth is broke with
the cleeves of the foot on either side, and then ye
can judge it for a great hart or a hart chaceable,
as I have said before by the treading of the grass ;
and if leaves or other things be within the form
that ye may not see at your ease, ye should take
away the leaves all softly or the other things with
your hands, so that ye undo not the form of the
foot and blow within and do the other things as I

háve before said.[1] (After I will tell you how a
man shall speak among good hunters of the office
of venery.) First he shall speak but a little, and
boast little, and well (work [2]) and subtlely, and he
must be wise and do his craft busily, for a hunter
should not be a herald of his craft. And if it
happen that he be among good hunters that
speaketh of hunting he should speak in this
manner. First if men ask him of pastures he
may answer as of harts and for all other deer,
sweet pastures, and of all biting beasts as of wild
boar, wolves, and other biting beasts he may
answer, they feed, as I have said before. And if
men speak of the fumes ye shall call fumes of a
hart, *croteying* of a buck, and of a roebuck in the
same wise of a wild boar and of black beasts and
of wolves ye shall call it lesses, and of hare and
of conies ye shall say they crotey, of the fox
wagging, of the grey the *wardrobe*, and of other
stinking beasts they shall call it drit, and that of
the otter he shall call sprainting as before is said.
And if men asketh of the beasts' feet, of the harts
ye shall say the trace of a hart *and also of a buck*,
and that of the wild boar and of the wolf also

---

[1] A whole line is missing here in our MS. The words in
brackets are taken from the Shirley MS. It runs : "Affter I
wal telle yowe a man howe he shal speke amonge good hunters
of y offyce of venerye."
[2] The word "work" has been omitted. "Et bien *ouvrer*
subtilement" (G. de F. p. 134).

they call traces *beyond the sea.* And that of the
stinking beasts that men call vermin, he shall call
them steps as I have said. And if he hath seen a
hart with his eyes, there are three kinds of hues
of them, that one is called brown, the other
yellow, and the third dun, and so he may call
them as he thinketh that they beareth all their
hues. And if men ask what head beareth the
hart he hath seen, he shall always answer by even
and not by odd, *for if he be forked on the right side,
and lack not of his rights [1] beneath, and on the
right [2] side antler and royal and surroyal and not
forked but only the beam, he shall say it is a hart
of ten at default,[3]* for it is always called even of
the greater number. And every buck's tines
should be reckoned as soon as a man can hang a
baldric or a leash [4] thereupon and not otherwise.
And when a hart beareth as many tines on the
one side as on the other, *he may say if he be but
forked that he is a hart of ten, and if he be troched
of three he is a hart of twelve, if he be troched of
four he is a hart of sixteen, always if it be seen
that he hath his rights beneath as before is said.
And if he lack any of his rights beneath he must*

---

[1] Brow, bay, and tray tines. See Appendix : Antler.
[2] In Shirley MS. it is "left."
[3] Instead of this original passage G. de F. says : "For if he
had on one side ten points and on the other only one, it should
be called summed of twenty" (p. 135).
[4] G. de F. has "spur" instead.

abate so many on the top, for a hart's head should begin to be described from the mule [1] *upwards, and if he hath more by two on the one side than on the other, you must take from the one and count up that other withal, as I shall more clearly speak in a chapter hereafter in describing a hart's head.* And if it be so that the hart's trace have other tokens than I have said and he thinks him a hart chaceable, and men ask what hart it is he may say it is a hart of ten and no more. And if it seem to him a great hart and men ask what hart it is, he shall say it is a hart that the last year was of ten and should not be refused. And if he happen to have well seen him with his eye or the before said tokens, so that he knoweth fully that it is as great a hart as a hart may be, if men ask him what hart it is, he may say it is a great hart and an old deer. And that is the greatest word that he may say as I have said before. And if men ask him whereby he knoweth it, he may say for, he hath good bones [2] and a good talon and a good sole of foot, *for these four* [3] *things makes the trace great,* or by fair lairs or the grass or the earth well pressed or by the high head, [4] or by the fumes or

---

[1] Burr, mule, from the Fr. *meule*.   [2] Dew claws.

[3] According to Shirley MS. and the sense, the "iiii" should be omitted.

[4] G. de F. (p. 136) says : "Ou belles portées"—portées being the branches, and twigs broken or bent asunder by the head of the deer, termed "entry" or "rack" in mod. Eng.—Stuart, vol. ii. 551.

else other tokens as I have said before. And if he see a hart that hath a well affected (fashioned) head after the height and the shape and the tines well ranged by good measure, the one from the other, and men ask him what he beareth he may answer that he beareth a great head and fair of beam, and of all his rights, and well opened ; and if a man ask him what head he beareth, he shall answer that he beareth a fair head by all tokens and well grown. And if he see a hart that hath a low head or a high, or a great, or a small, and it be thick set, high and low and men ask him what head he beareth he may answer he bears a thick set head after his making, or that he hath low or small or other manner whatever it be. And if he see a hart that hath a diverse head, or that antlers grow back or that the head hath double beams or other diversities than other harts commonly be wont to bear, and men ask what head he bears, he may answer a diverse head or a counterfeit (abnormal), for it is counterfeited. And if he see a hart that beareth a high head that is wide and thin tined with long beams, if men ask what head he beareth, he shall answer a fair head and wide, and long beams, but it is not thick set neither well affeted. And if he see a hart that hath a low and a great and a thick set (head) and men ask what head he beareth, he may say he beareth a fair head and well affeted.

And if men ask him by the head whereby he
knoweth that it is a great hart and an old, he may
answer, that the tokens of the great hart are by
the head, and so the first knowledge is when he
hath great beams all about as if they were set as
it were with small stones, and the mules nigh the
head and the antlers, the which are the first tines,
be great and long and close to the mule and well
apperyng (pearled) and the royals which are the
second tines, be nigh the antlers, and of such
form, save that they should not be so great; and
all the other tines great and long and well set,
and well ranged and the troching as I have said
before, high and great, and all the beams all along
both great and stony, as if they were full of
gravel, and that all along the beams there be small
vales that men call gutters, then he may say that
he knows it is a great hart by the head.

After I will tell you how ye should know a
great wild boar, and for to know how to speak
of it among hunters of beyond the sea.   And if a
man see a wild boar the which seemeth to him
great enough, as men say of the hart chaceable of
ten, he shall say a wild boar of the third year
that is without refusal, and whenever they be not
of three years men call them swine of the sounder,
and if he see the great tokens that I shall rehearse
hereafter he may say that he is a great boar.   Of
the season and nature of boar and of other beasts,

I have spoken here before. And if men ask him
of a boar's feeding, it is properly called of acorns
of oak's bearing, and of beechmast, the other
feeding is called worming and rooting of the roots
out of the earth that feed him. The other kind
of feeding is of corn and of other things that
come up out of the land, and of flowers and of
other herbs; the other kind of feeding is when
they make great pits, and go to seek the root
of ferns and of spurge within the earth. And if
men ask whereby he knoweth a great boar, he shall
answer that he knoweth him by the traces and by
his den, and by the soil (wallowing pool). And
if men ask whereby he knoweth a great boar from
a young, and the boar from the sow, he shall
answer that a great boar should have long traces
and the clees round in front, and broad soles of
the feet and a good talon, and long bones, and
when he steppeth it goeth into the earth deep
and maketh great holes and large, and long
the one from the other, for commonly a man
shall not see the traces of a . boar without
seeing also the traces of the bones, and so
shall he not of the hart, for a man shall see many
times by the foot, that which he will not see by
the ergots, but so shall he not see of the boar.
What I call the bones of the boar, of the hart I
call the ergots, and the cause that a man shall
not know as well by the ergots of the hart as

by bones of the boar is this, for the bones of
the boar are nearer the talon than those of a
hart are, and also they are longer, and greater
and sharper in front.   And therefore as soon as
the form of the traces of his foot is in the earth,
the form of the bones is there also, and commonly
a great boar maketh a longer trace with one of his
claws than with the other in front or behind, and
sometimes both.   And when a man seeth the
tokens beforesaid greater, he may deem him
greater, and the smaller the trace, the smaller
the boar. ´The sow from the boar ye may know
well, for the sow maketh not so good a talon as
a right young boar doth.   And also a sow's
claws are longer and sharper in front than a
young boar's.   And also her traces are more
open in front and straighter behind, and the sole
of the foot is not so large as of a young boar, and
her bones are not so large nor so long, nor so far
the one from the other as those of a young boar,
nor go not so deep in the earth, for they be
small, and sharp and short, and nearer the one to
the other, than a young boar's.   And these are the
tokens by the which men know a young boar so
that he be two year old from all sows, by the trace,
for that say I not of the young boars of sounder.
And if men ask him how he shall know a great
boar by his den, he may answer that if the den of
the boar be long and deep and broad, it is a token

K

that it is a great boar so that the den be newly
made and that he hath lain therein but once. And
if the boar's den is deep without litter, and if the
boar lie near the earth it is a token that it is no[1]
fat boar. And if men ask him how he knoweth
a great boar by the soil, then may he answer that
commonly when a boar goeth to soil in the coming
in or in the going out, men may know by the trace,
and so it may be deemed as I have said by his
wallowing in the soil. Nevertheless some time he
turneth himself from the one side upon the other,
and up and down, but a man shall evermore know
the form of his body. Also sometimes when the
boar parteth from the soil, he rubbeth against a
tree, and there a man may know his greatness
and his height. And some time he rubs his snout
and his head higher than he is, but a man may
well perceive which is of the chine and which is
of the head. For by his lesses, that is to say what
goes from him behind, nor by other judgment a
man cannot know a great boar unless he see him,
save that he maketh great lesses, and that is a
token that he hath a great bowel, and that he be
a great boar, and also by the tusks when he is
dead, for when the tusks of a boar be great as
of half a cubit or more and be both great and

---

[1] G. de F. (p. 139) says if "le senglier gise près de la terre,
c'est signe qu'il ait bonne venoison," so our MS. is evidently
wrong when it says "it is a token that it is *no* fat boar."

large of two fingers or more and there be small gutters along both above and beneath, these be the tokens that he is a great boar and old, and of a smaller boar the judgment is less. And also when the tusks be low and worn, by the nether tusks it is a token of a great boar.

CHAPTER XXVI

HOW THE ORDINANCE SHOULD BE MADE FOR THE HART HUNTING BY STRENGTH AND HOW THE HART SHOULD BE HARBOURED

WHEN the king or my lord the Prince or any of their blood will hunt for the hart by strength, the Master of the Game must forewarn on the previous evening the sergeant of the office, and the yeomen berners at horse, and also the lymerer.[1] *And then he must ordain which of them three shall go for to harbour the hart, and with them the lymerer for the morrow, and charge the foresters, or if it be in a park, the parkers to attend to him busily. And all the four must accord where the meeting shall be on the morrow, and he must charge the sergeant and one of the two yeomen, if the sergeant be not there, to warn all the yeomen and grooms of the office to be at the meeting at sunrise. And that the yeomen berners on foot and the grooms that are called Chacechiens bring with them the hart hounds and this done ask for the wine, and let them go after. And he that is charged to harbour the hart must*

[1] The man who leads the hound in leash when harbouring the hart.

*accord with the forester of the bailie in which they
seek him where they should meet in the grey dawning. Nevertheless it were good readiness to look if
they might see any deer at its meating (feeding) the
previous evening to know the more readily where to
seek and harbour him on the morrow. And on the
morrow when they meet the forester that well ought
to know of his great deer's haunts, he shall lead the
hunter and the lymerer thither, where he best hopes
to see him or find of him without noise. And if they
can see him and they be in the wind they ought to
withdraw from him in the softest manner they can,
for dread of frightening him out of his haunt, and
then go privily till they be under the wind. And as
he stereth (stalks) and paceth forth feeding, they are
to draw nigh him as readily and warily as they can
so that the deer find them not. And when he has
entered his covert, and to his ligging, they ought to
tarry till they know that he be entered two skilful
bowshots from thence. And then ought the lymerer
by bidding of the hunter to cast round with his
lymer the quarter that the deer is in, if it be in a
huge covert, and if it be in a little covert that the
deer is in, set¹ all the covert to know whether he is
gone away or abides there still. And if he abides,*

---

¹ To set the covert was for the huntsman or limerer with his
hound on a leash to go round the covert that he had seen the
deer enter, and to look carefully whether he could find any
signs of the stag having left the place. This in more modern
parlance is called making his ring walks.

then shall the lymerer go there where the hart went in, and take the scantilon (measure) of the trace for which he should cut off the end of his rod, and lay it in the talon of the trace, there where he went in hardest ground, in the bottom thereof, so that the scantilon will scarcely touch at either end. And that done he should break a bough of green leaves and lay it there where the hart went in, and cut another scantilon thereafter to take to the hunter that he may take it to the lord or to the Master of the Game at the meeting which some men call Assembly. But on the other side, if it be so that they cannot see him as before is said, the forester ought to bring him where most defoil is (tracks) *of great male deer within his bailiewick, and there where the best haunt is, and most likely for a hart. And when the harbourer and the lymerer be there, the lymer if he crosses the fues of a deer he will anon challenge it, and then shall the lymerer take heed to his feet to know by the trace what deer it is that the lymer findeth, and if he finds thereby that it is no hart he shall take up his hound and say to him softly, not loud,* "WARE RASCAL, WARE !" *And if it be of a hart that the lymer findeth, and that it be new he ought to sue* (hunt up) *with as little noise as he can contreongle* (hunting heel) *to undo all his moving* [1] *till he find his fumes* (excrements), *which he ought to put in the great end of his horn, and*

---

[1] Moving, moves. See Appendix : Move.

stop it with grass to prevent them falling out and reward his hound a little. And that done come again there where he began to sue and sue forth the right line till he comes to the entering of the quarter where he thinks that the hart is in. And always with little noise and cast round the quarters, if it be in a great covert as I said before. And also if it be in a little covert, to do of the scantilon and of all other things right as I have said before. And if he be voided (gone) to another quarter or wood, and there be any other covert near always to sue forth and cast round quarter by quarter, and wood by wood till he be readily harboured. And when he is harboured of the scantilon and of all other things do as before is said, and then draw fast to the meeting that men call assembly. And it is to be known that oftentimes a deer is harboured by sight of man's eye, but who should do it well it behoves him to be a skilful and wise hunter. Nevertheless to teach hunters the more readily to seek and harbour a hart according to the country that he is in, I have devised it in certain chapters as ye may hereafter hear.

CHAPTER XXVII

AFTERWARDS I shall show you how a man should
go in quest for the hart with his lymer or by himself. *This word quest for the hart is a term of
hunters beyond the sea, and means when a man goeth
to find a deer and to harbour him, and it is a fair
term and shorter said than our term of England to
my seeming.* And then shall the groom quest in
the country that shall be devised to him the night
before, and he shall rise in the dawning, and then
he must go to the meating (pasturing) of the deer
to look if he may see anything to his liking, and
leave his lymer in a certain place where he may
not alarm them. And thence he should go to the
newly hewn wood of the forest or other places where
he hopes best to see a hart, and keep always from
coming into the wind of the hart, he should also
climb upon a tree so that the hart shall wind
nothing of him, and that he can see him further.
And if he sees a hart standing stably he must look
well in what country he shall go to his lair, and
privily repair to some place where he can best see

HOW THE HUNTER SHOULD VIEW THE HART

(From MS. f. fr. 616, *Bib. Nat.*, Paris)

him and there break a bough for a mark.   But he
must remain a great while after, for some time a
hart will stall and look about a great while before
he will go to his lair, and specially when a great
dew is falling, or else sometimes he cometh out
again to look about, and to listen and to dry himself, and therefore he should stay long, so as not
to frighten him.   Then he should fetch his lymer
and cast round *as it is before said in the chapter of
the harbouring of a hart,* and take care that neither
he nor his hounds make but little noise for dread
lest he void.

CHAPTER XXVIII

HOW AN HUNTER SHOULD GO IN QUEST BETWEEN THE PLAINS AND THE WOOD

ALSO a man may go in quest in the fields in corn, in vines, in gardens, and in other places, where the harts go to their pasture in the fields out of the wood, and he must go forth right early so that he may look at the ground and judge well, and if he sees anything that pleases him he can break boughs and lay his mark and cast round as before is said.

CHAPTER XXIX

HOW A HUNTER SHOULD GO IN QUEST IN THE COPPICE AND THE YOUNG WOOD

Also a man may go in quest among young wood, and although he has been in the morning and (seen) nought, nevertheless he should not neglect to quest with his lymer when it is high day when all the deer have gone to their lairs, for peradventure the hart will sometimes have gone into the wood before the hunter and lymer came to quest for him.

CHAPTER XXX

HOW AN HUNTER SHOULD GO IN QUEST IN GREAT COVERTS AND STRENGTHS

ALSO a hunter may go in quest and put himself and his lymer in the great thickets by high time of day, as I have said, for it befalleth sometimes that harts are so malicious, that they pasture within themselves, that is to say within their covert, and go not out to the fields nor to the coppices nor to the young wood, especially when they have heard the hounds run before in the forest once or twice. He must have affeeted (trained) his lymer in such a manner that he neither opens nor quests[1] when he hunts in the morning, for he would make the hart void, and that must be by high noon, as I have said, when all beasts are in their lairs. And if his lymer find anything he should hold him short and lead him behind him, and look what deer it is, and if it be anything that pleases him, then he shall sue with his lymer till the time that he has brought it into some thicket, and then he shall break his boughs *and take the scantilon and cast round as is before said, and then return home again to the assembly that in England is called a meeting or gathering.*

[1] Should not give tongue.

CHAPTER XXXI

HOW A HUNTER SHOULD QUEST IN CLEAR SPIRES AND HIGH WOOD [1]

ALSO I will tell you how a hunter should go in quest among clear spires, and among high trees, and specially when it has rained the night before and in the morning. Eke in the time when the heads of the harts be tender, commonly they abide among clear spires and in high woods, for a thick country peradventure would do harm to their heads which be tender. If he meets rain as I before have said, or when their heads (are tender, and he meeteth [2]) anything that pleaseth him, he should not follow it with his lymer, for they remain in such a country as I have said in that time, that is to say in rain and when their heads are tender, for he might make the deer void into some other place of the quests as it is before said. And whoso meets him in the wood in sight of his

---

[1] In the text of our MS. (the Vespasian) no break occurs here, but in the table of chapters at the beginning of the MS. the chapter as here given is enumerated, and this corresponds also with the Shirley and other MSS.

[2] The scribe who copied the Vespasian MS. omitted the bracketed words.

eyes, then he must set his lymer in his fues.   And
if it be a deer that enter-changeth,[1] that is to say
if a deer puts his hind feet in the trace of the fore-
feet without passing on, it is no good token, but if
he sets his hinder feet far from the fore feet it is a
good token, for when a hart entre-marcheth it is a
token that he is a light deer and well running and
of great flight, for if he had a side belly and great
flanks he could not entre-marche, but the contrary
would he do.[2]   And sometimes when the hart
makes a long stride with the hind foot, commonly
they cannot fly well, and have been little hunted.
And if he has of the fumes, he should put them in
his horn with grass, or in his lap [3] with grass, for
a man should not bear them in his hand, for they
would all break.   And when he should meet in
the fields anything that pleaseth him, he should
draw towards his covert, for to make him draw
the sooner to his stronghold, and when he findeth
where he goeth in, then he should break a bough
towards the place where the hart is gone, and
take the scantilon, and follow him no further in
the wood.   Then he should make a long turn and

---

[1] See Appendix: Hart.
[2] The explanation of this sentence is that a stag which entre-
marched or sur-marched, or in other words placed the hind
foot on the track or beyond the track made by the front foot,
was a thin or light deer, and therefore not a fat stag, which
latter was what the hunter would be looking for.
[3] Lappet of his coat.

cast round about by some ways or by-paths, and if he sees that he hath not passed out of his turn, he may return again to the gathering, and make them his report, and if it be so that he pass there where he would umbicast (cast round) and make his turn, and his lymer before him, then he should look if it is the same hart he had umbicast (cast round), and if he cannot well see at his ease, then he should reconnoitre the country till he can see easily and plainly, but have a care that his lymer open not, *and if his lymer be dislave* [1] (be wild), *let him investigate it with his eye.* And if he seeth that it is his first hart he should not follow him, but then he should take another turn and umbicast. He must look that he go not along the ways, for it is the worst sueing that is : for the lymer commonly overshoots. But he should go a little way off the paths on one side or the other, until he (the hart) be within his turn, for then he is most securely harboured and the search shall be shorter. But if he see that it be too late to run him with strength, and if he see that the hart goes but softly pacing towards his stronghold he need not do all these things. And I pray him where he hath met with the hart, or harboured him in his stronghold or in coppices or in other thickets, that he take all his blenches (tricks) and his ruses

[1] Shirley MS. *Dislavee*—obsolete word meaning going beyond bounds, immoderate.

before said, to be more secure, and to make a shorter search, if he hath time to do as I have said. Thus I have rehearsed the readiness that belongs to the harbouring of the hart. *And now will I devise where men will best find them in bellowing time. It is known that they begin to bellow fifteen days before grease time [1] ends, especially old deer, and also if the end of August and the beginning of September be wet and rainy.*

[1] *After* grease time. See Appendix: Grease Time.

CHAPTER XXXII

HOW A GOOD HUNTER SHALL GO IN QUEST
TO HEAR THE HARTS BELLOW

ALSO a good hunter should go before daybreak to
hear the harts bellow which peradventure bellow
in the forest in divers parts, and to look by the
bellowing of the harts which seemeth to him the
greatest. And always hearkening nearer and nearer
under the wind, in such wise that when he will
begin to sue, that he need nothing but to bring
the lymer to the fues. And anon when he seeth
that it is a hart that he findeth, uncouple the
finders, but not too many, and this, for fear of
falling in danger (of losing the right deer), should
be done right early as soon as men can see day-
light, for in that time the harts chase the hinds,
and go hither and thither and abide no while in one
place as they do in the right season. And because
a man cannot come nigh him with a lymer, it is
good to uncouple the hounds, for the hounds will
get nigh them quicker and the bolder hounds will
soon dissever (separate) the harts from the hinds.
The harts bellow in divers manners, according as
they be old or young, and according whether they

be in a country where they have not heard the hounds, or where they have heard them. Some of them bellow with a full open mouth and often cast up their heads. And these be those that have heard the hounds only a little in the season, and that are well heated and swelled. And sometimes about high noon they bellow as before is said. The others bellow low and great and stooping with the head, and the muzzle towards the earth, and that is a token of a great hart, and an old and a malicious, or that he hath heard the hounds, and therefore dare not bellow or only a few times in the day, unless if it be in the dawning. And the other belloweth with his muzzle straight out before him, bolking and rattling in the throat, and also that is a token of a great and old hart that is assured and firm in his rut. In short all the harts that bellow greatest and mightiest by reason should be greatest and oldest.

CHAPTER XXXIII

THE assembly *that men call gathering* should be
made in this manner: the night before that the
Lord or the Master of the Game will go to the
wood, he must cause to come before him all the
hunters and the helps, the grooms and the pages,
and shall assign to each one of them their quests
in a certain place, and separate the one from the
other, and the one should not come into the quest
of the other, nor do him annoyance or hinder
him. And every one should quest in his best
wise, in the manner that I have said; and should
assign them the place where the gathering shall
be made, at most ease for them all, and the
nearest to their quests. And the place where the
gathering shall be made should be in a fair mead
well green, where fair trees grow all about, the
one far from the other, and a clear well or beside
some running brook. And it is called gathering
because all the men and the hounds for hunting

gather thither, for all they that go to the quest should all come again in a certain place that I have spoken of. And also they that come from home, and all the officers that come from home should bring thither all that they need, every one in his office, well and plenteously, and should lay the towels and board clothes all about upon the green grass, and set divers meats upon a great platter [1] after the lord's power. And some should eat sitting, and some standing, and some leaning upon their elbows, some should drink, some laugh, some jangle, some joke and some play—in short do all manner of disports of gladness, and when men be set at tables ere they eat then should come the lymerers and their grooms with their lymers the which have been questing, and every one shall say his report to the lord of what they have done and found and lay the fumes before the lord he that hath any found, and then the Lord or the Master of the hunting by the counsel of them all shall choose which they will move and run to and which shall be the greatest hart and the highest deer. And when they shall have eaten, the lord shall devise where the relays shall go and other things which I shall say more plainly, and then shall every man speed him to his place, and all haste them to go to the finding.

[1] G. de F. (p. 151) says "in great plenty," not "upon a great platter."

HOW TO QUEST FOR THE HART IN COVERTS

(From MS. f. fr. 616, *Bib. Nat.*, Paris)

CHAPTER XXXIV

HOW THE HART SHOULD BE MOVED WITH THE LYMER AND RUN TO AND SLAIN WITH STRENGTH

WHEN the hart is harboured as before is said and they before named come to the meeting that some men call the assembly, and also the scantilon,[1] and the fumes well liked by the Lord and Master of the Game, then shall the Master of the Game choose oj the sergeants or of the yeoman at horse, which of them shall be at the finding, or all, or some. Nevertheless, if the deer be likely to fall among danger it were good to assign some of the horsemen among the relays to help more readily the hounds, if they fall upon the stint,[2] and when the hunters on horseback be assigned then he must assign which of the yeomen berners on foot shall be finders, and which hounds he shall have with him to the finding, and the lymerer and the pages to go with him. And after that to assign the relays by advice of them that know the country and the flight of the deer.

[1] Measure of the deer's footprint. In old English, a measure (Stratmann).

[2] Wrong scent, or check.

And there where most danger is, there set the readiest hunters and the best footers with the boldest hounds with them. And at every relay sufficeth two couple of hounds or three at the most. And see that amid the relays, somewhat toward the hinder-most relay, especially if it be in danger, that one of the lymerer's pages be there with one of the lymers. And the more danger (there is) *the older and the readier, and the most tender nosed hound. And when all is ordained then shall the Lord and the Master of the Game, if he liketh better to be at the finding than with a relay, shall go thither where the deer is harboured, and set ready waits about the quarter of the wood that the deer is in, to see what cometh out, or to see if the deer that is harboured would start and steal away ere the lymer moved him. And this done, then should the Lord and Master of the Game bid the lymerer bring them there where he marked that the hart went in, and when they be there the lymerer should take away the boughs he laid over the trace at the harbouring, and set his lymer in the fues, and then shall the Lord if he can blow, blow three motes, and after him the Master of the Game, and after the hunters, as they be greatest in office, that be at the finding, and then the lymerer. And after that if the lymer sue boldly and lustily the lymerer shall say to him loud ; " Ho moy, ho moy, hole hole hole." And ever take good heed to his feet, and look well about him. And as oft as he findeth the fues, or if it be in thick spires,[1] boughs or branches broken, where the deer hath walked, he should say aloud—" Cy va—cy va—cy va," and rally with his horn, and always should the yeoman berner the which is ordained to be finder, follow the lymer and be as nigh him as he might with the raches that he leadeth for the finding, and if the lymer as he sueth, overshoot and be out of the fues, the lymerer should always, till his hounds be fallen in again, speak to him, calling his name, be it Loyer, or Beaumont, or Latimer or Bemond according to what the hound is named, and anon as he falls in again and finds the fues or branches as before is said he shall say loud, " Cy va " as before and rally and so forth at every time that he findeth thereof, until that the lymer move him. Nevertheless I have seen when a lymer sueth long and could not so soon move him as men would, that they have taken up the lymer and uncoupled one or two hounds, to have him sooner found, but this truly no skilful hunter ought to do, unless the lymer cannot put it forth, nor bring it any further, or that the deer be stirring in the quarter, and hath not waited for the moving of the lymer. Or else that it be so far advanced in the day, that the sun hath dried up the fues, and that they have little day enough to run him and hunt him with strength. But now to come again to the lymer, it is to wit that when the lymer*

---

[1] Shoots, fresh-growing young wood.

hath moved him, if the lymerer can see him he shall blow a mote,[1] *and rechace* (recheat),[2] *and if the deer be soule* (alone) *the Berners shall uncouple all the finders, and if he be not alone two hounds sufficeth till he be separated, and if the lymerer saw him* (not) *at the moving he should go to his lair and look thereby whether it be a hart or not, and if he see by the lair or by the fues that it is the same deer, that he hath sued* (hunted) *and alone he should rechase without a long mote, for the mote should never be blown before the rechasing,*[3] *unless a man seeth that which he hunteth for. And then the Berner should do as I have said before, and if he be not alone the Berner should do as above is said, for it is to wit that the mote before rechasing* (recheating) *shall never be blown but when a man seeth what he hunteth for, as I have said. Now furthermore, when the hart is moved and the finders cast off, then should the lymerer take up his hounds and follow after, and foot it in the best wise that he can. And the Berner also and every horseman go that can go, so that they come not into the fues* (across the line) *nor in front of the hounds, and shape* (their course) *as often as they can to meet him. And as often as any man see him or meet him, he should go to the fues and blow a mote and rechace and then holloa*

---

[1] A long note.
[2] Recheat, a hunting signal on the horn.
[3] Recheating. See Appendix: Hunting-Music.

to the hounds to come forth withall, and this done, speed him fast in the manner that I have said to meet with him again. And the relay that he (the hart) cometh to first should take good heed that he vauntlay¹ not, if other relays be behind for dread of bending out from the relay. But he should let the deer pass and go to the fues, and there blow a mote, and rechace and rally upon the fues. And the hunter ought to be advised that his hounds catch it (the scent) well in couple, ere he relay, that they run not counter.² For that might make the hounds that come therewith and the hunters to be on a stynt (at fault), and peradventure not recover it all the day after. And if it so be that the hunter that hath relayed, see that the deer be likely to fall into danger, that is to say among other deer, and else it needeth not, he should when he hath relayed stand still in the fues, and holloa the hounds that come forth therewith and take up the hindermost, and if it be in a park go stand again with them at his place, and if it be out of park in a forest or other wood follow after as well as he is able. And in this wise ought every relay to do till he come among the back relays. For if they at the back see by the spreading of the clees (claws) by setting fast and deep his ergots (dew claws) in the earth, and if

---

¹ Vauntlay, to cast off the relay before the hounds already hunting have passed. See Appendix: Relays.

² Do not hunt heel: *contre*, counter.

they see him also cast his chaule,[1] *then they ought to vauntlay for advantage of the hounds, for so shall they sooner have him at bay, and from then he is but dead if the hunters serve aright the hounds. Nevertheless men have seen at the first finding or soon after, deer turn the head (to bay), and oftenest in rutting time, but I mean not of deer that turneth so to bay, but I mean of hunted deer when men have seen of them the tokens said before that he stand at bay. And if it be so that the hounds have envoised* [2] *or have overshot, or that they be on a stynt by any other ways, those hunters on horseback or on foot to whom belongs the right, first should blow the stynt as I shall devise in a chapter that shall be of all blowing.*[3] *And after that he should fall before the hounds as soon as he can and take them up, and if so be that they have envoysed two deer of antler* [4] *they should not be rated badly, but get in front off them and take them off in the fairest way that men can. And if they run ought else they should be got in front of and rated and well lashed. And what hounds they may get up, bring them to the next rights (right line) if they know where, or else there where he (the hart) was last seen. And if it be great danger they ought to blow a mote for the lymer and let him sue till he hath retrieved him*

[1] Drop his jaw. (?)   [2] Gone off the right line.
[3] This chapter does not exist.
[4] If the hounds have gone away after two stags.

*or else till he hath brought him out of danger. And
as oft as he findeth or seeth that he is in the rights
the lymerer should say loud, " Cy va " twice or
thrice—and recheat, and so should the hunters as
oft as they lust to blow. And if the lymer overshoot or cannot put it forth, every hunter that is
there ought to go some deal abroad for to see if he
may find the rights by vesteying* (searching) *thereof.
And whoso may find it before the lymer be fallen in
again, he should recheat in the rights, and blow
after that a mote for the lymer and sue forth as is
said before. And if the lymer gave it up, and
cannot and will not do his devoire* (duty), *then
should they blow two motes for the raches and cast
them off there where they were last in the rights.
And if the hunters hear that the hounds run well
and put it lustily forth they should rout and jopey* [1]
*to them lustily and often and recheat also. And
if there be but one hound that undertaketh it lustily
they shall hue and jopey to him, and also recheat.
As oft as they be on a stynt they should blow the
stynt and do as before is said. And if any of the
aforesaid hounds retrieve him so that men may
know and hear it by the doubling of their menee,* [2]
*but if they hear any hunter above them that hath
met* (the deer) *that bloweth the rights and holloaeth*

[1] Call to the hounds encouragingly.
[2] Shirley MS.: "doubling of their mouths," from the Fr.
menee. See Appendix : Menee.

else (where) they should haste them thither where they thought the hounds retrieved it; or else to meet with the hounds for to see the fues whether it be the hunted deer or not.   And if it is not he, they should do as above is said when they be on a stynt, and if it be he every man shall speed him that speed may, and every relay do as before is said. And if any of the hunters happen while they be on a stynt to see a hart that he thinketh to be the hunted deer he ought to blow a mote and recheat and after that blow two motes for the hounds and stand still before the fues till the Berner with the hounds do come.   And if they suppose that they may not hear him he should draw to them till they have heard him.   And when any of the Berners or the lymerer hear a man blow for them, they should answer blowing in this wise in their horn : "trut trut trut," but he should know readily by the fues after the tokens that have been said before, whether it be the hunted deer or not.   And in the same wise shall a hunter do that findeth an hart quat (couched), and he thinketh it to be the hunted deer, and he sees that his fellows and the hounds be on a stynt, he should well beware that he blow not too nigh him, lest he start, and go away, before the hounds come. Nevertheless for to wit whether it be the hunted deer or no, the tokens have been rehearsed before—and when he hath been so well run to and enchased and retrieved, and so oft relayed and vauntelayed to, and that he seeth that (neither) *by beating up the rivers nor brooks nor foiling him down, nor going to soil, nor rusing to and fro upon himself, which is to say in his own fues, can help him, then turns he his head and standeth at bay. And then as far as it may be heard every man draweth thither, and the knowing thereof is that the hunter that cometh first, and the hunters* (one) *after the other they holloa all together, and blow a mote and rechace all at once. And that they never do but when he is at bay or when bay is made for the hounds, after he is dead, when they should be rewarded or enquerreyde.*[1] *And when the hunters that held the relays be there, or that they be nigh the bay, they should pull off the couples from the hounds' necks and let them draw thither. And the hunters should break the bay as often as they can for two causes ; the one lest he* (the stag) *hurt the hounds, if he stand and rest long in one place ; another is that the relays that stand far can come up with their hounds the while he is alive, and be at the death. And it is to be known that if any of the hunters have been at any time while the deer hath been run to out of hearing of hound and horn, he should have blown the forloyne,*[2] *unless he were in a park, for there it should never be blown. And whoso first heard him so blow*

---

[1] See Appendix : Curée.

[2] A horn signal denoting that the chase is being followed at a distance by those who blow. From the Fr. *fortloin*, written forlonge. See Appendix : Forlonge.

should blow again to him the " perfect," [1] if it so be that he were in his rights, and else not. For by that shall he be brought to readiness and comfort who before did not know where the game or any of his fellows were. And when it so is, that they have thought that the bay has lasted long enough, then should he whoso be the most master bid some of the hunters go spay [2] him behind the shoulder forward to the heart. But the lymerer should let slip the rope while he (the deer) *stood on his feet, and let the lymer go to* (him), *for by right the lymer should never* (go) *out of the rope, though he* (be let) *slip from ever so far. And when the deer is dead, and lieth on one side then first it is time to blow the death, for it should never be blown at hart hunting till the deer be on its side. And then should the hounds be coupled up and as fast as a man can. One of the Berners should encorne him, that is to say turn his horns earthwards and the throat up-wards, and slit the skin of the throat all along the neck, and cut labelles* (small flaps) *on either side of the skin, the which shall hang still upon the head, for this belongeth to an hart slain with strength, and else not. And then should the hunter flay down the skin as far as he can, and then with a sharp trencher cut as thick as he can the flesh down to the neck bone, and this done every man stand abroad and*

---

[1] A note sounded only by those who are on the right line.
[2] To kill with a sword or hunting knife. See Appendix : Spay.

blow the death, and make short bay for to reward the hounds. And every man (shall) have a small rod in his hand to hold the hounds that they should the better bay and every man blow the death that can blow. And as oft as any hunter beginneth to blow every man shall blow for the death to make the better noise, and make the hounds better know the horns and the bay, and when they have bayed a while let the hounds come to eat the flesh, to the hard bone from in front of the shoulders right to the head, for that is their reward of right. And then take them off fair and couple them up again. And then bring to the lymers and serve each by himself, and then should the Lord if he list or else the Master of the Game, or if he be absent whoso is greatest of the hunters, blow the prise at coupling up, and that should be blown only of the aforesaid, and by no others. Nevertheless it is to wit that if the Lord be not come soon enough to the bay, while the deer is alive they ought to hold the bay as long as they can, without rebuking the hounds, to await the Lord, and if the Lord remains away too long, when the deer is spayed and laid on one side, before they do ought else, the Master of the Game, or which of the horsemen that be there at the death, should mount their horses and every man draw his way blowing the death till one of them hath met with him, or heard of him, and brought him thither. And if they cannot meet with him, and that they

*have word that he is gone home, they ought to come
again, and do, whoso is greatest master, as the Lord
should do, if he were there, and right so should they
do to the Master of the Game in the Lord's absence.
Also if the Lord be there all things should be done
of the bay and rewarding as before is said, and
then he should charge whom he list to undo the deer,
if the hounds shall not be enquyrid thereon, for
if they should, there needeth no more but to caboche [1]
his head, all the upper jaw still thereon, and the
labelles aforesaid; and then hold him and lay the
skin open, and lay the head at the skin's end right
in front of the shoulders.   And when the hounds are
thus inquirreide the lymers should have both the
shoulders for their rights, and else they should not
have but the ears and the brain whereof they should
be served, the hart's head lying under their feet.
But on the other hand if the lord will have the deer
undone, he that he biddeth as before is said, should
undo him most woodmanly and cleanly that he can
and wonder ye not that I say woodmanly, for it is a
point that belongeth to woodmanscraft, though it be
well suiting to an hunter to be able to do it.   Nevertheless it belongeth more to woodmanscraft than to
hunters, and therefore as of the manner he should be
undone I pass over lightly, for there is no woodman
nor good hunter in England that cannot do it well*

---

[1] Cut off the head close behind the antlers. Shirley MS. :
"Cabache."

*enough, and well better than I can tell them. Never-
theless when so is that the paunch is taken out clean
and whole and the small guts, one of the groom
chacechiens should take the paunch and go to the
next water withal, and slit it, and cast out the
filth and wash it clean, that no filth abide therein.
And then bring it again and cut it in small gobetts
in the blood that should be kept in the skin and the
lungs withal, if they be hot and else not, and all the
small guts withal, and bread broken therein according whether the hounds be few or many, and all this
turned and meddled together among the blood till it
be well brewed in the blood, and then look for a
small green, and thither bear all this upon the skin
with as much blood as can be saved, and there lay
it, and spread the skin thereupon, the hair side
upward, and lay the head, the visage, forward at
the neck end of the skin. And then the lord shall
go take a fair small rod in his hand, the which one of
the yeomen or of the grooms should cut for him, and
the Master of the Game and other, and the sergeants,
and each of the yeomen on horse, and others, and
then the Lord should take up the hart's head by
the right side between the surroyal and the fork
or troche whichever it be that he bear, and the
Master of the Game, the left side in the same wise,
and hold the head upright that the nose touch the
earth. And then every man that is there, save the
berners on foot and the chacechiens and the lymerers*

which should be with their hounds and wait upon them in a fair green where there is a cool shadow, should stand in front on either side of the head, with rods, that no hound come about, nor on the sides, but that all stand in front. And when it is ready the Master of the Game or the sergeant should bid the berners bring forth their hounds and stand still in front of them a small quoit's cast from thence, as the bay is ordained. And when they be there the Master of the Game or sergeant should cry skilfully loud: "Devour" and then holloa every wight, and every hunter blow the death. And when the hounds be come and bay the head, the Berners should pull off the couples as fast as they can. And when the Lord thinketh the bay hath lasted long enough, the Master of the Game should pull away the head and anon others should be ready to pull away the skin and let the hounds come to the reward, and then should the Lord and Master of the Game, and all the hunters stand around all about the reward, and blow the death. As oft as any of them begin every man bear him fellowship till the hounds be well rewarded, and that they have nought left. And right thus should be done when the hounds should be enquyrreied of the whole deer. And when there is nought left then should the Lord, if he wishes, or else the Master of the Game or in his absence whoso is greatest next him, stroke (blow) in this wise, that is to say *blow four motes and stynt* (stop) *not* (for the time of) *half an Ave Maria and then blow other four motes a little longer than the first four motes. And thus should no wight stroke, but when the hart is slain with strength, and when one of the aforesaid hath thus blown then should the grooms couple up the hounds and draw homewards fair and soft. And all the rest of the hunters should stroke in this wise :* " *Trut, trut, tro-ro-row, tro-ro-row,*" *and four motes all of one length not too long and not too short. And otherwise should no hart hunter stroke from thenceforth till they go to bed. And thus should the Berners on foot and the grooms lead home the hounds and send in front that the kennel be clean and the trough filled with clean water, and their couch renewed with fresh straw. And the Master of the Game and the sergeant and the yeoman at horse should come home and blow the menee at the hall door or at the cellar door as I shall devise. First the master, or whoso is greatest next him, shall begin and blow three motes* [1] *alone, and at the first mote* [2] *the remnant of the aforesaid should blow with him, and beware that none blow longer than another, and after the three motes even forthwith they should blow the recoupling as thus :* " *Trut, trut, trororo rout,*" *and that they be advised that from the time they fall in to blow together, that none of them begin before* (the)

[1] Shirley MS. says four notes.
[2] Should read : "at the last moot."

other nor end after (the) *other. And if it be the first hart slain with strength in the season, or the last, the sergeant and the yeoman shall go on their office's behalf and ask their fees of the which I report me to the old statutes and customs of the King's house. And this done the Master of the Game ought to speak to the officers that all the hunters' suppers be well ordained, and that they drink not ale, and nothing but wine that night for the good and great labour they have had for the Lord's game and disport, and for the exploit and making of the hounds. And also that they may the more merrily and gladly tell what each of them hath done all the day and which hounds have best run and boldest.*

CHAPTER XXXV

HOW AN HUNTER SHOULD SEEK AND FIND THE HARE WITH RUNNING HOUNDS AND SLAY HER WITH STRENGTH

Ere I speak how the hare should be hunted, it is to be known that the hare is king of all venery, for all blowing and the fair terms of hunting cometh of the seeking and the finding of the hare. For certain it is the most marvellous beast that is, for ever she fumeth or croteth and roungeth and beareth tallow and grease. And though men say that she fumeth inasmuch as she beareth tallow, yet that which cometh from her is not called fumes but croteys. And she hath teeth above in the same wise as beneath. It is also to be known that the hare is at one time male and another time female. When she is female sometimes she kindles in three degrees, two rough, two smooth and two knots that afterwards should be kindles, but this happeneth but seldom. Now for to speak of the hare how he shall be sought and found and chased with hounds. It is to be known what the first word (should be) that the hunter should speak to his hounds when he lets them out of the kennel. When the door is opened he shall say

loud : " *Ho ho arere*,"[1] *because that his hounds
will come out too hastily.   And when he uncoupleth
his hounds, he shall say to them when he comes into
the field : " Sto mon amy sto atrete*," *but when he
is come forth into the field he shall blow three motes
and uncouple the hounds, then he shall speak twice
to his hounds in this wise, " Hors de couple, avaunt
cy avaunt* "[2] *and then he shall say thrice " So how "
and no more ; afterward he shall say loud " Sa say
cy avaunt* " *and then " Sa cy avaunt, sa cy avaunt
so how*," *and if he see the hounds draw fast from
him and would fain run, he shall say thus to them
here : " How amy—how amy*," *and then shall he
say " Swe mon famy swef* "[3] *for to make them go
softly, and between always blow three motes.   And
if any of his hounds find and own to the hare where
he hath been, he shall say to them in this wise :
" Oyez a Beaumont le vaillant*," *or what the hound
is called.   And if he seeth that the hare hath been
at pasture in green corn or in any other place and
his hounds find of her and that they fall well in
enquest*[4] (hunt) *and chase it well, then he shall say
" La Douce, la il a este* "[5] *and therewith "So
howe* " *with a high voice, and if his hounds chase*

---

[1] " Back there ! " from the Fr. *arrière.*
[2] " Out of couples, forward there, forward ! " (Precisely the
same instructions are given by the ~~later~~ Twety and Gyfford.)
[3] " Gently, my friend, gently ! "
[4] Quest, hunt, seek, also challenge.
[5] " Softly, there he has been ! "

earlier

HARE-HUNTING WITH GREYHOUNDS AND RUNNING HOUNDS

(From MS. f. fr. 616, *Bib. Nat.*, Paris)

not well at his pleasure and they grede (hunt) *there
where he has not pastured, then shall he say " Illeoqs
illeoqs "* [1] *in the same place while they seek her.
And then he should cast and look about the field, to
see where she hath been and whether she hath pastured or not, or whether she be in her form, for she
does not like to remain where she hath pastured
except in time of relief. If any hounds scent her,
and she hath gone from thence to another place, he
shall say thus to his hounds as loud as he can : " Ha
cy douce cy et venuz arere, so howe."* [2] *And if he
see that she be gone to the plain or the field or to
arable land or into the wood, if his hounds get well
on her scent, then he shall say : " La douce amy, il
ad est illeoqs "* [3] *and therewith he shall say : " so-
how illeoqs, sy douce cy vayllant "* [4] *and twice
" so-howe," and when he is come there where he
supposeth the hare dwells then shall he say thus :*

----

[1] " In this place," or "here, here." This passage, which
reads somewhat confusedly in our MS., is clearer in Twety and
Gyfford (*Reliquiæ Antiquæ*, vol. i. p. 149). It reads as follows :
"And then ye shall blowe iij notes, yf yowr hund ne chace not
well hym, there one ther another, as he hath pasturyd hym, ye
shall say ' *Illeosque, illeosque, illeosque,*'" meaning that 3 motes
should be blown where the hare has pastured to bring your
hounds to the place, *illeosque* meaning here, in this place.

[2] " Softly there, here she has been, back there." Following
this the Shirley MS. and Twety and Gyfford contain a passage
which our MS. has not got : "And thenne *sa cy, a este sohow,*
and afterwards *sa cy avaunt.*"

[3] " Softly, my friend, she has been here."

[4] " Here gently, here valiantly."

"*La douce la est il venuz*" and therewith thrice
"*so-howe*" and no more. And if he thinks he is
sure to find her in any place then he shall say:
"*La douce how-here, how-here, how-here, how-here,
douce how-here how-here*," and when she is found
and started he shall blow a mote and rechase[1] and
holloa as often as he wishes and then say loud:
"*Oyez! a Beaumond*" or what the hound is
named, "*le vailaunt oyez, oyez, oyez, who-bo-
lowe*," and then "*Avaunte assemble, avaunte*."
And then should the horsemen keep well to one
side and some way to the front with long rods in
their hands to meet with her, and so blowe a mote
and rechace and holloa and set the hounds in the
rights if they see her, and also for to prevent any
hound following sheep, or other beasts, and if they
do to ascrie (rate) them sorely and dismount and
take them up and lash them well, saying loud "*Ware
ware ha ha ware*" and lash them back to their
fellows, and if it happens that the hare be seated in
her form in front of the hounds, and that they
cannot find her as soon as they would, then shall he
say : "*How-sa amy sa sa acouplere, sa arere, so-
how*," but not (blow) the stynt too soon. And if
he seeth that his hounds cannot put her up as soon as
he would, then shall he blow the stynt, and say loud :
"*ho ho ore swef a la douce, a lui, a lui, so how*

---

[1] To call back the hounds from a wrong scent, the same as
"recheat."

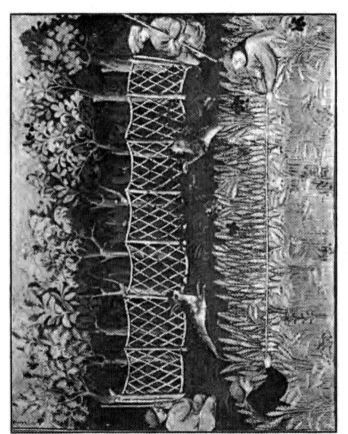

HARE-DRIVING WITH LOW BELLS

(From MS. f. fr. 616, *Bib. Nat.*, Paris)

*assamy, assamy, la arere so-howe, venez acouplere,"
and thus as oft as the aforesaid case happeneth.
And as oft as any hound catcheth it (the scent) he
should hue to him by his name, and rout him to his
fellows as before is said, but not rechace till the
hare be found, or that some man meet it and blow
the rights and holloa, or else that he findeth her
pointing or pricking whichever it be, for both
mean the same, but some call it the one and some
the other. And if he find that he can well blow
the rights and holloa and jopey three or four times
and cry loud " le voy, le voy," till the hounds
come thither and have well caught it. And (when)
she is retrieved blow and holloa and rout to the
hounds as it is said you should do at the finding, and
follow after and foot it who can foot it. And if it
happen when men hunt her and hounds chase her
that she squat anywhere before the hounds, and that
any hunter find her squatting, if the hounds be nigh
about, he should blow a mote and rechace and start
her, and then halloa and rout to them as above is
said. And if he find her squat, and the hounds be
far from him, then should he blow as I last said
before, and after two motes for the hounds, and the
berners that hear him should answer him thus
" trut, trut, trut," and draw all towards him with
the hounds as fast as they can, saying to their
hounds : " so-how, mon amy, so-howe." And when
they be there and the hounds have all come up, they*

should check them with one of their rods, and when she is started, blow, holloa and rout as before is said, and according to what the case requireth, do as before is said and devised. And when she hath been well chased and well retrieved, notwithstanding her rusing and squatting and reseating, so that by strength at last she is bitten by the hounds, whoso is nearest should start to take her whole from them, and hold her in his one hand over his head high, and blow the death that men may gather thither, and when they be come, then should she be stripped, all save the head, and the gall and the paunch cast away, and the remnant should be laid on a great staff or on a board, whoso hath it, or on the earth, and then it should be chopped as small as it can be, so that it hang together ; and when it is so done then should one of the berners take it up with the head and hold it as high as he is able in his hands, and then whoso is most master, blow the death, and anon as he beginneth every man help and holloa. And when the hounds have bayed, as long as is wished by the aforesaid most master, then should the berner pull as high as he can every piece from the other and cast to every hound his reward. And then should the most master blow a mote and stroke, if so be that he thinks that the hounds have done enough, and else he should rest awhile, if the hounds be hot, till they be cooled, and then led to the water to lap. And then if he wish blow three motes and

NETTING HARES IN THEIR "MUSES"

(From MS. f. fr. 616, *Bib. Nat.*, Paris)

*uncouple and speak and so do as before is said.
And if they will seek a covert for the hare and set
greyhounds without, they should blow and seek and
speak in the manner as before is said, save that
if the hounds find anything what so ever it be, he
shall rally and jopey till he has seen it, or that he
knows what it is (and if it be an hare do as above is
said),[1] and if it be ought else he shall blow drawing
with his horn and cry loud " So-how mon amy,
so-how, sto arere, so-how, so-howe," and seek forthwith again with three long motes till the hare be
found. Yet nevertheless if they be hart-hunters
that seek a covert for the hare, and their hounds
find a fox, whoso meeteth with him should blow out
upon him to warn the fewterers[2] that there is a
thief in the wood. And if they run at the hare and
the hare happen to come out to the greyhounds in
front of the raches and be killed, the fewterer that
let run should blow the death and keep it as whole
as he may till the hunters be come, and then should
they reward the hounds as before is said.*

[1] The words in brackets are in the Shirley MS.
[2] Huntsman holding hounds in leash.

CHAPTER XXXVI

OF THE ORDINANCE AND THE MANNER OF HUNTING WHEN THE KING WILL HUNT IN FORESTS OR IN PARKS FOR THE HART WITH BOWS AND GREYHOUNDS AND STABLE

The Master of the Game should be in accordance with the master forester or parker where it should be that the King should hunt such a day, and if the tract be wide, the aforesaid forester or parker should warn the sheriff of the shire where the hunting shall be, for to order sufficient stable,[1] and carts, also to bring the deer that should be slain to the place where the curées at huntings have been usually held. And thence he should warn the hunters and fewterers whither they should come, and the forester should have men ready there to meet them, that they go no farther, nor straggle about for fear of frightening the game, before the King comes. And if the hunting shall be in a park all men should remain at the park gate, save the stable that ought to be set ere the King comes, and they should be

[1] Men and hounds stationed at different places, usually on the boundaries of the district in which the game was to be roused and hunted, or at convenient passes from whence the hounds could be slipped at the game.

*set by the foresters or parkers. And early in the
morning the Master of the Game should be at the
wood to see that all be ready, and he or his lieutenant
or such hunters that he wishes, ought to set the greyhounds and who so be teasers*[1] *to the King or to the
Queen, or to their attendants. As often as any
hart cometh out he should when he passes blow a
mote and recheat, and let slip to tease it forth, and
if it be a stag, he should let him pass as I said and
rally to warn the fewterers what is coming out.
And to lesser deer should no wight let run, and if he
hath seen the stag, not unless he were commanded.*[2]
*And then the master forester or parker ought to show
him the King's standing if the King would stand
with his bow, and where all the remnant of the
bows would stand. And the yeoman for the King's
bows ought to be there to keep and make the King's
standing, and remain there without noise, till the
King comes. And the grooms that keep the king's
dogs and broken greyhounds should be there with
him, for they belong to the yeomen's office, and also
the Master of the Game should be informed by the
forester or parker what game the king should find
within the set,*[3] *and when all this is done, then*

[1] Teasers, a small hound to tease forth or put up the game.

[2] A difficult sentence to unravel. In the Shirley MS. it
runs: "and yif hit have eseyne nought to ye stagge, but yif he
were avaunced."

[3] "Within the set" means within that quarter of the forest
or park around which are set or stationed the men and hounds,
called the stable.

should the Master of the Game *worthe* (mount) upon (his) horse and meet the King and bring him to his standing and tell him what game is within the set, and how the greyhounds be set, and also the stable, and also tell him where it is best for him to stand with his bow or with his greyhounds, for it is to be known that the attendants of his chamber and of the queen's should be best placed, and the two *fewterers* ought to make fair lodges of green boughs at the *tryste* to keep the King and Queen and ladies, and gentlewomen and also the greyhounds from the sun and bad weather. And when the King is at his standing or at his tryste, whichever he prefers, and the Master of the Game or his lieutenant have set the bows and assigned who shall lead the Queen to her tryste, then he should blow the three long motes for the uncoupling. And the hart hounds and the harriers that before have been led by some forester or parker thither where they should uncouple, and all the hounds that belong to both the *mutes* (packs) waiting for the Master of the Game's blowing. Then should the sergeant of the mute of the harthounds, if there be much rascal within the set, make all them of office, save the yeomen of the horse, *hardel*[1] their hounds, and in every hardel two or three couple of hounds at the most suffice. And then to stand abroad in the woods for relays, and then blow three motes to the uncoupling. And then

---

[1] To tie the couples of hounds together.

*should the harrier uncouple his hounds and blow
three motes and seek forth saying loud and long,
" hoo sto ho sto, mon amy, ho sto " and if they draw
far from him in any unruly manner he should
speak to them in that case as when he seeketh for
the hare. And as oft as he passes within the set
from one quarter to another, he should blow drawing,
and when he is passed the boundary of the quarter,
and entered into a new quarter, he should blow three
motes and seek forth, but if so be, that his hounds
enchace anything as he wishes, and if any hound
happen to find of the King's (game), he should hue
to him by his name and say loud : " Oyez a
Bemond, oyez-oyez, assemble, assemble," or what
the hound is named, " assemble, assemble" and
jopey and rally. And if it be an hart and any of
the hart hounds meet with it they should blow a
mote and rechace and relay, and go forth therewith
all rechacing among. And if it come to the bows
or to greyhounds and be dead, he should blow the
death when he is come thither, and reward his
hounds a little, and couple them up and go again to
his place. And if the hart has escaped he should no
longer rechace, but blow drawing and draw in again,
and in the best way that he can, take up his hounds
and get in front of them. And after that the harriers have well run and well made the rascal void,[1]
then should the sergeant and the berners of the hart*

---

[1] Made the smaller deer clear out of the forest.

hounds blow three motes, the one after the other and uncouple there where they suppose the best ligging (lair) is for a hart, and seek as before is said ; unless it be the season when the hart's head is tender, then he shall use some of the aforesaid words of seeking to the hounds : " Le doulez, mon amy, le doulez, le doules," and if his hounds find anything do as before is said, and if it be a hart, do as above is said, as he may know by his fues or by men that meet with him.   And if it be ought else, the berner ought to blow drawing, and who meeteth with him (the hart) call to them, and the berner should say " Sto arere so how, so how."   And if the lymerer meet withal, or see by the fues that it is an hart, he should sue thereto till he be dead.   If it go to the greyhounds and if it go to the bows, and be smitten anon, as he findeth blood he should take up his hounds and lead them thence and reward them a little, and then if he escape out of the set, he should reward his hounds, and take them up and go again to the wood and look if he may meet with anything. And as often as he meeteth and findeth, or his hounds run on a fresh scent, do as before is said. And one thing is to be known, that the hart-hounds should never be uncoupled before any other, unless a hart be readily harboured, and that he may be sued to and moved with the lymer, or else that they be uncoupled to a herd of great male deer at the view, namely within a set in a forest or in a park,

THE "UNDOING" OR GRALLOCHING OF THE HART

THE MASTER INSTRUCTING HIS HUNTERS HOW IT IS DONE

(From MS. f. fr. 616, *Bib. Nat.*, Paris)

there where there is a great change of rascal. And that is the cause why the other hounds shall be first uncoupled to make the rascal void, for small deer will sooner leave their covert than will a great hart, unless it be a hind that hath her calf in the wood, and hath lately calved. And when the rascal is thus voided then the hart hounds are uncoupled and they find the great old wily deer that will not lightly void, and they enchace him well and lustily and make him void both to bows and to greyhounds, so that they fully do their duty. And all the while that the hunting lasteth should the carts go about from place to place for to bring the deer to the curée. And there should the server[1] of the hall be to arrange the curées, and to lay the game in a row, all the heads one way—and every deer's feet to the other's back. The harts should be laid in two or three rows (by themselves) according to whether there be many or few, and the rascal in the same way by themselves, and they should take care that no man come within the curées till the King come, save the Master of the Game. And when the covert is well hunted and cleared, then should the Master of the Game come to the King to know if he would hunt any more. And if the King say yea, then shall the Master of the Game if the greyhounds or bows or stable need not to be

---

[1] The beginning of this sentence relating to the " server of the hall " is not in our MS. but in the Shirley MS.

N

removed, blow two long motes for the hounds, and forthwith blow drawing with three long motes that men should stand still, and the hunters may know that they should come to a new seeking with their hounds. And when the hounds be come there where they should uncouple blow three long motes and do and seek and blow, as is before said. And if the bows and greyhounds and stable should be removed, then should he blow a mote and stroke, without the mote in the middle, for to draw men together, and thereby may men know that the king will hunt more ere he go home. And when men come together, then should the Master of the Game see to the placing of the King and of the Queen and of the bows and of the greyhounds and of the stable, as I have said here before, and the hunters to their seeking, and of all other things do in the same manner as I have said. And if the king will hunt no more, then should the Master of his Game, if the King will not blow, blow a mote and stroke with a mote in the middle and the sergeant or whoso bloweth next him, and no man else, should blow the first mote but only the middle, and so every man as oft as he likes to stroke, if they have obtained that which they hunted for. And the middle mote should not be blown save by him that bloweth next the master. And thereby may men know as they hear men stroke homeward whether they have well sped or not. And this way of stroking should serve in the manner I have re-hearsed for all hunting save when the hart is slain with strength. And when the mote is blown and stroked, then should the Master of the Game lead the King to the curée, and show it him, and no man as I have said above should come within it, but every man (keep) *without it. And then the King shall tell the Master of the Game what deer he would were* (given away) *and to whom, and* (after this) *if the King wishes to stay he may. Nevertheless he usually goes home when he hath done this. And then should the Master of the Game begin at one row and so forth, and tythe all the deer right as they lie, rascal and others, and deliver it to the proctors of the church that ought to have it. And then* (separate) *the deer that the king commandeth him to deliver, and if any of them that should have part of the deer be not there he should charge the master forester to send it home, and then he should deliver a certain* (part) *of the remnant to the afore said sewers and to the sergeant of the larder and the remnants should be given by the Master of the Game, some to the gentlemen of the country by the information of the forester or parker, as they have been friendly to the bailie, and the remnant to the officers and hunters as he liketh best. And it is to be known that every man bow and fewterer that hath slain anything should mark it*

*that he might challenge his fee, and have it at the
curée, but let him beware that he marks no lord's
mark nor (other) fewterers nor hunters, or he will
lose his fee. And also it is to be known that the
fees of all follies belong to the master of the harriers,
if so be that he or his deputy be at the hunting, and
blow three motes and else not, in which case the
Master of the Game can give it to whom he wishes
save what the King slayeth with his bow or the
Queen or my lord the prince, or that which they
bid with their own mouth to let run to. And all
shall be judged folly of red deer which is beneath
the hart, and of fallow deer which is beneath the
buck, nevertheless if the harrier would challenge
the deer for folly, and it is not folly, if there be a
strife with him who asketh the fee, the Master of
the Game shall judge it, and right so shall he do
of all these strifes for fees between bow and bow,
and fewterer and fewterer, and of all other strifes
and discords that belong to hunting. And when all
the deer be delivered, and the hunters and the
fewterers of the kennel be assigned to undo the deer
that be delivered for the king's larder, then should
the grooms chacechiens of the hart-hounds gather
the paunches and small guts together and do with
them as is advised in the chapter of the hart hunting
with strength, and get them a skin to lie thereover,
and do as in the same chapter described with the*

HART-HUNTING WITH GREYHOUNDS AND RACHES

(From MS. f. fr. 616, *Bib. Nat.*, Paris)

greatest and best head (antlers) *that they can find
in all the curée. Save the blowing of the prise and
the stroking and the menee, the bay should wait till
the curées be done, and the flesh taken away, and
there should the Master of the Game be, and the
sergeant and all the yeomen and grooms of the
office. And if the greyhounds* [1] *shall be rewarded
it should be done right as is devised in the aforesaid
chapter, except that the blowings above described
shall be left out. And also whosoever slew the
deer the yeomen of the office should have the skin
that lyeth upon the deer when the hounds are rewarded. And also it is to know that the harriers
when they have run shall be rewarded with the
paunches and guts, but there is no need to make a
long bay with the hart's head to them, for they are
made to run and chase all game that one wishes, and
that is the cause why the master of them has the fees
of all deer save the hart and the buck, unless it be
in the certain case before mentioned. And when
the curée is done, and the bay made, then is the
time for every man to draw homeward to his supper
and to make himself as merry as he can. And when
the yeomen berners and grooms have led home the
hounds and set them well up and supplied them
with water and straw according to what they need,
then should they go to their supper and drink well*

[1] Shirley MS., "harthounds."

and make merry. And of the fees it is to be known
that the man whoever he be, who has smitten a deer
while posted at his tree with a death-stroke so that
the deer be got before the sun goes down, he shall
have the skin. And if he be not posted or has gone
from his tree, or has done otherwise than is said, he
shall have none. And as of the fewterers, if they
be posted, the first teaser and receiver [1] that draweth
the deer down shall divide the skin.[2] Nevertheless
in other lord's hunting whoso pincheth first and
goeth therewith to the death he shall have the
skin. And all the deer's necks are the hunters, and
one shoulder and the chine is his that undoeth the
deer, and the other shoulder is the forester's or the
parker's fee that keepeth the bailie that is hunted.
And all the skins of harts slain with strength of the
hart-hounds, belong to the master of the hart-hounds
as his fee, that is to say he that hath the wages of
twelve pence a day for the office. It is to be known
that when the king hunteth in the park or in the
forest with bows and greyhounds, and it happens
that any hart be slain with strength of hart-hounds,
all the hart hunters after the King or the Master of
his Game have blown a mote and stroked, all day
they should stroke the assise that belongeth to the

[1] Shirley MS. has "resteynour."
[2] This means that the men in whose charge the teasers and
receivers were placed were given the skin or fee.

THE "CURÉE" OR REWARDING OF THE HOUNDS

(From MS. f. fr. 616, *Bib. Nat.*, Paris)

hart slain with strength, but not with eight long motes, but with four short and four long motes, as is in the aforesaid chapter plainly devised. And all the other hunters should stroke the common stroking as is above described and said.

END OF THE BRITISH MUSEUM MS.
VESPASIAN B. XII.

THE FOLLOWING IS THE CONCLUDING PASSAGE
OF THE SHIRLEY MANUSCRIPT (Add. MS.
16, 165) IN THE BRITISH MUSEUM :—

*Now I pray unto every creature that hath heard
or read this little treatise of whatever estate or
condition he be that there where there is too little
of good language that of their benignity and grace
they will add more, and there where there is too
much superfluity that they will also abridge it as
may seem best by their good and wise discretion.
Not presuming that I had over much knowledge
and ability to put into writing this royal disportful
and noble game of hunting so effectually that it
might not be submitted to the correction of all gentle
hunters. And in my simple manner as best I
could and as might be learned of old and many
diverse gentle hunters, I did my business in this
rude manner to put the craft and the terms and the
exercise of this said game more in remembrance
and openly to the knowledge of all lords, ladies,
gentlemen and women, according to the customs and
manners used in the high noble court of this Realm
of England.*

FINIS

APPENDIX

ACQUILLEZ, Fr., to take, to hold at bay, to gather. "Et s'il voit que les chiens heussent acueili le change" (G. de F., p. 156)—"if he sees that the hounds have taken the change." It also denotes : "owning to the scent" (Senechal, p. 8 ; Roy Modus, xxix. v).

Twici says : "Les chevereaus ne sunt mie enchacez ne aquyllees," which Dryden translates, "the roebuck is not chased nor hunted up," from *enquiller* or *aquiller*, O. Fr. a form of *accuellir*, to push, put in motion, excite. "The word in English which is nearest to it is 'to imprime,' which was afterwards used for the unharbouring of the hart" (Twici, p. 26).

In the old English translation of Twici (Vesp. B. XII.) *aquylees* is construed "gadered," which is certainly one sense, but not the one here required (Twici, p. 53).

The "Master of Game" translates *ils accueillent* in G. de. F., p. 112, by "they run to them" (p. 111. *See also* Godefroy).

AFFETED, Mid. Eng., *affaiten;* O. Fr. *affaitier*, to trim, to fashion. A well-affaited or affeted head, a well-fashioned or good-shaped head. In speaking of stags' antlers, means regularly tined and well grown.

Affeted also meant trained or tamed, reclaimed, made gentle, thoroughly manned. *Affaiter* is still in use in M. Fr., as a term of falconry.

We find this word employed in this sense in the Vision of Piers Plowman (1362) : "And go affayte the

Fawcons, wilde fowles to kill." And in O. Fr. sporting literature one constantly reads of " Chiens bien,
affaities" (well-broken dogs); "oiseaux bien affaities"
(well-trained hawks). Roy Modus, lxxix.; Bormans,
p. 52; *La Chace dou Cerf*, Jub. 157; T.M. vol. ii.
p. 933.

ALAUNTES, *Allaunts, Canis Alanus;* Fr. *alans.*
Also spelt *alande, alaunt, allaundes, Aloundys* (MS. Brit.
Mus., Egerton, 1995). *See also* Twici, p. 56.

A strong, ferocious dog, supposed to have been brought
to Western Europe by a Caucasian tribe called Alains
or Alani. This tribe invaded Gaul in the fourth century, settling there awhile, and then continued their
wanderings and overran Spain. It is from this country
that the best *alans* were obtained during the Middle
Ages, and dogs that are used for bull- or bear-baiting
there are still called *Alanos.* Gaston de Foix, living on
the borders of this country, was in the best position to
obtain such dogs, and to know all about them. His
description, which we have here, tallies exactly with
that written in a Spanish book, *Libro de la Monteria*,
on hunting of the fourteenth century, written by
Alphonso XI.

Alauntes were used as war dogs, and it was said that
when once they seized their prey they would not loose
their hold.

Cotgrave (Sherwood's App.) says that the mastiff
resembles an Alan, and also Wynn in his book on the
" British Mastiff" (p. 45) says that he is inclined to
think that the Alan is the ancient name for mastiff, and
thinks it possible that the Phœnicians brought this breed
to the British Isles. He cannot have known the description given us of the Alan by the " Master of Game,"
nor can he have been acquainted with the work of
Gaston Phœbus, for he says that the Alan is not mentioned among any of the earlier dogs of France and
Germany. There is ample evidence that they existed

in France from very early days. Probably they were relics left there by the Alani in their wanderings through Gaul. About the same period as our MS. we find Alans mentioned by Chaucer, who in the "Knight's Tale" describes Lycurgus seated on his throne, around which stand white *Alaunts* as big as bulls wearing muzzles and golden collars.

The ancient Gallo-Latin name of *veltrahus*, or *veltris*, which in the first instance denoted a large greyhound used for the chase of the bear and wild boar, passed later to a different kind of dog used for the same purpose. These *veltres*, *viautres*, or *vautres* were also known under the name of Alan, and resembled the Great Dane or the German Boarhound (De Noir., vol. ii. p. 295–7).

ANTLER, O. Fr. *auntilor*, *antoiller*, or *andoiller*, derived from a Teutonic root; Anglo-Saxon *andwlit*; Frank. *antlutt* or *antluzze*; Goth. *andawleiz*; O. Ger. *antliz*; face. Gaston Phœbus and Roy Modus and other old French authors almost invariably use *teste*, or head, when referring to a hart's antlers, but English writers did not observe time-hallowed terms of venery so rigorously, and our author frequently uses the jarring and, from every point of view, incorrect term "horns" when speaking of the hart's attire or head. The substance of deers' antlers is true bone, the proportion of their constituents differing but very slightly from ordinary bones. The latter, when in a healthy condition, consist of about one-third of animal matter or gelatine, and two-thirds of earthy matter, about six-sevenths of which is phosphate of lime and one-seventh carbonate of lime, with an appreciable trace of magnesia. The antlers of deer consist of about thirty-nine parts of animal matter and sixty-one parts of earthy matter of the same kind and proportion as is found in common bone. Later on, a more sportsmanlike regard for terms of venery is observable, and Turbervile in one of his few original passages impresses upon his fellow-sportsmen : "Note that

when you speake of a harts hornes, you must terme them
the Head and not the Hornes of a hart.   And likewise
of a bucke ; but a Rowes hornes and a Gotes hornes are
tollerable termes in Venery " (1611, p. 239).

Up to the end of the seventeenth century it was customary when speaking of a stag's head to refer only to
the tines " on top," or the " croches " or " troches," leaving unconsidered the brow, bez and trez tines, which
were called the stag's " rights," and which every warrantable hart was supposed as a matter of course to possess.
When referring to the number of tines a head bore, it
was invariably the rule to use only even numbers, and
to double the number of tines borne by the antler which
had most.   Thus, a stag with three on each top was a
head of " twelve of the less " (or " lasse ") ; " twelve of
the greater " when he had three and four on top, or,
counting the rights, six and seven tines, or, as a modern
Scotch stalker would call it, a thirteen-pointer.   The
extreme number of tines a hart was supposed to bear
was thirty-two.

BERCELET, barcelette, bercelette, is a corruption of
the O. Fr. *berseret*, a hunting dog, dim. of *bersier*, a
huntsman ; in Latin, *bersarius*, French, *berser*, *bercer*, to
hunt especially with the bow.   *Bercel*, *biercel*, meant a
butt or target.   Italian, *bersaglio*, an archer's butt, whence
bersagliere, archer or sharpshooter (Oxford, and Godefroy
Dict.).

Given the above derivation, it may be fairly accepted
that *bercelet* was a dog fitted to accompany a hunter who
was going to shoot his game—a shooting dog.   The
" Master of Game's " allusion also points to this.   He
says some mastiffs (*see* Mastiff) become " *berslettis*, and
also to bring well and fast a wanlace about."   We might
translate this sentence : " There are nevertheless some
(mastiffs) that become shooting dogs, and retrieve well
and put up the game quickly " (*see* Appendix : Wanlace).

Jesse conceives *bracelettas* and *bercelettus* to come from *brache*, but that can scarcely be so, as we see the two words used together, as the following quotations will show :

> " Parler m'orez d'un buen brachet.
> Qens ne rois n'ont tel berseret."
>
> T. M. i. 14404.

When the fair Ysolt is parting from her lover Tristan she asks him to leave her this same brachet, and says that no huntsman's shooting dog will be kept with more honour :

> " Husdent me lesse, ton brachet.
> Ainz berseret à vénéor
> N'ert gardeé à tel honor
> Comme cist sera."
>
> *Ibid.* i. 2660.

Jesse quotes Blount's "Antient Tenures" : "In the 6th of John, Joan, late wife of John King, held a ser-jeantry in Stanhow, in the county of Norfolk, by the service of keeping 'Bracelettum deymerettum of our Lord the King,' " and Jesse thinks these might have been a bitch pack of deerhounds, overlooking the fact that it was only in later days that the words *brache* and *rache* were used for bitch hounds. As *deymerettum* meant fallow deer, the *bracelettum* or *bercelettum deymerettum* may be taken, I think, to mean those hounds that were used for buck-shooting (Jesse, ii. 21).

BERNER, bernar ; O. Fr. *bernier, brenier*, a man who has the charge of hounds, a huntsman, or, perhaps, would be more accurately described as a kennelman. The word seems to have been derived from the French *brenier* or *bernier*, one who paid his dues to his feudal lord in bran of which bread was made for the lord's hounds. *Brenage, brennage*, or *bernage* was the tenure on which land was held by the payment of bran, and the refuse of all grains, for the feeding of hounds. Berner in its first sense meant finder of bran, then feeder of hounds. This word seems to have remained in use in England long after it had disappeared from the language of French venery. Gaston no longer uses the word *berner*, but has *valet de chiens*.

BISSHUNTERS, furhunters. Our MS. (p. 74) declares that no one would hunt conies unless they were bisshunters, that is to say rabbits would not be hunted for the sake of sport, but only for the sake of their skins. Bisse, bys, byse was a fur much in vogue at the period of our MS., as its frequent mention in contemporaneous records testifies.

BLENCHES, trick, deceit; O. N. *blekkja* (Strat.). Blanch, or blench, to head back the deer in its flight. Blancher or blencher, a person or thing placed to turn the deer in a particular direction.

BOCE, from the French *bosse*, O. Fr. *boce*, boss, hump or swelling. Cotgrave says : " Boss, the first putting out of a Deere's head, formerly cast, which our woodmen call, if it bee a red Deere's, the burle, or seale, and, if a fallow Deeres, the button."

BOUGHS, bowes (*brisées*). When the huntsman went to harbour the deer he broke little branches or twigs to mark the place where he noticed any signs of a stag. Also, at times during the chase he was instructed to do the same, placing the twigs pointing towards the direction the stag had gone, so that if the hounds lost the scent he could bring them back to his last markings, and put them on the line again. In harbouring the stag a twig was broken off and placed in front of the slot with the end pointing in the direction in which the stag was going ; each time the harbourer turned in another direction a twig was to be broken and placed so as to show which way he took ; sometimes the twig was merely bent and

left hanging on the tree, sometimes broken off and put
into the ground (in French this was called making *brisées
hautes* or *brisées basses*). When making his ring-walks
round the covert the harbourer was told to put a mark
to every slot he came across; the slot of a stag was to
be marked by scraping a line behind the heel, of a hind
by making a line in front of the toe. If it was a fresh
footing a branch or twig should be placed as well as the
marking, for a hind one twig, for a stag two. If it be a
stale trace no twig must be placed. Thus, if he returned
later, the hunter would know if any beast had broken
from or taken to covert since he harboured his stag in
the morning. When the harbourer went to "move"
the stag with his limer he was to make marks with
boughs and branches so that the berners with their hounds
should know which way to go should they be some
distance from the limer (Roy Modus, x. v; xii. r;
xiii. r; Du Fouilloux, 32 r). Blemish is the word used
by Turbervile for *brisées* (Turbervile, 1611, p. 95, 104,
114).

CHANGE. The change, in the language of stag
hunting, was the substitution of one deer for another in
the chase. After the hounds have started chasing a stag,
the hunted animal will often find another stag or a hind,
and pushing it up with its horns or feet will oblige it to
get up and take his place, lying down himself in the spot
where he found the other, and keeping quiet, with his
antlers close over his back, so that the hounds will, if
care is not taken, go off in chase of the substitute. Sometimes a stag will go into a herd of deer and try to keep
with them, trying to shake off his pursuers, and thus give
them the change.
A hound that sticks to the first stag hunted, and re-
fuses to be satisfied with the scent of another deer, is
called a staunch hound, one who will not take the
change, which was considered one of the most desirable
qualities in a staghound. G. de F., in speaking of the

different kinds of running hounds, says that there were some that, when they came to the change, they would leave off speaking to the scent, and would run silently until they found the scent of their stag again (G. de F., p. 109).

CURÉE, Kyrre, Quyrreye, or Quarry. The ceremony of giving the hounds their reward was thus called because it was originally given to the hounds on the hide or *cuir* of the stag.

Twici, the huntsman of Edward II., says that after the stag is taken the hounds should be rewarded with the neck and bowels and the liver. ("Et il se serra mange sur le quir. E pur ceo est il apelee quyrreye.") When the hounds receive their reward after a hare-hunt he calls it the hallow. In the "Boke of St. Albans" we find the quarry given on the skin, and it is only in the "Master of Game" that it is expressly stated that a nice piece of grass was to be found on which the hounds' mess was to be put, and the hide placed over it, hair-side upwards, the head being left on it and held up by the antlers, and thus drawn away as the hounds rush up to get their share. According to Turbervile, in his day the reward was placed *on* the hide; at least he does not in his original chapter on the breaking up of the deer notice any such difference between the French and English customs. In France, it is as well to expressly state, the *curée* was always given on the hide until the seventeenth century, but after that it seems the hide was placed over it just as described in our text (De Noirmont, vol. ii., p. 458). Preceding the quarry came the ceremonial breaking up of the deer. The stag was laid on its back with feet in the air, slit open, and skinned by one of the chief huntsmen, who took a pride in doing it according to laws of woodmanscraft. They took a pride in not turning up their sleeves and performing everything so daintily that their garments should show no bloodstains; nobles, and princes themselves, made it a point of honour to be well versed in this art. After the skinning was done, it was customary to give the huntsman who was "undoing" the deer a drink of wine; "and he must drinke a good harty draught: for if he should break up the dear before he drinke the Venison would stink and putrifie" (Turb., 1611, p. 128).

In the "Master of Game" the limers were rewarded after the other hounds, but they were never allowed to take their share with the pack.

The bowels or guts were often reserved, and put on a large wooden fork, and the hounds were allowed to have this as a sort of dessert after they had finished their portion. They were halloaed to by the huntsman whilst he held the fork high in the air with cries of *Tally ho!* or *Tiel haut!* or *Lau, lau!* This tit-bit was then thrown to them. This was called giving them the *forhu*, from the word *forthuer*, to whoop or holloa loudly. Probably our term of giving the hounds the holloa was derived from this. It was done to accustom the hounds to rally round the huntsman when excited by a similar halloaing when they were hunting, and had lost the line of the hunted beast.

In some instances the daintiest morsels were reserved for the King or chief personage, and for this purpose placed on a large wooden fork as they were taken from the deer. The vein of the heart and the small fillets attached to the loins (Turbervile says also the haunches, part of the nombles and sides) should also be kept for the lord, but these were generally recognised as the perquisites of the huntsmen, kennelmen, foresters, or parkers.

EXCREMENTS, fumes, fewmets, obs. term for the droppings of deer. From the Fr. *fumées*. G. de F. says that the droppings of all deer, including fallow and roe deer, are to be called *fumées*. The "Master of Game," no doubt following the custom then prevalent in England, says the droppings of the hart only are to be called fumes, and of the buck and the roebuck croties. The following names are given to droppings by—

GASTON DE FOIX	AND	MASTER OF GAME
Of the hart } ,, buck } Fumées. ,, roebuck }		Of the hart—Fumes. ,, buck } Croteys. ,, roebuck }

Of the hart }
  ,,   buck } Fumées.
  ,,   roebuck }
  ,,   bear }
  ,,   wild boar } Laisses.
  ,,   wolf }
  ,,   hare and conies—Crotes.
  ,,   fox, badger, and } Fiantes.
      stinking beasts }
  ,,   otter—Spraintes.

Of the hart—Fumes.
  ,,   buck } Croteys.
  ,,   roebuck }
  ,,   wild boar }
  ,,   black beasts and } Lesses.
      wolves }
  ,,   hare and Conies—Croties.
  ,,   fox—The wagging.
  ,,   grey or badger—The Wardrobe.
  ,,   stinking beasts—The Drit.
  ,,   otter—Spraintes.

Other forms of this term are : fewmets, fewmishing, crotels, crotisings, freyn, fuants, billetings, and spraits.

FENCE MONTH. The month so called began, according to Manwood, fifteen days before and ended fifteen days after midsummer. During this time great care was taken that no men or stray dogs should be allowed to wander in the forest, and no swine or cattle were allowed to feed within the precincts, so that the deer should be absolutely undisturbed during three or four weeks after the fawning season. He tells us that because in this month there must be watch and ward kept with men and weapons for the fence and defence of wild beasts, for that reason the same is called fence or defence month (Man., p. 76, ed. 1598).

FEWTE, fuite, fute (M. E.), O. Fr. fuite (*voie de cerf qui fuit*), track, trace, foot. Gawaine : feute. Will of Palerne (90) : foute. Some beasts were called of the sweet *fute*, and some of the stinking *fute*. The lists of the beasts which should come under either heading vary somewhat ; some that are placed by the "Boke of St. Albans" under "Swete fewte" coming under the other category in the MS. Harl., 2340.

In " Boke of St. Albans."	In Harl. MS. 2340, fol. 50b.

Beasts of " Swete fewte."

The Buck, the Doo, the Beere, the Reynd, the Elke, the Spycard, the Otre, and the Martwn.	The Buke, the Doo, the Ber, the Reyne der, the Elke, the Spycard.

Beasts of the " Stinking fewte."

The Roobucke, the Roo, the Fulmard, the Fyches, the Bauw, the Gray, the Fox, the Squirrel, the Whitecat, the Otyr, the Stot, the Pulcatt.	. . . . . The Fulmard, the Fechewe, the Catt, the Gray, the Fox, the Wesyll, the Marteron, the Squirrel, the Whyterache, the Otyr, the Stote, the Polcatte.

In Roy Modus the beasts are also divided into *bestes doulces* and *bestes puans*. The reasons for doing so are also given (fol. lxii.): " *Les bestes doulces sont : le cerf, la biche, le dain, le chevreul et le lièvre. Et sont appelées doulces pour trois causes : La première si est que d'elles ne vient nulle mauvais senteur ; la seconde, elles ont poil de couleur aimable, lequel est blond ou fauve ; la tierce cause, ce ne sont mie bestes mordans comme les autres cincq, car elles n'ont nulz dens dessus ; et pour ces raisons puent bien estre nommées bestes doulces.*" Under the *bestes puans* are classed the wild boar, the wild sow, the wolf, the fox, and the otter.

FEWTERER, the man that lets loose the greyhounds (Blome, p. 27); from *veltraria*, a dog leader or courser; originally one who led the dogs called *veltres*, *viautres* (*see* Veltres). In Gallo-Latin, Veltrahus. It has been asserted that the word fewterer is a corruption

of *vautre* or *viautre*, a boarhound, but although both
evidently owe their origin to the same parent-word,
fewterer can scarcely be derived from *vautre*, a boarhound. It was only in the Middle Ages in France that
the word *vautre*, from originally meaning a powerful
greyhound, was applied to a large boarhound. Fewterers
in England appear invariably as attendants on greyhounds, not boarhounds. Another derivation has been
also given from fewte, foot or track, a fewterer being,
according to this, a huntsman who followed the track of
the beast. But *venator* was the contemporary designation for a huntsman, and as far as we can ascertain the
fewterer was always merely a dog-leader.

FORLONGE, forloyng, forlogne, from the Fr. *fort
loin*. G. de F. says, "flies far from the hounds," *i.e.*
having well distanced them ("*Fuit de fort longe aux chiens,
c'est a dire que il les ait bien esloinhes*"). Hounds are said
to be hunting the forlonge when the deer is some way
in front of them, or when some of the hounds have got
away with the deer and have outpaced the rest. As our
MS. (p. 173) says, the forlogne should be blown if the
stag has run out of hearing of hound and horn, but it
should not be blown in a park. In old French hunting literature it is an expression one constantly comes
across.

Twici, writing almost a hundred years earlier than
the Duke of York, says: "The hart is moved and I do
not know where the hart is gone, nor the gentlefolk, and
for this I blow in that manner. What chase do we call
this? We call that chase The chase of the forloyng."

Forloyneth: "When a hound meeteth a chase and
goeth away with it far before the rest then we say he
forloyneth" (Turber., ed 1611, p. 245).

FOX. According to the laws of Canute the fox was
neither reckoned as a beast of venery nor of the forest.
In Manwood's Forest Laws he is classed as the third

beast of chase (p. 161), as he is also in Twety and Gyfford, and the "Boke of St. Albans."

Although early records show that the English Kings kept their foxhounds, we hear nothing of their having participated in this sport, but they seem to have sent their hounds and huntsmen about the country to kill foxes, probably as much for the value of the pelt as for relieving the inhabitants of a thievish neighbour.

In Edward's I.'s Wardrobe Accounts, 1299–1300, appear some interesting items of payments made to the huntsman for his wages and the keep of the hounds and his *one horse* for carrying the nets. These allusions to nets throw an interesting light on the fox-hunting of those days. William de Blatherwyke, or, as he is also called, *William de Foxhunte*, and *William Fox-dog-keeper*, had besides their wages an allowance made to them for clothes and winter and summer shoes (*see* Appendix : Hunt Officials). As only one horse was provided, and that to carry the nets, the huntsman, we must presume, had to hunt on foot, not such an arduous undertaking when we remember that the country was so much more thickly wooded than at present, and that every possible precaution was taken to prevent Reynard's breaking covert.

We see by our text (p. 65) that it was usual to course foxes with greyhounds, and although the passages referring to this are translated from G. de F. we know from many old records that this fox-coursing was as usual in England at this time as in France.

In the earlier days hounds used for the chase of the fox one day, probably hunted hare, or even buck or stag, on another—such as the harriers, which, if we can believe Dr. Caius, were entered to any animal from stag to stoat (*see* Appendix : Harriers). The first real pack of foxhounds is said to be the one established by Thomas Fownes, Esq., of Stepleton, in Dorsetshire (1730). They were purchased at an immense price by Mr. Bowes, of Yorkshire. A very amusing description is given in

"Cranbourne Chase" of the first day's hunting with
them in their new country. There must have been
several packs entered to fox only about the end of the
eighteenth century, for an erstwhile Master of the Cheshire
Foxhounds had in his possession a horn with the following inscription : "Thomas Boothby Esqre. Tooley Park
Leicester. With this horn he hunted the first pack of
foxhounds then in England 5 years : born in 1677 died
1752." This pack, which was purchased by "the great
Mr. Meynell" in 1782, had been hunted both in Hamp-
shire and in Wiltshire previously by the ancestors of Lord
Arundel (Bad. Lib., "Hunting," p. 29).

FRAYING-POST, the tree a stag has rubbed his
antlers or frayed against.
By the fraying-post the huntsman used to be able to
judge if the stag he wished to harbour was a warrantable
stag or not. The greater the *fraying-post* the larger the
deer (Stuart, vol. ii. p. 551).

FUES, "not find his fues," not to find his line of
flight, his scent ; Gaston says : "Ne puissent deffaire ses
esteurses" : literally, "cannot unravel his turnings."
Fues, flight, fuite, track. Gaston calls these sometimes
voyes. *Voyes* was written later *Foyes* (Fouilloux).
FUE. "Se mettre a la fue" (var. *fuie*), (to take flight)
(Borman, p. 89).

GLADNESS, glade. The original sense is a smooth,
bare place, or perhaps a bright, clear place in a wood.

GREASE. One of the important technical terms of
venery, related to the fat of game ; for in the Middle Ages,
when game was hunted to replenish the larder as much as
for sport, it entered largely into the economy of even the
highest households. The fat of the red deer and fallow
deer was called *suet*, occasionally *tallow*. That of the roebuck was bevy-grease. Between that of the hare, boar,

wolf, fox, marten, otter, badger, and coney no difference was made—it was called grease; and in one sense this general term was also used for deer: "a deer of high grease," or "a hart in the pride of grease," were phrases used for the season of the year when the stag and the buck were fattest (*see* Appendix : Seasons of Hunting).

GREASE TIME, not *Grace Time* or *Grass Time*, as Strutt and others have it. It did not include the whole season when the hart or buck could be killed, but meant to indicate the time when they were fat and fittest for killing. As pointed out already by Dryden (p. 25), the *Excerpta Historica* (Lond. 1831) contains an interesting example of the use of this word. This is a letter written (p. 356) about 1480 by Thomas Stonor, Steward of the Manor of Thame. He was in Fleet Prison at the time he writes to his brother in the country concerning some property of his own in his brother's neighbourhood. "No more to youe at thys tyme but . . . more ovr I entende to kepe my gresse tyme in yat countre, where fore I wolle yat no mane huntte tylle I have bene ther."

In the privy-purse expenses of Henry VIII. (1532) is an entry of a payment for attendance on the king during the last *grece-time*. Cavendish in his Life of Wolsey says : "My lord continued at Southwell until the latter end of *grease time.*" Both these passages refer to the month of June. In the laws of Howel the Good, King of Wales, a fine of 12 kine was imposed on whoever kills a hart in grease time (*kylleic*) of the kings.

Confusion arose occasionally owing to the similarity of the words as formerly spelt, grass being sometimes spelt "grysse" (Dryden, p. 25). Manwood, also, misinterprets Grease time. In the agreement between the Earl of Winchester and the Baron of Dudley of 1247, in which their respective rights of hunting in Charnwood Forest and Bradgate Park, Leicestershire, were defined, and which agreement Shirley has given (in a translation) in his "English Deer Parks," the time of the fallow buck season (*tempus pinguedinis*) or grease time or the fat season, is fixed between the Feast of St. Peter ad Vincula (August 1) and the Exaltation of Holy Cross (September 6, 14), while the time of the doe season (*tempus firmationis*) was fixed between the Feast of St. Martin (November 11) and the Purification of the Blessed Virgin (February 2).

GREYHOUND, Fr. *levrier*, Lat. *leporarius*. Under this name a whole group of dogs were included, that were used for the chase of big and small game. They were swift hounds, hunting chiefly and in most cases by sight only. For in the Middle Ages the name greyhound, or *levrier*, denoted such seemingly different dogs as the immense Irish wolfhound, the Scotch deerhound, and the smaller, smooth-coated, elegant Italian greyhound. The powerful greyhound used for the chase of stag, wolf, and wild boar were known in France as *levrier d'attache*, and the smaller, nervous harehound as *petit levrier pour lievre*. In our illustrations we can see what are intended to be portraits of both the larger and the smaller kinds, some being smooth- and some rough-coated. The bigger hounds were considered capable of defending their masters against their armed enemies, as is shown by numerous legends of the Middle Ages, which, although they may not be strictly historical facts, showed the reputation these dogs enjoyed in those days (Jesse, p. 19).

Greyhounds were the constant companions of their masters during journeys and wars, and at home. In the houses they were allowed the greatest liberty, and seem to have ranged at will in both living- and bedrooms; one sees them at the board when their owners are at meals, at the fireside, and they even accompanied their masters as good Christians to mass.

No hound seems to belong so peculiarly to the epoch of chivalry as the greyhound, and indeed one can scarcely picture a knight without one. A Welsh proverb declared that a gentleman might be known " by his hawk, his horse, and his greyhound." By a law of Canute, a greyhound was not to be kept by any person inferior to a gentleman ("Greyhounds," by a Sportsman, p. 28; and Dalziel, vol. i. p. 25).

Canis Gallicus was the name used by the Gauls for their coursing dogs, which were most probably greyhounds, and Arian says they were called *Vertragia*, from a Celtic word denoting swiftness. In Gallo-Latin the name for a large greyhound was *Veltrahus* or *veltris* (De Noir., ii. 295). They were also called *Veltres leporarii* (Blane, p. 46). There is some difference of opinion as to the derivation of our word greyhound. In the early Anglo-Norman days they retained their French name of *levrier*, or Latin *leporarius*. When our MS. was penned the English word *grei*, *gre*, or *grewhound* was in general use; it is thought by some to be derived from Grew hound or Greek hound, as they were supposed to have been originally brought from Greece. Others, again, consider that the name was simply taken from the prevalent colour of the common greyhound. Jesse gives the most likely origin of the name. "Originally it was most likely *grehund*, and meant the noble, great, choice, or prize hound" (Jesse, ii. 71; and Dalziel, i. 23). Probably the Celtic denomination for a dog, *grech* or *greg*, stands in close connection with our word greyhound (Cupples, p. 230). White seems to have been the favourite colour, and to say one had *i levrier plus blanc que flors de lis* (*Heruis de Mes*, 107a, 44; Bangert, p. 172) would be the greatest tribute to the beauty of one's hound. *Co si sunt deus leveres nurit en ma meisun, cume cisne sunt blauns* (Horn, 613 f.).

When Froissart went home from Scotland he is depicted as riding a grey horse and leading *un blanc levrier*, perhaps one of the four he took from these isles and presented to the Comte de Foix at Orthéz, whose names have been preserved to us as Tristan, Hector, Brun, and Rolland (La Curne de la Palaye).

Greyhounds were used, as has already been mentioned, for all kind of hunting and every kind of game, in conjunction with limers who started the game for them. They were let slip as relays to a pack of running or scenting hounds, and they were used by themselves for coursing game in an open country, or were placed at the passes where game was likely to run and were slipped to turn the game back to the archer or to chase and pull down the wounded deer (*see* Appendix : Stables). In our illustrations we see them in the pictures of stag-, hare-, roe- and boar-hunting, to say nothing of badger-hunting, for which one would have thought any other dog more suitable.

They seem always to have been held in couples except when following their master and he not bent upon the chase. The collars to which these couplings were attached were often wonderful gems of the goldsmith's and silver-smith's art. Such an item appears in the Q. R. Ward-robe Acc. for 1400 (Wylie, iv. p. 196): "2 collars for greyhounds (*leverer*) ie tissue white and green with letters and silver turrets." Another one of "soy chekerey vert et noir avec le tret (? turret) letters and bells of silver gilt."

The ancient doggerel in the Book of St. Albans, "Heded like a snake, and necked like a drake. Foted like a cat. Tayled like a Rat, Syded lyke a Teme. Chyned like a Beme" ("Boke of St. Albans," f. iv.), was preceded by a very similar one written some time previously by Gace de la Buigne. Of these verses G. de F. gives, twenty-eight years later, a prose version, which our Master of Game has rendered into English.

HARDEL, hardeyl, to tie couples of hounds together. From the French word *harder*, which has the same meaning : *Harder les chiens*, and *harde*, the rope with which they are tied. It is derived from *hart*, *hard*, *art*, a binder of willow or other pliable wood used for fastening fagots together (Lit. and God.). The primitive way of tying hounds together was by passing such a small flexible branch through the couplings which bent back on itself, both ends being held. "*Les chiens . . . seront enhardez par les couples à genoivres ou à autre josne bois tors*" (Roy Modus, f. xlvii. recto). In France there used to be two *hardes* to each relay and not more than eight hounds in every harde (D'Yauville). In England there used to be about the same number. The term was still used in Blome's time (1686), for he writes in his "Gentleman's Recreation": "The huntsman on foot that hath the charge of the coupled hounds, and before that must have *hardled* them, that is, with a slip, for the purpose ready secured three or four couple together, that they may not break in from him, to run into the cry of the Finders" (p. 88).

Harling was a word used in Devonshire, and as it meant tying the hound together by means of a rope passed through the rings of the couples, it is undoubtedly a corruption of the word *hardeling*. "Until comparatively recent times the hounds in Devonshire were taken to the meet and held in this manner until the time came to lay the pack on" (Collyns).

Hardel, the technical O. E. term for binding together the four legs of the roebuck, the head having been placed between the two forelegs, in order to carry him whole into the kitchen.

HARE. Pliny records the fable that hares "are of many and various sexes." Topsell remarks that "the Hebrews call the hare 'arnebet,' in the feminine gender," which word gave occasion to an opinion that all hares were females (pp. 264, 266).

"In the Gwentian code of Welch laws supposed to be of the eleventh century, the hare is said not to be capable of any legal valuation, being in one month male and in another female" (Twici, p. 22).

Certainly in many of the older writings on hares the pronouns "her" and "him" are used indiscriminately in the same sentence. Sir Thomas Browne in his treatise on vulgar errors asserts from his own observation that

the sex of the hare is changeable, and that the buck hare
will sometimes give birth to young. Up to the end of
the eighteenth century there was a widespread and firm
belief in this fable (Brehm, ii. p. 626). Buffon describes
it as one of the animal's peculiar properties, and from the
structure of their parts of generation he argues that the
notion has arisen of hermaphrodite hares, that the males
sometimes bring forth young, and that some are alternately
males and females and perform the functions of either
sex.

"Master of Game" (copying G. de F.) states that
the hare carries her young for a period of two months,
but in reality the period of gestation is only thirty days.
Harting says that the adult hare will breed twice or
thrice in the year, but Brehm declares they breed as
many as four times, and but seldom five times (Encyclop.
of Sport, vol. ii. p. 504; Brehm, vol. ii. p. 626; G. de
F. p. 47).

G. de F. (p. 43) says of a hare, "*Elle oīt bien, mais elle
voit mal.*" "Master of Game" translates this simply as
She hath evil sight; but does not say she hears well. The
sense of hearing is most highly developed in the hare,
and every lightly breaking twig or falling leaf will disturb her. It is said that of old when warreners wished
to prepare hares for the market they filled their ears with
wax, so that, not being continually disturbed by noises,
they did not move about much, and grew sleek and fat
(Blome, p. 95). G. de F.'s assertion that the hare "has
evil sight" is also confirmed by Brehm, who, however,
says that they are endowed with a keen sense of smell,
whereas G. de F. says *elle sent pou.*

Attention has already been called to the Duke of
York's statement that "the hare hath great fear to run."
This arose probably from the similarity of the words
peur and *pouvoir* in the MSS., for it should read "hath
great power to run," the principal MSS. which we have
examined showing *pouvoir*. Verard in his first edition
of G. de F. also has the same rendering as the Duke of

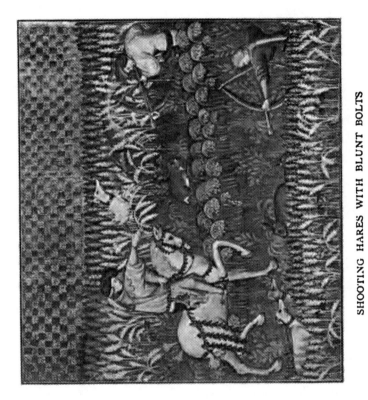

SHOOTING HARES WITH BLUNT BOLTS

(From MS. f. fr. 616, *Bib. Nat.*, Paris)

York, to which Lavallée draws attention as being one
of the many ludicrous mistakes in this edition (G.
de F., xli.).

Our text calls the hare the most marvellous beast
(p. 181), the reasons given being because she "fumeth
or croteth and rowngeth and beareth tallow and grease."
By "rowngeth" (Fr. *ronger*) it was meant that the hare
chewed the cud, as by the ancients it was generally supposed that the hare was a ruminant. Although this is
not the case, and the hare has not a compound stomach,
nevertheless this belief showed a close observation of
nature, for when a hare is seated she can bring up parts
of her food and give it a second mastication.

The hare and rabbit have little or no fat, but what
they do possess is called grease. Twici says: *Il porte
gresce* (pp. 1 and 21).

"She has teeth above in the same wise as beneath"
(p. 181) is another of the peculiarities noticed in our text,
which shows that the difference in dentition that dis-
tinguishes the hare from all other rodents had been re-
marked. Instead of two incisors in the upper jaw, the
hare has four, having two small rudimentary incisor teeth
behind the two large front ones, and five or six molars
in the upper jaw, with two incisors and five molars in the
lower jaw (Brehm, ii. p. 627; Cornish, "Shooting," ii.
p. 153).

It is difficult to know why the hare was considered a
"melancholy" beast, and how this curious reputation
was kept up during the whole of the Middle Ages.
It was thought that eating the flesh of the hare rendered
one also subject to melancholy. G. de F. does not
mention this, and altogether his book is comparatively
free of such superstitions, but he says the flesh of the
hare should not be given to the hounds after a day's
hunting, as it is indigestible: *quar elle est fastieuse viande
et les fet vomir* (p. 210). Therefore, when rewarding the
hounds, they should only have the tongue and the kidneys,
with some bread soaked in the blood of the hare.

In our MS., at the end of the chapter on the nature of the hare (p. 22), the Duke of York says that he "trows no good huntèr would slee them so," alluding to pockets, pursenets, and other poaching devices; and although G. de F. gives six ways of taking the hare, he does not approve of such methods for the true sportsman, but enters an amusing protest : "I would that they who take hares thus should have them [the cords] round their own necks" (p. 171). Snaring hares was never considered legitimate sport. In hare-hunting proper, the hounds were taken into the fields to find the hare, as at present ; or hare-finders were sent out early in the morning, and the tufts of grass or plants where the hare was likely to be seated were beaten, and the hounds uncoupled only when the hare was started. One of the chief differences in the sport between then and now was that often, when the hare was once on foot, greyhounds were also uncoupled, and our Plate, p. 182, shows greyhounds and running-hounds hunting seemingly happily together. It must have been rather discouraging for the old-fashioned, slow scenting-hound to have the hare he has been diligently hunting suddenly "bitten" in front of him by the swifter greyhound. Trencher-fed packs also existed as early as the fourteenth century, and we read in Gace de la Buigne that the small farmers would assemble together, bringing all told some forty hounds of different breeds and sizes, immensely enjoying their sport, and accounting for many hares.

HARNESS means in our text "paraphernalia wherewith animals can be caught or taken." It is frequently used in this sense by Gaston—*Hayes et autres Harnoys* (p. 126). In Julien's note to this same sentence occurring in *Le bon Varlet*, he says, *autres harnois, autres engins, instruments, procédés.*

HARRIER, spelt in early documents with many variations—*eirere, heyreres, heyrer, hayrers.* A hound which is described in modern dictionaries as "resembling a fox-hound but smaller, used for hare-hunting" (Murray). This explanation would not have been a correct one for our harriers of the fourteenth century, for as far as we can gather they were used to hunt all kinds of game and by no means only the hare. They were evidently a smaller kind of running hound, for as our MS. says, there are some small and some large running hounds, "and the small are called Kenettis (or small dogs—*see* Kenet), and these hounds run well to all manner of game and they that serve for all game men call them heirers" (p. 111). And in chapter 36 we see that *heyrers* were used to hunt up the deer in the forest, the herthounds and greyhounds meanwhile being held in leash till a warrantable deer was on foot, or till "the heyrer have well run and well made the rascal void" (made the smaller deer clear out of that part of the forest) (p. 191). Then the herthounds were to be uncoupled where the most likely "ligging is for an hert, and seek." The herthounds then put up the wary old stag and hunted him till he came to the tryst where the King would be with his long bow or cross-bow, or till the hert was pulled down by them or the greyhounds which had been slipped at him.

In the chapter on hare-hunting in our MS. the word harrier does not occur; only hounds, greyhounds, and raches are mentioned. So when Henry IV. paid for "*La garde de nos chiens appelez hayrers*" (Privy Seal, 20 Aug. 9th Henry, 1408, No. 5874), or Henry V. for the "*Custodiam Canum nostrum vocatorum hayreres*" (Rot. Pat. 1 Henry V. 1413), it was not because they were especially addicted to hare-hunting, but because they kept these useful hounds to "harry" game.

In 1407 we find one Hugh Malgrave "*servienti venatori' vocat' hayters p' c'vo (cervo)*," which we may accept as another proof that their office was to hunt the stag. The Duke of York also repeatedly says that "*heirers*" run at all game (see pp. 111, 196, 197). In 1423 Hugh Malgrave still held the "office of the hayrers" by grant from Henry IV. In the curious legal Latin of the thirteenth century, we find the word *canes heirettes*, and *heyrettor* (Wardrobe Accounts, 34 Ed. I.).

There are a great number of early records which show us that these hounds were used then for hunting red and fallow deer, sometimes in conjunction with greyhounds and sometimes without their aid.

Harriers were sometimes taken with buckhounds on hunting expeditions as well as with greyhounds. In some of the documents harriers are simply alluded to as *canes currentes*. As they were not a distinct breed, but were included under the designation "raches," or running hounds, a separate chapter is not given to them in our text, and neither Twici nor the Dame of St. Albans mentions these hounds. Gradually we find the spelling, although presenting still countless variations, bringing the *a* more constantly than the *e*; the "*heirers*" become *hayrers, hareres, hariers,* and after the sixteenth century *harriers*. It is also probable that the word was originally derived from the Anglo-Saxon *Hergian, herian*, to harry, to disturb, to worry; O. Fr. *harrier, herrier, herier*, to harry; F. *hare* and *harer*, to set a dog on to attack. The harrier, in fact, was a dog to "hare" the game. Although now obsolete, we find this word used late in the seventeenth century.

"Let the hounds kill the fox themselves and worry and *hare* him as much as they please" (Cox, "Gent. Rec.," p. 110). It is also in the sixteenth century that one comes across the first allusions to their use in hunting the hare.

HART. It is not necessary to dwell here at length upon the great esteem in which the hart was held by all devotees to sport in Europe during the Middle Ages. It was royal game, and belonged to the Prince or ruler of the country, and the chase was their prerogative. Few unconnected with the court were ever able to enjoy the chase of the stag unless in attendance on or by special licence granted by the sovereign. Those who had extensive property of their own and had permission to erect a fence could, of course, keep deer on it, but this did not enable them to enjoy the sport of real wild deer hunting, or *La chasse Royale* as the French called it.

The stag was one of the five beasts of venery, and was, according to the ancient French regulations, a beast of the sweet foot, although in the list of beasts of sweet and stinking foot given in the "Boke of St. Albans" the hart is included in neither category (*see* Appendix: Fewte).

One of the first essentials for a huntsman in the Middle Ages was to learn to know the different *signs* of a stag (according to German venery there were seventy-two signs), so as to be able to "judge well." These signs were those of the *slot*, the *gait*, the *fraying-post*, the *rack* or *entry* (*i.e.* the place where the stag entered covert), and the *fumes*. By recognising differences in these signs made by a young stag, a hind, and a warrantable stag, he was enabled to find out where the latter was harbouring, and by the slot and gait he could recognise when the chased stag was approaching his end.

There were many things that the huntsman of old had to learn regarding the stag before he could be considered as more than an apprentice—for instance, how to speak of a hart in terms of venery. The terms used were considered of the greatest importance, even to the manner in which the colour of the stag was spoken of, brown, yellow, or dun being the only permissible terms to distinguish the shade of colour. Special terms are given for every kind of head, or antlers, a stag might bear.

The huntsman spoke of the stag's *blenches* and *ruses* when alluding to the tricks of a deer when trying to rid himself of the hounds, of his *doubling* and *rusing to and fro upon himself* when he retraced his steps, of his *beating up the river* when he swam up-stream, and of *foiling down*, when he went down-stream, or of *going to soil* when he stood in water. When the deer lay down he was *quat*,

P

when he stood still in covert he was *stalling*. When he was tired he "*cast his chaule*," *i.e.* drooped his head, a well-known sign when the deer is done, as was his closed mouth when dead beat.

The hart was *meved* or moved, when he was started from his resting-place; he was *quested* or hunted for, and *sued* or chased; his resting-place was called his *ligging* or *lair*, his scent of line of flight, his *fues*. He was spoken of as *soule* or *soile* (F. *seule*) if unaccompanied by other deer, and in "*herd with rascal and folly*" if keeping company with lesser deer.

Besides many other quaint terms of venery the following were the designations given to the hart according to his age by :—

"Master of Game."	Twici, "Boke of St. Albans," Manwood, Turbervile.	Blome; Cox's "Gentleman's Recreations."
1st yr. A calf.	A calf.	A hinde-calf or calf.
2nd „ A bullock.	A brocket.	A knobler or knobber.
3rd „ A brocket.	A spayer, spayard, or spayd.	A brocket or brocke.
4th „ A staggart.	A staggart or stag.	A staggard.
5th „ A hart of ten.	A hart.	A hart.

Until he was a hart of ten our text tells us he was not considered a chaseable or warrantable deer. By the above one will see that the "Master of Game" is exceptional in calling a deer of the second year a bullock, brocket being the usual term.

In old French literature we occasionally find the word *broches* used for the tines of a deer's antlers; brochet would be the diminutive, *i.e.* a small tine, and hence perhaps brocket, a young stag bearing small tines. Any stag of ten or over if hunted by the king became a Hart Royal, and if hunted and not taken, but driven out of the forest, a proclamation was made to warn every one that no person should chase or kill the said hart, and he was then a "Hart Royal proclaimed" (Man., p. 180).

All stags not chaseable, such as young or lean stags and hinds, were classed as folly or rascal.

A young stag accompanying an old one was called his squire (F. *escuyer*).

Hinds also were called by different names from the first to the third year, but the "Master of Game" does not give these, nor do any of the earliest works. Manwood, Blome, and Cox give the following terms: first year, a calf; second year, a Hearse or brocket's sister; third year and ever after, a hind. A somewhat similar term was employed in France to denote a young stag between six months and a year old. *Haire*, also spelt *her* (G. de Champgrand Baudrillard), and *Harpaille*, was the term for a herd of young stags and hinds.

Hart's Age.—The fable that a stag can live a hundred years which the "Master of Game" repeats (p. 34) after G. de F. was not of the latter's invention, but one that had been current for many centuries before their day.

HORNS.—When the "Master of Game" was written hunting horns were the curved primitive shape of those made from the horns of animals, and most of them probably were still made of the horns of cattle, while those used by the richer gentry and nobles were fashioned from some rarer animals' trophy, such as the ibex, or carved of ivory, and some were made of precious metal. But whether of simple horn, ivory, or of wood, they were decorated with gold or silver ferrules, rings, and mouthpieces, and some being provided with a stopper, could be converted into drinking horns. Unfortunately the "Master of Game" does not tell us the material of which horns should be made. He simply says how they should "be dryve." They were to be two spans long (1 ft. 6 in.), slightly curved so that both ends were raised from three to four fingers' breadth above the centre; the larger end or the bell was to be as wide as possible, and the mouthpiece not too small. It was waxed thickly or thinly, whichever the huntsman thought produced the best sound. What effect the wax had can scarcely be judged, but it was evidently considered an improvement, as it is stated that for foresters "mene hornes and unwexid" are good enough for them. Besides the hunter's horn five different kinds of horns are mentioned in our MS.—the bugle, great abbots, ruets, small foresters, and mean horns. The bugle was not the trumpet we now understand by that name, but a simple curved horn, most probably deriving its name from the bugle, as the wild ox was called; although Dryden says from the German word *bugel*, a curve or bend. Ruets may have been the name for a much curved or almost circular horn, from French *rouette*, small wheel. The mean horns were probably the medium-sized, shrill-sounding horns made out of wood or bark, known as *ménuels, menuiaux, moienel, menuier*, &c. (Perc. 27,166 and 27,140).

A good length for a horn is mentioned as being "*une paume et demie*" (Perceval, 31,750). It is uncertain whether this length and that given by the "Master of Game" were measured round the inside of the bend or in a straight line between the two extremities. The famous Borstall horn, also known as Nigel's horn, is 2 feet 4 inches long on the convex and 23 inches on the concave bend; the inside measure of the bell end being 3 inches in diameter. The size of another noted horn, *i.e.* the Pusey horn, is 2 feet ½ inch long, the circumference at the widest end being 12 inches. The general length of these horns seems to have been somewhere between 18 inches and 2 feet. The above-mentioned specimens were horns of tenure, the first being a hunting-, the second a drinking-horn. The Borstall horn is said to have been given by Edward the Confessor to one Nigel, in reward for his killing an immense wild boar, and by this horn he and his successors for generations held lands of the crown.

The curved horn remained in fashion in England till about the latter half of the seventeenth century, then a straight one came into use about 1 ft. 6 in. to 2 ft. long, such as we see depicted in Blome. Of this shape, but a few inches shorter, is the hunting-horn still in use in England. The French hunting-horn was used in England in the eighteenth century, but did not remain long in fashion.

HUNTING CRIES. We can see that the hunting cries and the language used in speaking to the hounds when hunting in the days of the "Master of Game" were still those brought into Britain by the Normans, and in most instances the words can actually still be recognised as French. There are only a few examples given by him as to the manner a huntsman should speak to his hounds in the stag-hunting chapters, such as :—

Ho moy, ho moy, hole, hole, hole : To encourage the limer when drawing for a stag (p. 166).

Cy va, cy va, cy va : To call the hounds when any signs of the stag were seen (p. 167).

Le douce mon amy, le douce : "Softly, my friend, softly." To the hounds when they were uncoupled near to where the stag was supposed to be lying.

Sto arere, so howe, so howe : "Hark back," if the hounds were on a wrong scent.

Hoo sto, ho sto, mon amy, ho sto : To harriers drawing for a stag.

Oyez, à Beaumont, oyez, assemble à Beaumont : "Hark to Beaumont, hark, get to him." To the hound of that name who picks up the right line, and to bring the other hounds to him.

It is in the hare-hunting chapter that we have more of the "fayre wordis of venery," and here, if the "Master of Game" does not slavishly copy Twici, yet he employs the same cries, with a slight difference only in orthography. The "Boke of St. Albans" has also most of the following :—

Hoo arere : "Back there." When the hounds come too hastily out of the kennel.

So moun amy atreyt : Until they come into the field ;

these two are not given by Twici, but the following are identical in both books :—

Hors de couple, avaunt sy avaunt, and thrice *so howe :* When the hounds are uncoupled.

Sa sa cy avaunt, cy sa avaunt, sa cy avaunt (avaunt, sire, avaunt, in Twici) : Forward, sir, forward.

Here how, amy, how amy, and *Swef, mon amy, swef :* "Gently, my friend, gently " (*swef,* from Latin *swavis*), when the hounds draw too fast from the hunts- man.

Oyez, à Beaumont (in Twici : *Oyez, a Beaumont le vaillaunt que il quide trover le coward od la courte cowe*) : " Hark to Beaumont the valiant, who thinks to find the coward with the short tail."

La douce, la il ad este sohowe : " Softly, there—here he has been," if the place where the hare has pastured is seen.

Illoeques, illoeques : " Here, here," if the hounds hunt well on the line (*see* Appendix : Illoeques).

Ha sy toutz, cy est il venuz arere, so howe. Sa cy a este so howe. Sa cy avaunt : " Here, he has gone back. Here he has been. Forward there." When the hare has doubled.

La douce amy, il est venuz illoeques, sohowe : " Softly, friend, he is here." When the hounds hunt well in fields or arable land.

La douce, amy, la est il venuz (pur lue segere sohow) : " Softly, friend, here he has come to seat himself " (Mid. Eng., *sege*—a seat. Latin, *sedere*).

La douce, amy, la il est venuz (pur meyndir) : " Here he has been to feed " (*meyndir,* from Latin *manducare, mandere*).

The bracketed part of the last two cries are given in the MS. of Twety and Gyff., and the following are only in the " Master of Game " :—

Le valliant oyez, oyez who bo bowe, and then, *Avaunt, assemble, assemble, war war, a ha war,* for running riot. *How assamy assamy so arere so howe bloues acoupler.*

On seeing the pricking or footing of the hare: *Le voye, le voye* ("The view, the view").

In France, *Tallyho*, or a very similar sounding word, was employed in the early days when the huntsman was sure that the right stag had gone away, whether he only knew it by his slot, &c., or whether he had viewed him.

It was also a call to bring up the hounds when the stag had gone away, and at the end of the *curée*, when the huntsman held part of the entrails of the deer on a large wooden fork, and the hounds bayed it (which was called the *forhu*), the huntsman called out *Tallyho*.

We only find *Tallyho* in comparatively recent English hunting literature and songs—never, so far as I am aware, before the late seventeenth century, and it does not occur at all constantly until the eighteenth century. Neither Turbervile nor Blome nor Cox, in their books on the various chases, mention such a word, though we find instruction to the huntsman to say "Hark to him," "Hark forward," "Hark back," and "To him, to him"; besides the inevitable "So how sohow." Neither in Twici, "Master of Game," "Boke of St. Albans," Chaucer, or Shakespeare can we find an invigorating *Tallyho*. It would almost appear as if it were a seventeenth century importation from across the Channel, which is quite possible, for Henry IV. of France sent in that century three of his best huntsmen, Desprez, de Beaumont, and de Saint-Ravy, to the Court of King James I. to teach the royal huntsmen how to hunt the stag in the French way, English Court hunting having degenerated into coursing of stags within the park palings.

Taïaut in France was used solely in the chase of red, fallow, or roe deer.

HUNTING MUSIC. In the "Master of Game," as in all the earliest hunting literature, much importance is placed on the huntsman's sounding his horn in the proper manner in order, as Twici says, that "Each man who is around you, who understands Hunting, can know in which point you are in your sport by your blowing." The author of "Master of Game" (p. 170) says he will give us "a chapter which is all of blowing," but he omitted to fulfil this promise, so that we have only such information as we can gather in his chapters on stag and hare-hunting. The differences in the signals were occasioned by the length of the sound or note, and the intervals between each. Twici expresses these notes in syllables, such as *trout, trout, trourourout.* The first of these would be single notes, with an interval between them, blown probably with a separate breath or wind for each; the latter would be three notes blown without interval and with a single breath or wind. The principal sounds on the hunting horn were named as follows :—

A *Moot* or *Mote,* a single note, which might be sounded long or short.

A *Recheat.* To recheat, Twici says, "blow in this manner, *trourourourout, trourourourout, trourourourout,*" therefore a four-syllabled sound succeeded by an interval, blown three times. In the "Master of Game" we find the recheat preceded or followed by a moot, the most constantly recurring melody. When the limer has moved the stag, and the huntsman sees him go away, he was to blow a moot and recheat. If the stag is moved but not viewed, and the huntsman knows only by the slot that it is his stag that has gone away, he is to recheat without the moot, for that was only to be blown when the stag was seen. When the hounds are at fault and any one finds the slot of the deer, he should recheat "in the rightes and blow a long moot for the lymerer," or if he thinks he sees the hunted stag, he should blow a moot and recheat, and after that blow two moots for the hounds.

The *Forlonge.* A signal that the stag had got away far ahead of the hounds or that these had distanced some or all of the huntsmen (*see* Appendix : Forlonge).

The *Perfect* or *Parfit.* Twici says it began by "a

moot and then *trourourout, trout, trout, trourourout, trourourout, trourourout, trout, trout, trourourourout,*" "and then to commence by another moot again, and so you ought to blow three times. And to commence by a moot and to finish by a moot." This was only blown when the hounds were hunting the right line (*see* Appendix : Parfet).

The *Prise.* Twici says, blow four moots for the taking of the deer. According to the "Master of Game," "the prise or coupling up" was to be blown by the chief personage of the hunt only, after the quarry. It was only blown when the deer had been slain by strength, or hunted, and not when shot or coursed. He was to blow four moots, wait a short interval (half an Ave Maria), and blow another four notes a little longer than the first four.

The *Menée.* Twici says the *Menée* should only be blown for the hart, the boar, the wolf, and the male wolf, but he does not give us any analysis of this melody. In the "Master of Game" we are told that the *Menée* was blown at the hall-door on the return of the huntsmen. The Master first blew four moots alone, then at the end of the four moots the others joined him in blowing, and they all continued keeping time together (*see* Appendix : Menée).

The *Mort* or *Death* was another sound of the horn, but we have no description of the notes. Perhaps it is synonymous with the *Prise.*

The *Stroke* must have been another grouping of short and long notes, but of this we have no record.

Hardouin de Fontaines Guerin wrote a poem on the chase chiefly concerning the different manners of blowing such as obtained in his native country the provinces of Anjou and Maine. The poem was illustrated with fourteen miniatures showing the notes to be blown on as many different occasions during stag-hunting.

The notes are written in little squares : □ denoting a long note ; ◪ a short note ; ▢▢ a note of two long syllables; ▅🔳 a note of two short syllables; ▉🔲🔲 a note of one short and two long syllables; and ▉🔲🔲🔲 a note of one short, two long, and two short syllables. Of these six notes combinations were made for all the signals to be blown.

ILLOEQUES, "here in this place," from the L. *illo loco.* Sometimes it is spelt *illecques, iluec, illosques,* &c. It

FROM HARDOUIN DE FONTAINES GUERIN'S WORK, WRITTEN IN 1394

is constantly met with in Anglo-Norman, and the Provence dialects (Botman, pp. 90, 242; T. M., pp. 31, 93, 142; Roy Modus, lxix.; and in the will of the Duke of York, Nichols). It has been suggested that it is the origin of the familiar *yoicks.* In the "Boke of St. Albans" in the verses on hare-hunting it also occurs.

JOPEYE, synonymous with *jupper,* which, according to Cotgrave, is an old word signifying "to whoot, showt, crie out alowd." The French word *juper, jupper,* also spelt *joppeir,* had the same meaning, and we find it em-

ployed in the " Chace dou cerf " for a halloa in hunting
in a similar way to *jopeye* in our text :

> " *Et puis juppe ou corne i. lonc mot*
> *Chaucuns en a joie qui l'ot.*"

In the sense it is used in our " Master of Game " (p.
185) it means to halloa to the hounds, to encourage them
with the voice.

KENETTES, small hounds. Kenet is a diminutive
form of the Norman-French *kenet*, and the O. F. *chen*,
cienetes, chenet, a dog : *i veneour a ii cienetes, Ne mie grans*
mais petitetes, Et plus blans que n'est flors d'espine (Percival,
22,895). Derived from the Latin *canis* (*see* Appendix :
Harriers).

LIGGING, a bed, a resting-place, a lair. From O.
Eng. *licgan, licgean*, Goth. *ligan*, lie, lie down. The
ligging of the hart was what we now call his lair, spelt
also layer. In our MS. it is used for the dwelling of a
wild cat (p. 71).
·This old expression is not entirely obsolete, but can
be heard still among the country people of the northern
counties of England.

LIMER, lymer ; the name given to a scenting-hound
which was held in a liam or leash whilst tracking the
game. Limers never were any distinct breed of hounds,
but, of course, some breeds produced better limers than
others (De Noirmont, vol. ii. p. 350).
A dog used as a limer had to be keen on the scent,
staunch on the line, not too fast, and was taught to run
mute, for if the exact whereabouts of any game had to be
discovered, it would have been impossible, if the hound
gave tongue or challenged while on the scent. A likely
hound was chosen from the kennel at an early age,
G. de F. says at a year old (p. 157), and from that time
accompanied his master, sleeping in his room, and being

taught to obey him. He was continually taken out by
his master with collar and liam and encouraged to follow
the scent of hinds and of stags and other beasts, and
punished should he venture to acknowledge the scent of
any animal he was not being entered to, or should he
open on finding or following the line.

In England as well as on the Continent the huntsman
went out in the early morning to track the game to be
hunted to its lair, or den, before the pack and huntsmen
came into the field. Deer, wild boar, bear and wolves
were thus harboured by means of a limer. Twici makes
the apprentice huntsman ask: "Now I wish to know
how many of the beasts are moved by the lymer, and how
many of the beasts are found by braches?—Sir, all those
which are chased are moved by a lymer, and all those
which are hunted up (*enquillez*) are found by the braches"
(Twici, p. 12; *see* Appendix: Acquillez).

Limers were not only employed when a warrantable
stag was to be hunted by hounds, but a huntsman going
out with his bow or cross-bow would have his brachet on
a liam and let him hunt up the quarry he wished to shoot
(*see* Appendix: Bercelet). Also, the day before one of
the large battues for big game, the limers would be taken
out to ascertain what game there was in the district to
be driven.

A liam, *lyome*, or *lyame*, was a rope made of silk or
leather by which hounds were led, from O. F. *liamen*,
a strap or line, Latin *ligamen*. This strap was fastened
to the collar by a swivel, and both collar and liams were
often very gorgeous. We read of "A lyame of white
silk with collar of white vellat embrawdered with perles,
the swivell of silver." "Dog collors of crymson vellat
with vi lyhams of white leather." "A lieme of grene
and white silke." "Three lyames and colors with tirrett
of silver and quilt" (Madden, "Expenses of Princess
Mary").

A hound was said to carry his liam well when he just
kept it at proper tension, not straining it, for that would

show that he was of too eager temperament, and likely to overshoot the line ; if he trailed his liam on the ground, it showed that he was slack or unwilling (D'Yauville).

As soon as the stag was "moved" the limer's work was over, but only for the time being ; his master led him away, the other hounds were uncoupled, and the harbourer, mounting his horse and keeping his limer with him, rode as close to the chase as he could, skirting below the wind and being careful not to cross the line, but managing to be at hand in case the stag should run in company or give the hounds the change. In this case the huntsman had to check the hounds, and wait for the harbourer and limer to come up and unravel the change, and put the pack on the right scent once more.

The method of starting the stag with a limer was not done away with in France until the eighteenth century, although in Normandy a change had been made previously, and probably in England also. For our author says that some sportsmen even in his time, when impatient, would uncouple a few of the hounds in the covert, before the stag had been properly started by the limer, which practice he, however, was not in favour of except under the conditions he mentions.

This uncoupling of a few older hounds in covert to start the deer, coupling them again as soon as the deer was on foot, was later called *tufting*, and is still customary in Devon and Somerset.

The limer was not rewarded with the other hounds ; he received his reward from the hands of his master before or after the other hounds, and after he had bayed the head of the stag.

When not quoting or translating the old text the more modern spelling of *li*mer has been used.

MADNESS. Old Eng. and Mid. Eng. *Woodness,* *wodnesse,* and *wodnyss ;* mad, *wode.* The seven different sorts of madnesses spoken of by the "Master of Game" are also mentioned in nearly all subsequent works on old hunting dealing with "sicknesses of hounds." They are the hot burning madness, running madness, dumb madness, lank madness, rheumatic madness or slavering madness, falling madness, sleeping madness.

These are mentioned in Roy Modus, and the cure for rabies, of taking the afflicted dog to the sea and letting nine waves wash over him, as well as the cock cure mentioned in our English MS., were both taken by Gaston from Roy Modus, or both derived them from some common source (Roy Modus, fol. xlv. r).

The water cure is mentioned also by Albertus Magnus (Alb. Mag., 215, a 27).

It seems likely to have been to try the efficacy of this cure that King Edward I. sent some of his hounds to Dover to bathe in the sea, the following account for which is entered in his Wardrobe Accounts :

"To John le Berner, going to Dover to bathe six braches by the King's order and for staying there for 21 days for his expense 3. 6d" (6 Edward I. Quoted from MS. Philipps, 8676).

The means of recognising rabies by a cock is also mentioned in the recipe of the eleventh century given by Avicenna (957–1037), and it appears again in Vincentius Bellovacensis and is also to be found in Alexander Neckham. Although the manner of using the cock for this purpose varies, we see by the fact of its being mentioned in different works preceding our MS. that the cock enjoyed some legendary renown for at least a couple of centuries before Gaston (Werth, p. 55).

Nowadays only two varieties of rabies are recognised : furious and dumb rabies. The numerous divisions of the old authors were based on different stages of the disease and slight variations in the symptoms.

When a dog is attacked with rabies its owner often supposes that the dog has a bone in its throat, so that a report of this condition is regarded by veterinary surgeons with suspicion. This corresponds with the description in our text of dogs, with their mouths "somewhat gaping, as if they were *enosed* in their throat."

MASTIFF, from F. *metif*, O. F. *mestif*, M. E. *mastyf*, *mestiv*, mixed breed, a mongrel dog (Cent. Dict., Murray). Some etymologists have suggested that the word mastiff was derived from *masethieves*, as these dogs protected their master's houses and cattle from thieves (Manwood, p. 113). Others again give *mastinus*, i.e. *maison tenant*, house-dog, as the origin, but the first derivation given of *mestif*, mongrel, is the one now generally recognised.

Although it will be quite evident to any one comparing the mastiff depicted in our Plate, p. 122, with any picture of the British mastiff that the two are very different types, we must not therefore conclude that the artist was at fault, but that the French *matin*, which is what our MS. describes and depicts, was by no means identical with our present English breed of mastiffs, nor even with the old British mastiff or bandog. The French *matins* were generally big, hardy dogs, somewhat light in the body, with long heads, pointed muzzles, flattened forehead, and semi-pendant ears; some were rough and others smooth coated.

Matins were often used for tackling the wild boar when run by other hounds, so as to save the more valuable ones when the boar turned to bay.

In this chase, as well as when they were used to protect their master's flocks against wolves, huge iron spiked collars were fastened round the dog's neck. These spiked collars were very formidable affairs; one of very ancient make which I have measures inside nearly eight inches in diameter, and the forty-eight spikes are an inch long, the whole weighing without the padlock that fastened it together about two pounds.

In England the name Mastiff was not in general use till a much later date, even as late as the end of the eighteenth century, Osbaldiston in his Dictionary ignoring the term mastiff, and using, like a true Saxon, the old term bandog (Wynn, p. 72). In the seventeenth and eighteenth centuries the terms were generally synonymous, and it seems quite possible that the mastiff of the ancient forest laws was not our bandog, but denoted, as in France, any large house-dog capable of defending his master and his master's goods, watching his cattle, and, as frequently necessary, powerful enough to attack the depredatory wolf or the wild boar. These would in all likelihood be a very mixed breed, and thoroughly justify the name *mestif* or mongrel.

Cotgrave in his French-English Dictionary gives the following :—

"*Mastin*, a mastiue or bandog; a great country curre; also a rude, filthie, currish or cruell fellow."

We find the word *matin* in France used as a term of opprobrium, or a name of contempt for any ugly or distorted body or a coarse person : "*C'es un matin, un vilain matin.*" Many interesting facts about the mastiff have been collected by Jesse in his "History of the British Dog," but he also makes the mistake of considering that the "Master of Game" and Turbervile give us the description of the dogs then existing in England, whereas these descriptions really relate only to French breeds, although the characteristics may in many cases have tallied sufficiently; but in others a dire confusion has resulted from blindly copying from one another.

MENÉE, from Latin *minare*, something which is led, a following. This word frequently occurs in the mediæval romances, and usually denoted pursuit, either in battle or in the hunting field (Borman, p. 37).

There are various meanings attached to *menée* :—

1. The line of flight the stag or other game has taken, and *Chacier la menée* seems to have meant hunting with horn and hound by scent on the line of flight, in contradiction to the chase with the bow or crossbow, which was called *berser* (*Le Roman des Loherains*, 106, *c.* 30). In G. de F. (p. 157) it is used in the same sense. The

meaning in which Gaston de Foix uses the word menée
is explained by him : *Et puis se metre après, et chevauchier
menée : c'est à dire par où les chiens et le cerf vont* (G. de
F., pp. 43, 44, 171, 179). See also *Chace dou Cerf* and
Hard. de Font. Guer. Édit. Pichon).

2. The challenge of the hound when on the line.
Page 171, we read that a hunter should know whether
the hounds have retrieved their stag by the doubling of
their menée, *i.e.* the hounds would make more noise as
soon as they found the scent or line of flight of the stag
they were chasing. *Menée* evidently meant the sound
made by the hound when actually following the scent,
not when baying the game. Later the sense seems to
have been widened, and a musical hound was said to have
la menée belle (Salnove, p. 246).

3. A note sounded on a horn (*see* Appendix : Hunting
Music). It was the signal that the deer was in full
flight. It appears to be used in Twici to signify the
horn-signal blown when the hounds are on the scent of
hart, boar or wolf, to press the hounds onwards (Twici,
p. 23). This author says one cannot blow the menée
for the hare, because it is at one time female and another
male, and to this Dryden in his notes remarks that
Twici is perfectly right in saying a man ought not to
blow the menée for a hare ; for as every one knows, it
is but a rare occurrence for a hare to go straight on end
like a fox, for they commonly double and run rings, in
which case if the hounds were pressed, they would over-
run the scent and probably lose the hare. But he does
not explain why Twici says if it were always male the
menée could be blown at it as at other beasts, such as
the hart, the boar, and the wolf. Is it that a male hare
will occasionally run a long, straight course of several
miles, but that the female runs smaller rings and more
constantly retraces her steps, and therefore the menée
could never be blown at her ?

4. Menée was also used in the sense of a signal on a
horn.

The "Master of Game" says the *menées* should be sounded on the return of the huntsman at the hall or cellar door (p. 179). There was a curious old custom which occasioned the blowing of the horn in Westminster Abbey. Two *menées* were blown at the high altar of the Abbey on the delivery there of eight fallow deer which Henry III. had by charter granted as a yearly gift to the Abbot of Westminster and his successors.

METYNGE, here evidently means meating or feeding. As the "Master of Game" says: "or pasturing" as if the two words were synonymous, as *metinge* also was Mid. Eng. for *measure*, it might have been a deer of "high measure and pasturing." But anyhow the two were practically identical, for as Twici says: "Harts which are of good pasture. For the head grows according to the pasture; good or otherwise." See below: MEUTE.

MEUTE had several meanings in Old French venery.
1. The "Master of Game" translated G. de F.'s "grant cerf" as a hart of high feeding or pasture. But he omitted to render the following passage: "*Et s'il est de bonne meute, allons le laisser courre.*" The "*bonne meute*" is not translated by "high meating." It was an expression in use to indicate whether the stag was in good company or not. If a warrantable stag was accompanied by one or two large stags he was termed "*Un cerf de bonne mute*" (or *meute*), but if hinds and young stags (rascal) were with him he was designated as a "*cerf de mauvaise mute.*" In Roy Modus we read: "*La première est de savoir s'il est de bonne mute.*"
Perhaps *meute* when used in this sense was derived from the old Norman word *moeta*, *māēta*, from *mōt*, meet, come together. There was also an Old Eng. word *metta* or *gemetta*, companion.
2. Meute was also used in another sense which is translated by the "Master of Game" as *haunts*, probably

the place the deer usually moves in. G. says : " *Il prendra congé de sa meute*," and the " Master of Game " has : " he leaves his haunts." If a deer was harboured in a good country for hunting he was also called " *En belle meute* " (D'Yauville, voc. *Meute*).

It was in this sense that the "Sénéschal de Normandye " answers the question of his royal mistress about the stag he himself had harboured that morning ; he tells her the stag was *En belle meute et pays fort.*

3. MEUTE, MUTE, a number of hounds, now called a pack or kennel of hounds or a cry of hounds.

MEW, *Mue,* to shed, cast, or change. " The hart mews his horns," the deer casts his head, or sheds his antlers. From the French *muer,* and the Latin *mutare,* to change, of hawks to moult.

MOVE, MEU, Meue, mewe, meeve, old forms of move. To start a hart signified to unharbour him, to start him from his lair.

G. de F. says : *Allons le laisser courre ;* but the word *meu* or *meve* was also used in Old French in the same way as in English.

Twici says : *Ore vodroi ioe savoir quantez des betes sunt meuz de lymer, e quanz des bestes sunt trouez des brachez. . . . Sire, touz ceaus qe sunt enchaces ; sunt meuz de lymer. E tous ceaus enquillez sunt trovez de brachez.* (Now I would wish to know how many beasts are moved by a lymer and how many beasts are found by the braches. —Sir, all those which are chased are moved by a lymer. And all those which are hunted up are found by braches.) (Line 18 ; Tristan., i. 4337 ; Partonopeus de Blois, 607.)

MUSE, *Meuse.* An opening in a fence through which a hare or other animal is accustomed to pass. An old proverb says : " 'Tis as hard to find a hare without a muse, as a woman without scuse."

"A hare will pass by the same muses until her death or escape" (Blome, p. 92).

NUMBLES. M. E. *nombles, noumbles*; O. F. *nombles.* The parts of a deer between the thighs, that is to say, the liver and kidneys and entrails. Part, and sometimes the whole of the numbles were considered the right of the huntsman; sometimes the huntsman only got the kidneys, and the rest was put aside with the tit-bits reserved for the King or chief personage (Turb., pp. 128–129). Numbles by loss of the initial letter became umbles (Harrison, vol. i. p. 309), and was sometimes written humbles, whence came "humble pie," now only associated with the word humble. Humble pie was a pie made of the umbles or numbles of the deer, and formerly at hunting feasts was set before the huntsman and his followers.

OTTER. The Duke of York does not tell us anything of the chase of the Otter, but merely refers one at the end of the chapter on "The Nature of the Otter" to Milbourne, the King's Otter-hunter, for more information and says, "as of all other vermin I speak not" (p. 73). The Otter was evidently beneath his notice, as being neither regarded as a beast of venery nor of the chase (Twety and Gyfford, Brit. Mus. MS. Vesp. B. XII.). But the very fact that the King had an Otter-hunter shows that it was a beast not altogether despised, although probably hunted more for the value of its skin and for the protection of the fish than for the sport.

The Milbourne referred to by the Duke of York can scarcely be any other than the William Melbourne we find mentioned in Henry IV.'s reign as "Valet of our Otter-hounds" (Privy Seal, 674/6456, Feb. 18, 1410).

PARFET, *the perfect.* Twici says: *Une autre chasce il y ad qe homme appele le parfet. Dunkes covient il qe vous corneez en autre maneree. . . . E isse chescun homme qest en tour vous, que siet de venerie puet conustre en quel point vous estes en vostre dedut par vostre corneer* (line 111).

From comparing the various places where the word *parfait* is employed in connection with hunting, it may be concluded that to hunt the "*Parfet*" was when the hounds were on the line of the right stag, to sound the "*Parfet*" was to blow the notes that indicated the hounds were hunting the right line. Dryden in his notes to Twici suggests that the chase of the *parfet* was "in opposition to the chase of the *Forloyng*," that is, when the pack run well together "jostling in close array" (Twici, p. 43). But Perfect in the O. F. works seems to us to invariably be used, as already said, to indicate that the hounds have not taken the change, but are staunch to the right scent. Jacques de Brézé says the stag he is hunting joins two great stags, but although some of the hounds ran silent for awhile, they still continued staunch to their line, and here he uses the word "*parfait*" (Sen. de Nor., p. 13).

Modus also uses it in this sense : *Les chiens qui viennent chaçant après le parfait* (fol. xix. v). And what is most conclusive is the sense given to it in our text : "Should blow to him again the parfyt so that he were in his rightes and ellys nought," *i.e.* the parfyt should only be blown if the hound was on the right line (p. 174).

PARFYTIERES, the name given in the "Master of Game" to the last relay of hounds uncoupled during the chase of the stag. First came the "*vaunt chase*," and then the "*midel*," and then the "*parfytieres*." They may have been so called from being the last hounds to be uncoupled, being those that completed or perfected the pack—*i.e.* perfecters, or this relay may have derived its name from being composed of some of the staunchest hounds from the kennel, those not likely to follow any but the right line or the *parfyt*. It was customary in the old days to keep some of the slower and staunchest hounds in the last relay, and to cast them only when a

stag nearing its end rused and foiled, and sought by
every means to shake off his persecutors (*see* Appendix :
Relays). G. de F. gives the names of the three relays
simply as *La première bataille, la seconde,* and *la tierce*
(p 175).

POMELED ; spotted, from O. F. *pomelé,* spotted like
an apple. The young of the roedeer are born with a
reddish brown coat with white spots, which the " Master
of Game " calls *pomeled.* This term was also frequently
used in Ang.-N., O. F., and in the dog-Latin of our ancient
records to describe a flea-bitten or dappled horse. " *His
hakenei that was all pomeli gris* " (Strat.). " *Pommeli
liardus, gris pommele, Uno equo liardo pomele* " (Obs. Ward.
Acc. 28, Ed. I.). G. de F. does not use this word in
describing the young of the roedeer, but says they are
born " *eschaquettes* " (p. 40).

RACHES ; *ratches* or *racches,* a dog that hunts by
scent. A.-S. *raecc,* a hound, and O. F. and Ang.-N.
brache, brachet, bracon, braquet; Ger. *bracken.* Ang.-Lat.,
brachetus, bracketus.
Raches were scenting hounds hunting in a pack, later
called " running hounds," and then simply hounds. Although raches or brachets are frequently mentioned in
the O. F. and Ang.-N. metrical romances, and in various
early documents, we have never found any description of
them, but can only gather what they were from the uses
they were put to. We find that the bracco was used by
the early German tribes to track criminals, therefore
they were scenting hounds. There is plenty of evidence
that they were used for stag, wild boar, and buck hunting
during the Middle Ages. They were coupled together
and led by a *berner* or *bracennier* or *braconnier. Braconnier*
now means poacher, but this is only the later meaning ;
originally braconnier was the leader of the bracos, or
huntsman (Daurel, p. 337 ; Bangert, p. 173 ; Dol.
9188).

We gather that these brachets of the early Middle Ages were small hounds, sometimes entirely white, but generally white with black markings. Sometimes they were mottled (*bracet mautré*). One description of a *braces corant* says this hound was as white as a nut, with black ears, a black mark on the right flank, and flecked with black (Blancadin, 1271; Perc. 17,555, 22,585; Tristan M., 1475, 2261; Tyolet, 332).

In the early days in England we find that braches were used to hunt up such smaller game as was not unharboured or dislodged by the limer. Twici says: "*Sire, touz ceaus qe sunt enchaces, sunt meuz de lymer. E tous ceaus enquillez sunt trovez de brachez*" (*see* Appendix : Acquillez), *i.e.* All beasts that are enchased are moved by a limer, and all those that are hunted up are found by braches (Twici, pp. 2, 12). Raches are mentioned in the "Boke of St. Albans" among the "*Dyvers manere of houndes*," and the apprentice to venery is told he should speak of "A mute of houndes, a kenell of rachys." He is also informed that the hart, the buck, and the boar should be started by a limer, and that all "other bestes that huntyd shall be sought for and found by Ratches so free." John Hardyng in his Chronicle, speaking of an inroad into Scotland by Edward IV., in whose reign he was yet living, said, "And take Kennetes and Ratches with you and seeke oute all the forest with houndes and hornes as Kynge Edwarde with the long shanks dide." In the "Squyer of Low degree" we read that the huntsman came with his bugles "and seven score raches at his rechase."

RESEEYUOUR; the word the most approaching this to be found in any dictionary is under the head of receiver, M. E. *receyvour*, one who, or that which receives. The *reseeyuours* were most likely those greyhounds who received the game, *i.e.* pulled it down after it had been chased. We see in our text that *teasers* and *reseeyuours* are mentioned together (p. 198). The former

were light, swift greyhounds ; these were probably slipped
first ; and the latter (Shirley MS. spells *resteynours*) were
the heavy greyhounds slipped last, and capable of pulling
down a big stag.   De Noirmont tells us : *Ces derniers
étaient surnommés receveours ou receveurs* (ii. p. 426, and G.
de F., p. 177).

RELAYS.   In the early days of venery the whole
pack was not allowed to hunt at the commencement of
the chase.   After the stag had been started from his lair
by a limer, some hounds were uncoupled and laid on, the
rest being divided off into relays, which were posted in
charge of one or more *berners* along the probable line of
the stag, and were uncoupled when the hunted stag and
the hounds already chasing him had passed.   There were
usually three relays, and two to four couples the usual
number in each relay, though the number of couples depended, of course, on the size of the hunting establishment and the number of hounds in the kennel.   G. de
F. calls these relays simply, première, seconde, and tierce.
The "Master of Game" calls the first lot of hounds uncoupled the "finders" (p. 165), though this seems rather a
misnomer, as the harbourer with his limer (*see* Limer)
found and started the deer.   The *vauntchase* for the first
relay, and the *midel* speak for themselves, but we have little
clue to the origin of *parfitieres* for the third relay.   Were
they so called because they perfected or completed the
chase, or because they were some of the staunchest
hounds who could be depended upon to follow the *parfit*,
i.e. the right line of the stag or animal hunted ? (*see*
Appendix : Parfet).   Old authorities seem to have differed
in opinion as to whether the staunchest and slowest
hounds should have been put in the first cry or in the
last (Roy Modus, fol. xvi. ; G. de F., p. 178 ; Lav.,
Chasse à Courre, pp. 297–8).
In the "Boke of St. Albans" we read of the *vauntlay,
relay,* and *allay.*   The first was the name given to
hounds if they were uncoupled and thrown off between

the pack and the beast pursued, the relay were the hounds uncoupled after the hounds already hunting had passed by ; the *allay* is held :

> "Till all the houndes that be behynd be cum therto
> Than let thyn houndes all to geder goo
> That is called an *allay*."

Instructions concerning when relays should be given always warn the *berner* not to let slip the couples till some of the surest hounds have passed on the scent, and till he be sure that the stag they are hunting is the right one and not a substitute, *i.e.* one frightened and put up by the hunted stag. The "Master of Game" is careful also to say : "Take care that thou *vauntlay* not " (p. 169).

The discontinuing of relays seemed to have been begun first in Normandy and probably about the same time in England.

In France the three relays of greyhounds which were used were called *Levriers d'estric—i.e.* those which were first let slip ; *levriers de flanc,* those that attacked from the side ; and *levriers de tête,* those that bar the passage in front of the game or head it, terms that correspond with our vauntlay, allay, and relay. In the "Master of Game's" chapter on the wolf these relays of greyhounds are indicated (p. 59).

RIOT. The "Master of Game's" statement on p. 74 that no other wild beast in England is called ryott save the coney only has called forth many suggestions as to the origin of this name being applied to the rabbit, and the connection between riot, a noise or brawl, and the rabbit. The word riot is represented in M. E. and O. F. by *riote,* in Prov. *riota,* Ital. *riotta,* and in all these languages it had the same signification, *i.e.* a brawl, a dispute, an uproar, a quarrel (Skeat).

Diez conjectures the F. *riote* to stand for *rivote,* and refers to O.H.G. *riben,* G. *reiben,* to grate, to rub (orig.

perhaps to rive, to rend). From German, *sich an einem reiben*, to mock, to attack, to provoke one; lit. to rub oneself against one.

Rabbit, which is in O. Dutch robbe, has probably the same origin from *reiben*.

The etymology and connection, if any, between the two words rabbit and riot is difficult to determine. It is very probable that the rabbit was called *riot* from producing a brawling when the hounds came across one. The term "running *riot*" may well be derived from a hunting phrase.

ROE. The error regarding the October rut into which G. de F. and the Duke of York fell was one to which the naturalists of much later times subscribed, for it was left to Dr. Ziegler and to Dr. Bischoff, the Professor of Physiology at Heidelberg, to demonstrate in 1843 the true history of the gestation of the roe, which for more than a century had been a hotly disputed problem. On that occasion it was shown with scientific positiveness that the true rut of the roe takes place about the end of July or first week in August, and that the ovum does not reach the uterus for several months, so that the first development of the embryo does not commence before the middle of December.

RUNNING HOUNDS AND RACHES (F. *chiens courants*). Under this heading we include all such dogs as hunted by scent in packs, whatever the game they pursued might be. They appear in the early records of our kings as *Canes de Mota, Canes currentes,* and as *Sousos* (scenting hounds) (Close Rolls 7 John; Mag. Rot. 4, John Rot. 10; 4 Henry III.), and are mentioned specifically as *cervericiis, deimericiis,* as *Heyrectorum* (harriers) or *canes heirettes,* and foxhounds as *gupillerettis* or *wulpericiis* (Close Rolls, 15 John).

The Anglo-Saxon word *Hundas,* hound, was a general name for any dog; the dog for the chase in Anglo-Saxon times being distinguished by the prefix *Ren*, making *ren hund*.

Gradually the word dog superseded the word hound, and the latter was only retained to designate a "scenting" dog. Dr. Caius, writing to Dr. Gesner, remarks in his book: "Thus much also understand, that as in your language *Hunde* is the common word, so in our naturall tounge dogge is the universall, but *Hunde* is perticular and a speciall, for it signifieth such a dogge onely as serveth to hunt" (Caius, p. 40). (*See* Appendix: Raches.) Running hounds was a very literal translation of the French *chiens courants*, and as the descriptive chapter given in our text is as literal a rendering from G. de F. there is no information that helps us to piece together the ancestry of the modern English hound. We do not know what breed were in the royal kennels in the reign of Henry IV., but probably some descendants of those brought to this country by the Normans, about the origin of which breed nothing seems known.

Keep of Hounds. The usual cost of the keep of a hound at the time of our MS. was a halfpenny a day, of a greyhound three farthings, and of a limer or bloodhound one penny a day.

However for the royal harthounds an allowance of three farthings a day was made for each hound (Q. R. Acc. 1407), and we also find occasionally that only a halfpenny a day was made for the keep of a greyhound. In Edward I.'s reign a halfpenny a day was the allowance made for fox- and otter-hounds (14, 15, 31, 32, 34, Edward I. Ward. Acc.), and sometimes three farthings and sometimes a halfpenny a day for a greyhound. The Master of Buckhounds was allowed a halfpenny a day each for his hounds and greyhounds.

In the reign of Richard III. the Master of Harthounds was allowed 3s. 3d. a day "for the mete of forty dogs and twelve greyhounds and threepence a day for three limers" (Rolls of Parl., vol. v. p. 16).

The "Boke of Curtasye" (fourteenth century, Percy

Society, iv. p. 26), gives us information which quite
agrees with the payments entered in the Wardrobe and
other accounts of the King's hunting establishment.
And under the head of *De Pistore* we find the baker is
told to make loaves for the hounds :

> " Manchet and chet to make brom bred hard
> ffor chaundeler and grehoundes and huntes reward."

Chet, a word not in use since the seventeenth century,
meant wheaten bread of the second quality, made of flour
more coarsely sifted than that used for manchet, which
was the finest quality.

Brom bread was oaten bread, and probably was very
much the same as a modern dog biscuit.

One of the ancient feudal rights was that of obtaining
bran from the vassals for the hounds' bread, known as
the right of brennage, from bren, bran.

Although bread was the staple food given to hounds,
yet they were also provided with meat. At the end of
a day's hunting they received a portion of the game
killed (*see* Curée), and if this was not sufficient or it was
not the hunting season game was expressly killed for
them. In a decree from King John to William Pratell
and the Bailiffs of Falke de Breaut of the Isle of Ely,
the latter are commanded to find bread and paste for the
hounds as they may require, "and to let them hunt sometimes in the Bishops chase for the flesh upon which they
are fed" (Close Roll, 17 John). In an extract from the
Wardrobe Accounts of 6 Edward I. we find a payment
was made of 40s. by the King to one Bernard King for
his quarry for two years past on which the King's dogs
had been fed (MS. Phillipps, 8676).

We find also that "Pantryes, Chippinges and broken
bread" were given to the hounds, *Chippings* being frequently mentioned in the royal accounts as well as meat
for the hounds (Liber Niger Domus Ed. IV.; Collection
of Ordinances of the Royal Households; Jesse, ii. 125;
Privy Purse Expenses Henry VIII. 1529–1532).

The cost of the keep of some of the King's hounds were paid for out of the exchequer, others were paid from the revenues and outgoings of various counties, and an immense number were kept by subjects who held land from the crown *by serjeantry* or *in capite* of keeping a stated number of running hounds, greyhounds, and brachets, &c., for the King's use (Blount's Ancient Tenures, Plac. Chron. 12, 13 Ed. I.; Issue Roll 25 Henry VI.; Domesday, tom. i. fol. 57 v).

We see by the early records of our kings that a pack of hounds did not always remain stationary and hunt within easy reach of their kennels, but were sent from one part of the kingdom to another to hunt where game was most plentiful or where there was most vermin to be destroyed. As early as Edward I.'s reign we find conveyances were sometimes provided for hounds when they went on long journeys. Thomas de Candore or Candovere and Robert le Sanser (also called Salsar), huntsmen of the stag and buckhounds (Close Rolls 49 Henry III.; 6, 8 Ed. I.), were paid for a horse-litter for fifty-nine days for the use of their sixty-six hounds and five limers (Ward. Acc. 14, 15 Ed. I.). And as late as Henry VIII.'s time the hounds seemed to travel about considerable distances, as in the Privy Purse expenses of that King the cart covered with canvas for the use of his hounds is a frequently recurring item.

SCANTILON, O. F. *eschantillon*, Mid. Eng. *Scantilon*, Mod. Eng. scantling, mason's rule, a measure; the huntsman is continually told to take a *scantilon*, that is, a measure, of the slot or footprint of the deer, so as to be able to show it at the meet, that with this measure and the examination of the droppings which the huntsman was also to bring with him the Master of the Game could judge if the man had harboured a warrantable deer (*see* Appendix : Slot and Trace).

SEASONS OF HUNTING. In mediæval times

the consideration for the larder played a far more important part in fixing the seasons for hunting wild beasts than it did in later times, the object being to kill the game when in the primest condition. Beginning with the—

Red deer stag: according to Dryden's Twici, p. 24 (source not given), the season began at the Nativity of St. John the Baptist (June 24), and *ended* Holyrood Day (September 14). Our text of the "Master of Game" nowhere expressly states when the stag-hunting begins or terminates, but as he speaks of how to judge a hart from its fumes in the month of April and May (p. 30), and further says that harts run best from the "entry of May into St. John's tide" (p. 35), we might infer that they were hunted from May on. He also says that the season for hind-hunting begins when the season of the hart ends and lasteth till Lent. But as this part of the book was a mere translation from G. de F. it is no certain guide to the hunting seasons in England. The Stag-hunting season in France, the *cervaison*, as it was called, began at the *Sainte Croix de Mai* (May 3rd) and lasted to *la Sainte Croix de Septembre* (Holyrood Day, Sept. 14), the old French saying being : "*Mi Mai, mi teste, mi Juin, mi graisse ; à la Magdeleine venaison pleine*" (July 22) (Menagier de Paris, ii.). And although the stag was probably chiefly hunted in England between Midsummer and the middle of September, when they are in the best condition, and it was considered the best time to kill them, they were probably hunted from May on in the early days in England as they were in France. Had this not been customary we imagine the Duke of York would have inserted one of his little interpolations in the text he was translating, and stated that although the season began in May *beyond the sea*, it only began later in England.

In Twety and Gyfford we read that the "tyme of grece, begynnyth alle way atte the fest of the Nativyte of Saynt Johan baptist." Later on, according to Dryden,

the season of the stag began two weeks after Midsummer
(July 8).

Red deer hind, Holyrood Day (Sept. 14) to Candlemas
(Feb. 2) (Twici, p. 24; Man., p. 181). According to
others the hind and the doe season ends on Twelfth-day
or Epiphany (Jan. 6).

Fallow deer buck. According to the Forest Laws the
season began at the Nativity of St. John (June 24) and
ended on Holyrood Day (Sept. 14). Dryden adds a
second date, *i.e.* two weeks after Midsummer, to the
former, but does not quote the source.

Fallow doe was hunted from Holyrood Day (Sept. 14)
to Candlemas (Feb. 2).

Roe deer buck was hunted from Easter to Michaelmas
(Sept. 29).

Roe doe, Michaelmas to Candlemas.

Hare. According to the Forest Laws (Man., 176) the
season commenced Michaelmas (Sept. 29) and ended at
Midsummer (June 24); Dryden in his notes in Twici
states that it commenced at Michaelmas and ended at
Candlemas (Feb. 2), while the "Boke of St. Albans" gives
the same date as the first-named in Manwood. According to the "Master of Game" the hare seems to have
enjoyed no close season, as G. de F.'s assertion that the
hunting of the hare "lasteth all the year" is also translated without comment (p. 14): *Et le peut chassier toute
l'année, en quelque temps que ce soit quar touzjours sa sayson
dure* (G de F., p. 204).

In Twety and Gyfford we also find that "The hare
is alway in season to be chasyd."

In the sixteenth century in France the hare-hunting
season was from the middle of September till the middle
of April (Du Fouilloux, p. 51; De Noir., ii. p. 476).
In England the same season seems to have been observed
(Blome, p. 91).

Wild boar. According to the Forest Laws (Manwood
and Twici), the boar was hunted from Christmas Day
to Candlemas (Feb. 2), but we have evidence that boar-

hunting usually began earlier. The boar was in his
prime condition when acorns, beechmast, and chest-
nuts were plentiful, and was considered in season from
Michaelmas to St. Martin's Day (Roy Modus, xxxi.),
and by some even from Holyrood Day (Bornam, p. 100;
Part. de Blois, 525).

The huntsmen of King John of England were sent
to hunt in the forest of Cnappe in order to take two
or three boars a day in November. King John's letter
giving instructions on this point to one Rowland Bloet
is dated 8th November 1215 (Jesse, ii. 32).

Wolf. According to the Forest Laws, in the book
already quoted, the season during which the wolf was
hunted began at Christmas and ended at the Annunciation (March 25), but considering the destruction wrought
by this beast it is far more likely that it was hunted
throughout the year.

Fox. According to the Forest Laws the season opened
on Christmas Day and ended on March 25, but nevertheless the fox was hunted early in the autumn, for we
have it on Twety and Gyfford's authority that "the
sesoun of the fox begynneth at the natyvite of owre
Lady, and durryth til the Annunciacion" (Sept. 8 to
March 25).

The "Boke of St. Albans" gives the season of the
fox and wolf from the Nativity to the Annunciation of
Our Lady and that of the boar from the Nativity to
the Purification of Our Lady. Manwood and other
accepted authorities quote the above as alluding to the
Nativity of Christ, whereas the Nativity of Our Lady,
Sept. 8, was intended, thereby creating some confusion.

According to the Wardrobe Accounts of Edward I.
the foxhunting season began on 1st September (Ward.
Acc. Ed. I. 1299–1300).

No doubt one of the reasons why the fox was not
hunted earlier in the year was on account of the fur,
which was of course of less use or value if obtained in
summer.

Otter. The Forest Laws give the season as from Shrove Tide (Feb. 22) to Midsummer (June 24), but we find that in King John's reign the otter was hunted in July (Close Rolls 14 John I.).

Martin, badger, and rabbit were hunted at all seasons of the year.

SNARES. No work dealing with the chase of wild animals in mediæval times would be complete were it to omit all reference to snares, traps, gins, pitfalls, and other devices to take game other than by hunting. The "Master of Game" mentions the subject but briefly, saying, "Truly I trow no good hunter would slay them so for no good," but "Gaston Phœbus" contains seventeen short chapters in which the author as well as the miniaturist describe the various contrivances then in use, although the same disdain of these unsportsmanlike methods is expressed by G. de F. that marks the Duke of York's pages. In the first edition of the present work will be found descriptions of the principal snares used in the Middle Ages.

SPANIEL. It is difficult to say at what date these dogs were first introduced into our country; we only know that by the second half of the sixteenth century spaniels were a common dog in England. In Dr. Caius's time the breed was "in full being." He mentions land spaniels, setters, and water spaniels, besides the small spaniels which were kept as pet and lap dogs. That the breed was not then a recent importation we may infer from the fact that, when speaking of the water spaniel and giving the derivation of the name, Dr. Caius says: "Not that England wanted suche kinde of dogges (for they are naturally bred and ingendered in this country). But because they beare the general and common name of these dogs synce the time when they were first brought over out of Spaine."

The chapter in the "Master of Game" on this dog,

R

being translated from G. de F., unfortunately throws no
light on the history of the spaniel in England, although
we imagine that, had there been no such hounds in our
island at the time, the Duke would have made some
such remark as he has in other parts of his book of their
being a "manner of" hound as "men have beyond the
sea, but not as we have here in England."

In his time the spaniel had enjoyed popularity in
France for some two centuries, and there was such con-
tinual communication between France and England in
the fourteenth and fifteenth centuries that it would
have been indeed strange if this most useful dog for
the then favourite and universal sport of hawking had
not been brought to England long before his time.
We may conclude that the "gentle hounds for the
hawk" of which he speaks in his Prologue were not
spaniels.

SPAY. The usual meaning of this word (castrating
females) given in all dictionaries is clearly inapplicable
on this occasion (p. 174), where it undoubtedly means
killing a stag with a sword, probably derived from the
Italian *spada*. When the velvet was once off the antlers
the stag at bay was usually despatched with the bow, for
it was then dangerous to approach him close enough to
do so with the sword. When achieved by bold hunters,
as it occasionally was, it was accounted a feat of skill and
courage.

STABLES. O. F. *establie*, a garrison, a station.
Huntsmen and kennelmen with hounds in leash, whose
duty it was to take up a post or stand assigned to them
during the chase, were called stables. We have *Stabili-
tiones venationis* that are mentioned in Domesday (i. fol.
56b and fol. 252). In Ellis's introduction to Domesday
he says : "*Stabilitio* meant stalling the deer. To drive
the Deer and other Game from all quarters to the centre
of a gradually contracted circle where they were com-

pelled to stand, was *stabilitio*." Malmesbury, Scriptores, post Bedam, edit. 1596, p. 44, speaking of the mildness of Edward the Confessor's temper, says, "*Dum quadam vice venatum isset, et agrestis quidam Stabulata illa, quibus in casses cervi urgentur, confudisset, ille sua nobili percitus ira, per Deum, inquit, et matrem ejus tantundem tibi nocebo, si potero*" (Ellis, i. 112).

We see, however, at a later date from Twici and the "Master of Game" that the watchers or stables they allude to were stationary—and did not drive the game as described in above.

These stations of huntsmen and hounds were placed at intervals round the quarter of the forest to be driven or hunted in with hounds to move the game, so that the hounds could be slipped at any game escaping; sometimes they were to make a noise, and thus blench or head the game back. In French such a chase was called a *Chasse à titre* (Lav. xxviii.), the word *titre* meaning net or tape, but in this case used figuratively. Our "Master of Game" evidently placed these stations to keep the game within the boundaries so as to force it to pass the stand of the King. Twici describes these stations of huntsmen, using the word *establie*. "The bounds are those which are set up of archers, and of greyhounds (*lefrers et de establie*) and watchers, and on that account I have blown one moot and recheated on the hounds. You hunter, do you wish to follow the chase? Yes, if that beast should be one that is hunted up (*enquillee*), or chased I will follow it. If so it should happen that the hounds should be gone out of bounds then I wish to blow a moot and stroke after my hounds to have them back" (Twici, p. 6).

It was the duty of certain tenants to attend the King's hunts and act as part of the stable. In Hereford one person went from each house to the stand or station in the wood at the time of the survey (Gen. Introduction Domesday, Ellis, i. 195). From Shrewsbury the principal burgesses who had horses attended the King when he went hunting, and the sheriff sent thirty-six men on foot to the deer-stand while the King remained there.

Stable-stand was the place where these *stables* were posted or "set," and the word was also used to denote the place where archers were posted to shoot at driven game. Such stands were raised platforms in some drive or on some boundary of the forest, sometimes erected between the branches of a tree, so that the sportsman could be well hidden. A good woodcut of what was probably intended to represent a "stand" is in the first edition of Turbervile's "Arte of Venerie," representing Queen Elizabeth receiving her huntsman's report.

There is no mention made of raised stands in our text, but with or without such erections the position taken up by the shooters to await the game was called his *standing* or *tryste*, and a bower of branches was made, to shelter the occupant from sun and rain, as well as to hide him from the game. Such arbours were called *Berceau* or *Berceil* in Old French, from the word *berser*, to shoot with a bow and arrow ; they were also called *ramiers* and *folies*, from rames or branches, and folia, leaves, with which they were made or disguised (Noir., iii. p. 354).

Manwood tells us that *Stable-stand* was one of four "manners in which if a man were found, in the forest, he could be arrested as a poacher or trespasser," and says : "Stable-stand is where one is found at his standing ready to shoot at any Deer, or standing close by a tree with Greyhounds in his leash ready to let slip" (Man., p. 193).

STANKES, or layes ; tanks or pools, large meers. Gaston says : *Estancs et autres mares ou marrhès* (G. de F., p. 21). Stank house was a moated house. A ditch or moat filled with water was called a tank.

TACHE, or tecche, Mid. Eng. for a habit, especially a bad habit, vice, freak, caprice, behaviour, from the O. F. *tache*, a spot, a stain, or blemish ; also a disgrace, a blot on a man's good name. In the older use it was applied both to good as well as bad qualities, as in our text.

TAW, to makes hides into leather; tawer, the maker of white leather. In the fourteenth and early fifteenth centuries, in the days of the strict guilds, a sharp line was drawn between tawers and tanners, and a tawer was not allowed to tan nor a tanner to taw (Wylie, vol. iii. p. 195). No tawers were allowed to live in the Forest according to the ancient forest laws.

"If any white Tawer live in a Forest, he shall be removed and pay a Fine, for they are the common dressers of skins of stolen deer" (Itin. Lanc. fol. 7, quoted by Manwood, p. 161).

TEAZER, or *teaser*. "A kind of mongrel greyhound whose business is to drive away the deer before the Greyhounds are slipt," is the definition given by Blome (p. 96). These dogs were used to hunt up the game also when the deer was to be shot with the bow. The sportsmen would be standing at their trysts or stablestand in some alley or glade of the wood, and the hounds be put into the covert or park "*to tease them forth.*"

TRACE, slot, or footprint of deer. In O. F. and Ang.-N. literature the word trace seems to have been used indifferently for the track of the stag, wild boar, or any game (Borman, notes 147, 236, 237). G. de F. expressly says that the footprint of the deer should not be called *trace* but *voyes* or *piés* (view or foot), yet the "Master of Game" in his rendering says: "Of the hart ye shall say 'trace,'" so evidently that was the proper sporting term in England at the time. When slot entirely superseded the word trace amongst sportsmen it is difficult to determine. Turbervile uses slot, and in the beginning of the seventeenth century it seems the general term for the footprint of deer (Man., p. 180; Stuart Glossary, vol. ii.; Blome, p. 76). Slot, it may be contended, is as old a word as trace, but in Mid. Eng. it was employed as a general term for a foot-track or marking of any animal. The trace or slot was one of the signs of a stag, that is the mark by which an experienced huntsman could recognise the age, size, and sex of the deer.

The old stag leaves a blunter print with a wider heel than a hind, but it is difficult to distinguish the slot of a hind from that of a young stag. Although the latter has invariably a bigger heel and makes deeper marks with his dewclaws, yet his toes are narrow and pointed, their edges are sharp, and the distance between his steps is somewhat unequal, all of which may lead his slotting to be mistaken for the tracks of a hind. "He has found what he wanted," says Dr. Collyns, when speaking of the harbourer, "the rounded track, the blunted toe point, the widespread mark, the fresh slot, in short, of a stag" ("Chase of the Red Deer").

The huntsman of old used to consider that any slot into which four fingers could be placed with ease belonged to a warrantable stag (some declared a stag of ten). That would mean that the slot would be about three inches wide, if not more. I believe two and a half inches is considered a fair measurement for mark of the heel by Devonshire stag-hunters, who alone in England concern themselves with the differences in the slot, as they only chase the wild deer. No such woodcraft is necessary for the chase of the carted deer, and as long as the master and huntsman can distinguish the footprint of a deer from that of any other animal, that is all that is required of them in this matter. The stepping or gait of a stag is also a sign that was taken into consideration. The old stag walks more equally, and generally places the point of his hind feet in the heel of his fore feet. The gait of a hind is more uncertain; it is said she misprints, that is sometimes the hind foot will be placed beside the fore foot, sometimes inside or in front of it. She is not even so regular in her gait as a young stag, unless she is with fawn, when she will place her hind feet constantly outside her fore feet. A hind walks with wide-spreading claws, so does a young stag with his fore feet, but those of his hind feet will be closed. The larger the print of the fore feet are in comparison to the hind feet the older the stag.

The underneath edge of the claws round the hollow of the sole was called the *esponde* (sponde, edge or border). In older stags they were blunter and more worn, and in hinds and younger deer sharper, unless indeed the stag inhabited a damp and mossy country, where the *esponde* would not be so much worn down as if he lived on a rocky or stony ground. (G. de F., 155, 129–145; Lav., p. 246; Stuart, p. 58; Fortescue, p. 133). And thus did the woodmen of old study the book of nature, which told them all they wished to know, and found for them better illustrations than any art could give.

TRYST, in the language of sport, was the place or stand where the hunter took up his position to await the game he wished to shoot. The game might be driven to him by hounds, or he might so place himself as to shoot as the game went to and from their lair to their pasturing (*see* Appendix : Stables and Stable-stand). In French it was called shooting *à l'affut*, from *ad fustem*, near the wood, because the shooter leant his back to, or hid behind a tree, so that the game should not see him.

In our MS. we are told that Alaunts are good for hunting the wild boar whether it be with greyhounds, at the "tryst," or with running hounds at bay within the covert. The tryst here would be the place where a man would be stationed to slip the dogs at the wild boar as soon as he broke covert, or after the huntsman had wounded the boar with a shot from his long or cross-bow (p. 118).

VELTRES, *velteres, veltrai*. A dog used for the chase, a hound. Probably derived from the Gaelic words *ver*, large or long, and *traith*, a step or course, *vertragus* being the name by which according to Arian, the Gauls designated a swift hound (Blanc, 52).

WANLACE. Winding in the chase (Halliwell). In the sentence in which this word is used in the chapter on the Mastiff (p. 122) we are told that some of these dogs "fallen to be berslettis and also to bring well and fast a wanlace about." Which probably means that some of these dogs become shooting dogs, and could hunt up the game to the shooter well and fast by ranging or circling. *Wanlasour* is an obsolete name for one who drives game (Strat.).

In Brit. Mus. MS. Lansdowne 285 there is an interesting reference to setting the forest "with archers or with Greyhounds or with Wanlassours."

WILD BOAR. These animals were denizens of the British forests from the most remote ages, and probably were still numerous there at the time our MS. was penned. For although the Duke of York has only translated one of the eleven chapters relating to the natural history, chase, or capture by traps of the wild boar, and does not give us any original remarks upon the hunting of them, as he has of the stag and the hare, still it was most likely because he considered these two the royal sport *par excellence*, and not because there were none to hunt in England in his day. If the latter had been the case, he would in all probability have omitted even the chapter he does give us, as he has done with those written by Gaston de Foix on the deer, the reindeer, and the ibex and chamois (p. 160).

In some doggerel verses which are prefixed to "Le venery de Twety and Gyfford" (in Vesp. B. XII.), the wild boar is classed as a beast of venery. In the "Boke of St. Albans" the wild boar is also mentioned as a beast of venery.

When Fitzstephen wrote his description of London in

1174, he says wild boars as well as other animals frequented the forests surrounding London, and it would certainly be a long time after this before these animals could have been extirpated from the wild forests in more remote parts of the country.

Sounder is the technical term for a herd of wild swine. "How many herdes be there of bestes of venery? Sire of hertis, or bisses, of bukkes and of doos. A soundre of wylde swyne. A bevy of Roos" (Twety and Gyfford). In the French Twici we have also *Soundre dez porcs.*

Farrow (Sub.) was a term for a young pig, in Mid. Eng. *farh, far*, Old Eng. *fearh* (Strat.). Farrow (verb) was the term used when sows gave birth to young.

G. de F. says that wild boars can wind acorns as far as a bear can (p. 58), and turning to his chapter on bears, we find that he says that bears will wind a feeding of acorns six leagues off!

Routing or rooting. A wild boar is said to root when he is feeding on ferns or roots (Turb., pp. 153, 154).

Argus, as our MS. calls the dew-claws of the boar, were in the later language of venery called the *gards* (Blome, p. 102). Twety and Gyfford named the dew-claws of the stag *os* and of the boar *ergos*. "How many bestis bere *os*, and how many *ergos*? The hert berith *os* above, the boor and the buk berith *ergos*."

Grease, as the fat of the boar or sow was called, was supposed to bear medicinal qualities. "And fayre put the grece whan it is take away, In the bledder of the boore my chylde I yow pray, For it is a medecine : for mony maner pyne" ("Boke of St. Albans").

WILD CAT (*Felis Catus*), which at one time was extremely common in England, was included among the beasts of the chase. It is frequently mentioned in royal grants giving liberty to enclose forest-land and licence to hunt therein.

It was probably more for its skin than for diversion that the wild cat was hunted, as its fur was much used for trimming dresses at one time.

The wild cat is believed to be now extinct, not only in England and Wales, but in a great part of the South of Scotland. A writer in the new edition of the *Encyclopædià Britannica* (art. "Cat") expresses the opinion that the wild cat still exists in Wales and in the North of England, but gives no proof of its recent occurrence there.

Harvie-Brown in his "Vertebrate Fauna of Argyll" (1892) defines the limit of the range of the wild cat by a line drawn from Oban to Inverness; northward and westward of this line, he states, the animal still existed. But there is no doubt that of late years the cessation of vermin trapping in many parts of Scotland, which has caused a marked increase in the golden eagle, has had the same effect upon the wild cat.

The natural history chapter of the wild cat is taken by the Duke of York from G. de F.; did we not know this, some confusion might have arisen through the fact being mentioned that there are several kinds of wild cat, whereas only one was known to the British Isles. G. de F. says there were wild cats as large as leopards which went by the name of *loups-serviers* or *cat wolves,* both of which names he declares to be misnomers. He evidently refers to the *Felis Lynx* or *Lynx vulgaris,* which he properly classes as a "manner of wild cat," although some of the ancient writers have classed them as wolves (Pliny, Lib. viii. cap. 34).

WOLF. For a long time it was a popular delusion that wolves had been entirely exterminated in England and Wales in the reign of the Saxon King Edgar (956–957), but Mr. J. E. Harting has by his researches proved beyond doubt that they existed some centuries later, and did not entirely disappear until the reign of Henry VII. (1485–1509).

WORMING A DOG. This was supposed to be a preventive to the power of a mad dog's bite. It was a superstition promulgated in very early times, and seems to have been believed in until comparatively recent times. We find it repeated in one book of venery after another, French, English, and German : in England by our author, Turbervile, Markham, and others.

Pliny suggests this operation, and he quotes Columna as to the efficacy of cutting off a dog's tail when he is very young (Pliny, chap. xli.).

G. de F. and the Duke of York are careful to say that they only give the remedy for what it is worth, the latter saying : " Thereof make I no affirmation," and further on : " Notwithstanding that men call it a worm it is but a great vein that hounds have underneath their tongue" (p. 87).

LIST OF SOME BOOKS CONSULTED

AND ABBREVIATIONS USED IN TEXT

Albertus Magnus. *De Animalibus.* Ed. 1788.
—— *The Secrets of.* London, 1617.
Ancient Laws and Institutes of Wales. 1841.
—— *of Cambria.* E. Williams. 1823.
Anc. Ten., for *Ancient Tenures of Land.* By Thomas Blount. London, 1874.
Andreæ, E. C. A. *Die Geschichte der Jagd.* Frankfurt, 1894.
Archæologia. Pub. by Soc. of Antiq. Beginning 1770.
Arcussia, Ch. d'. *La Conference des Fauconniers (Cab. de Venerie,* vii.). 1880.
Arkwright, for *The Pointer and his Predecessor.* By William A. London, 1902. 4to. See Bibliog. in 1st edit.
Arrow Release, The. By Ed. S. Morse. 1885.
Aymon, for *Le Roman des quatres fils Aymon.* Edit. P. Tarbé. 1861.

Bad. Lib. Hunt., for " Badminton Library." Volume on Hunting by the Duke of Beaufort and Mowbray Morris. Ed. 7. London, 1901. Errors in, see Bibliog. in 1st edit.
—— vol. on *The Poetry of Sport.* London, 1896. Errors in, see Bibliog. in 1st edit.
Bangert, for *Die Tiere des Altfranz. Epos.* Von Fried. Bangert. Marburg, 1885.
Barrière-Flavy, C. *Censier du pays de Foix.* Toulouse, 1898.
Barthold, F. W. *Georg von Frundsberg.* 1833.
Bastard, A. de. *Libraire du duc de Berry.* Paris, 1834.
Baudrillart, for *Traite des Eaux et Forêts, Chasse et Pêches.* Par M. B. Paris, 1834.
Beckford, for *Thoughts upon Hare and Fox Hunting.* By Peter B. London, 1796.

Beltz, G. F. *Memorials of the Garter.* 1841.

Berg, L. F. Freiherr. *Gesch. der deutschen Wälder.* Dresden, 1871.

Bertheleti, T., *General Collections of Statutes,* 1225–1546. London, 1543–51.

Bib. Accip., for *Bibliotheca Accipitraria.* By James Edm. Harting. London, 1891.

Blancandin, ed. *H. V. Michelant.* 1867.

Blane, for *Cynegetica, or Observations on Hare Hunting.* By W. B. London, 1788.

Blaze, Elezear. *Catalogue d'une Collection.* Paris, 1852.

—— *Le Livre du Roy Modus.* Paris, 1839.

Blome, for *The Gentleman's Recreation.* By Richard Blome. London, 1686.

Blount, T. *A Law Dictionary and Glossary.* 1717.

Bodl. MS. 546, for the MS. of the "Master of Game" in the Bodleian Library at Oxford. See "Existing MSS. of the 'Master of Game'"; see Bibliog. in 1st edit.

Borman, for *Die Jagd in den Altfranz. Artus und Abenteuer Romanen.* Von Ernst Borman. Marburg, 1887.

Boldon Book, for *Chronicles and Memorials of Great Britain and Ireland* (vol. iii.). By Sir Th. Duffus-Hardy. London, 1875.

B. of St. Albans, for *The Boke of St. Albans.* Edit. by William Blades. London, 1881. See Bibliog. in 1st edit.

"*B. of C.*" for *Boke of Curtasye.* 14th cent. poem. Pub. by I. O. Halliwell. Percy Soc. vol. iv.

Bonney, for *Historic Notices on Fotheringhay.* By Rev. H. K. B. Oundle, 1821.

Borel, P., *Dictionnaire des termes du vieux François.* 2 vols. 1882.

Bouton, Victor. *L'Auteur du Roy Modus.* Paris, 1888.

Brachet, Ang. *An Etymological Dictionary of the French Language* (Clarendon Press). 1866.

Brehm, for B.'s *Tierleben.* 3. ed. Von Dr. Pechuel-Loesche. Leipzig and Wien, 1891.

Brèzé, Jacque de. *La Chasse du grand Sénéschal de Normandye.* Paris, between 1489 and 1494.

Brière, L. de la. *Livre de Prières par Gaston Phébus* (1835). Paris, 1893.

Broebel, P. *Die Fährte des Hirsches.* Halle, 1854.

Browne, for *Pseudoxia Epidemica.* By Sir Ths. B.
1650.

Brut., for *Le Roman de Brut.* By Wace. Ed. by Le Roux
de Lincy. Rouen, 1836–38.

Budé. *Traitte de la Venerie.* Par B. Ed. H. Chevreul
(Paris). 1861.

Burrows, Montagu, Prof. *The Family of Brocas.* 1886.

Caius, for *Englishe Dogges.* By Johannes Caius. Reprint
of ed. of 1576. 1880.

Camden, W. *Britannia.* 1586.

Canterbury Tales, Chaucer's. Ed. Furnivall. 1868.

Castellamonte, A. di. *La Venaria reale.* Torino,
1674.

*Catalogue of the Duke of Marlborough's Library at White
Knight.* London, 1819.

—— London, 1881–83.

—— Oxford, 1772.

"Cecil," for *Records of the Chase.* By "Cecil," edit.
London, 1877. See Bibliog. in 1st edit.

Chaffourt, Jacques de. *Instructions.* Paris, 1609. (2nd ed.)

Champgrand, for *Traité de Venerie et Chasse.* Par Goury
de C. Paris, 1769.

Champollion-Figeac, Aimi. *Louis et Charles, ducs d'Orleans.*
Paris, 1844.

Charles d'Orleans, for Charles de Valois. *Les poésies du
duc Charles d'Orleans.* Edit. Champollion-Figeac. Paris,
1842.

—— *Charles of Orleans' Poems.* Roxburgh Club. Ed.
G. W. Taylor. London, 1827.

—— Edit. by Charles d'Héricault. Paris, 1874.

Chassant, Alphonse. *L'Auteur du Livre du Roy Modus.*
1869. See Bibliog. in 1st edit.

Chaucer, *Minor Poems.* Ed. Furnivall. 1871.

Chézelles, H. de. *Vieille Vénerie.* Paris, 1894.

Chronique de la traïson de Richard II. Eng. Hist. Soc.
1846.

Cla., for *Li Romans de Claris et Laris.* Ed. by Dr. Alton.
1884.

Clam. *La Chasse du loup.* Par Jean de Clamorgan.
Paris, 1566.

Close Rolls, for *Calendars of the Close Rolls preserved in the Pub. Rec. Office.*

Codorniu, J. *Etude historique sur Gaston Phœbus.* Floraux, 1895.

Cogho. *Des Erstlings Geweih.* Leipzig, 1886.

Collyns, C. P. *The Chase of the Wild Red Deer.* London, 1862.

Compleat Angler. See Walton.

Com. Sports., for *The Complete Sportsman.* By T. Fairfax. London.

Corneli, R. *Die Jagd.* Amsterdam, 1884.

Cornish, Ch. J. *Shooting.* Ed. by Horace G. Hutchinson. 2 vols. (Newnes). London, 1903.

Cotgrave. *Dictionary.* 1679.

Cotgrave and Sherwood's *Dictionary.* 1632.

———   ———   ——— 1673.

Cox, Nich. *The Gentleman's Recreation.* London, 1674.

Cran. Ch., for *Anecdotes and History of Cranbourne Chase.* By Wm. Chafin. London, 1818.

Culemann, L. *Delineatio Venatus.* Hanover, 1564.

Cupples, George. *Scotch Deerhounds and their Masters.* London, 1894.

Curmer, L. *Verure de J. Foncquet.* Paris, 1866.

Curtasye, Boke of. Ed. by Halliwell. Percy Soc. Pub. Vol. iv.

Cynegetica. London, 1788.

Dalton, Michael. *The Country Justice.* 1666.

Daniel, W. B. *Rural Sports.* London, 1801.

D. et B., for *Daurel et Beton.* Ed. by Paul Meyer. Paris, 1880.

Dalziel, for *British Dogs.* By Hugh Dalziel. 3 vols. London, 1887–96.

Daurel et Beton. Ed. Paul Meyer. Paris, 1880.

Duc d'Aumale, for *Recueil de la Philobiblion Society.* Vol. ii. London, 1855–56.

Delacourt, for *Le Chasse à la Haie.* Par Peigne Delacourt. Péronne, 1872.

Delisle, L. *Inventaire des MSS. de la Biblioth. Nationale.* Paris, 1876, &c.

De Noir., for *Histoire de la Chasse.* Par le Baron Dunoyer
de Noirmont. Paris, 1876. 3 vols.
Dillon, Viscount. *Fairholt's Costumes in England.* London,
1885.
Ditschfield, R. H. *Old English Sport.* London, 1891.
Doebel, H. W. *Neueröffnete Jäger Practica.* Leipzig, 1783.
Dolopathos, for *Li Romans de D.* Ed. by Brunet et Mon-
taiglon. 1856.
Dombrowski, E. von. *Die Lehre von dem Zeichen.* 1836.
Dombrowski, R. von. *Allgemeine Encyklopadie der
gesammter Forst und Jagdwissenschaft.* Wien, 1886.
Domesday Book. By Henry Ellis (2 vols.). London, 1833.
Drake, Francis. *Eboracum.* London, 1736.
Dryden, Alice. *Memorials of Northamptonshire.* 1903.
Dryden, Sir Henry. *Twici's Art of Hunting.* Middle Hill
Press. 1840. See Bibliog. in 1st edit.
—— *Daventry.* 1843.
—— *Gaston III. Le livre de la Chasse.* Daventry, 1844.
Dudik. *Kaiser Maximilian's II. Jagdordnung.* Wien, 1867.
Du Fouil., for *La Venerie.* Par Jacques du Fouilloux.
Niort, 1864.
Dugdale Bar., for *The Baronage of England.* 1675.

Eglamoure, for *The Romance of E. of Artoys.* Camden
Soc. 1844.
Ellis. See *Domesday Book.*
Elyot, Sir Thomas. *The Boke named the Governour.* Ed.
H. H. S. Croft. 1880.
Emmanuel John, Infant of Spain. *El libro de la Caza.*
Edit. by G. Baist. Halle, 1880.
Ency. of Sport, for *Encyclopædia of Sport.* London, 1897.
Enslin, Th. Ch. Fr. *Bibliotheck der Forst and Jagdwissen-
schaft.* Leipzig, 1823.
Essenwein, Augst. *Quellen zur Geschichte der Feuerwaffen.*
1872.
Estlander, T., for *Pièces inedites du Roman de Tristan.*
Ed. by C. G. E. Helsingfors. 1867.
Evans, D. S. *An English and Welsh Dict.* 1852–58.
Ex. Brit. An., for *Extinct British Animals.* By J. E.
Harting. London, 1880.
Excerpta Historica. London, 1831.

Fleming, H. F. von. *Der Volkommene Teutsche Jäger*
Leipzig, 1719.
Fortescue, Hon. J. W. *Records of the Stag-hunting on
Exmoor.* London, 1887.
Foudras, Marquis de. *Recits de Chasseurs.* Bruxelles,
1858.
Fourtier, A. *Les grands Louvetiers de France.* Paris.
Frederic II. *Reliquæ liborum Frederici II.* August. Vindob.
1596.
Frunsberg, G. v. *Schlacht bei Pavia.* 1525.

Gace de la Buigne. *Bulletin du Bibliophile*, 13th series,
by the Duc d'Aumale ; also in Philobiblion Society, vol. ii.
London. See Bibliog. in 1st edit.
Garin de Loh. Die Geste der Loherains. A. Feist. 1884.
Garnier, P. *Chasse du Sanglier.* 1876.
Gaucheraud, H. *Histoire de C. de Foix.* 1834.
Gawaine, A Collection of Ancient Romance Poems. Edit. by
Sir Fred. Madden. 1839.
G. de F. stands for Joseph Lavallée's edition of Gaston de
Foix's *La Chasse de Gaston Phœbus.* Paris, 1854.
G. de P., for *Roman de Guillaume de Palerne.* Ed. H.
Michelant. Paris, 1876.
G. de St., for *Gottfried von Strassburg.* Ed. by P. A. Leh-
mann. Hamburg, 1703.
Gentleman's Magazine. 1752.
Gent. Recreation, for *Gentleman's Recreation.* By Nicholas
Cox. London, 1686.
God. de Bouill., for *Godefroi de Bouillon.* C. Hippeau.
Paris, 1877.
Goechhausen, H. F. von. *Notabilia Venatoris.* Weimar,
1751.
Goury de Champgrand. *Traité de Venerie.* Paris, 1769.
Graesse, J. G. T. *Jägerbrevier.* Wien, 1869.
—— *Literaturgeschichte.* Dresden, 1845.
Greyhounds. By a Sportsman. London, 1819.

Halliwell, for J. O. H.'s *A Selection from the Minor Poems of
Lydgate.* Pub. by the Percy Society. Vol. ii. 1842.
—— *Carols.* Pub. by the Percy Society. Vol. iv. 1842.
—— *Dictionary of Provincial and Archaic Words.* 1850.

Hammer-Purgstall, Jos. von. *Falkner Klee.* Wien und Pest, 1840.

Hard. de Font.-G. *Le Trésor de la Venerie.* Par Hardouin de Fontaines-Guérin. Ed. by Baron J. Pichon. Paris, 1855.

—— Ed. by Michelant. Metz, 1856.

Hardyng, for *The Chronicles of John Hardyng.* Ed. 1543. London.

Harewood, H. *A Dictionary of Sport.* London, 1835.

Harrison, for *Harrison's Description of England* (Holinshed). Edit. by F. J. Furnivall. London, 1877.

Hartig, G. L. *Lehrbuch fin Jäger.* Tübingen, 1810.

Harting, James Ed. See *Bib. Accip.* and *Ex. Brit. An.*

—— *Zoologist.* 1878–80.

H. de B., for *Huon de Bordeaux.* Ed. by F. Guessard and C. Grandmaison. Paris, 1866.

Hartopp, E. C. C. *Sport in England.* London, 1894.

Hearne, T. *Liber Niger Scaccarii.* 1728.

Heresbach, Conrad. *Rei rusticæ libri quatuor . . . Item de Venatione. . .* 1570.

Historical Review. Jan. 1903.

Hollinshed, R. (Harrison). Ed. F. G. Furnivall. London, 1877.

Hore, J. P. *History of the Buckhounds.* 1893.

Horn., for *Das Anglonormannische Lied vom Ritter Horn.* Ed. by E. Stengel. Marburg, 1883.

Houdedot, C. F. A. d'. *Les Femmes Chasseresses.* Paris, 1859.

Jesse, for *Researches into the History of the British Dog.* By G. R. Jesse. 2 vols. London, 1866.

Journal des Chasseurs. Vols. 27, 28, 29, and 30. Paris.

Jubinal, Michel. *Nouveau Recueil de Conte*, &c. (*La Chace dou Serf.*) 1839.

Jullien, E. *La Chasse, son Histoire et sa Législation.* Paris, 1868.

—— *La Chasse du Loup.* Paris, 1881.

Karajan, T. G. von. *Kaiser Maximilian's Geheimes Jagdbuch.* Wien, 1858.

Kellar, for *Thiere des Class. Alterthums.* Von Otto Kellar. Innsbruck, 1887.

Kennet, White. *Parochial Antiquities.* 1695.
Kobell, F. von. *Der Wildanger.* Stuttgart, 1859.
Kreiger, Otto von. *Die hohe und niedere Jagd.* Trier, 1879.
Kreysig, G. C. *Biblioteca Scriptorum Veneticorum.* Altenburg, 1750.
Kroeger, C. *The Minnesinger of Germany.* Camb. (Mass.), 1873.

Laborde, Leon E. S. J. de. *Glossaire Français du Moyen Age.* 1872.
—— *Les ducs de Bourgogne.* 1847.
La Chace dou Serf. Edited by Baron Jerome Pichon. Paris, 1840. *See also* Jubinal. See Bibliog. in 1st edit.
La Chasse Royal, for *La Chasse Royale, composée par le Roy Charles IX.* Ed. by H. Chevreul. Paris, 1857.
La Croix, P. *La Moyen Age.* Paris, 1848–51.
La Curne de Sainte Palaye: *Memoires sur l'ancienne Chevalerie.* Paris, 1781.
La Ferrière, Hector Conte. *Les Chasses de François I.* Paris, 1869.
Lallemand. *Bibliothèque historique . . . de la Chasse.* Rouen, 1763.
Lancaster, Henry, Earl of. *Expenses of John of Brabant.* Camden Soc., 1847.
Landau, G. *Beiträge zur Geschichte der Jagd.* Kassel, 1849.
Latini, Brunetto. *Li livres dou Tresor.* Edit. by Chabaille. Paris, 1835.
Lauchert, Prof. Fr. *Das Weidwerk der Römer.* Rottweil, 1848.
Lavallée, for *La Chasse à Courre en France par Joseph La Vallée.* Paris, 1859.
—— *Technologie Cynégétique, Journal des Chasseurs.* 1863.
—— *La Chasse à tir en France.* 1854.
Le Coulteux de Cauteleu, Baron. *La Venerie Française.* Paris, 1858.
Leguina, Enrique de. *Estudios bibliográficos La Caza.* 1888.
Lenz, J. O. *Zoologie der Alten Griechen und Römer.* Gotha, 1856.
Le Verrier de la Conterie. *L'Ecole de la Chasse aux Chiens Courans.* Rouen, 1783.
Liber Niger. See Hearne.

Lib. de la Mont., for *Biblioteca Venatoria de Gutierres de la Vega, Libro de la Monteria del Rey Alfonso XI.* Del D. Jose G. d. l. V. Madrid, 1877. See Bibliog. in 1st edit
Liebermann, Felix. *Constitutionis de Foresta.* Halle, A. S. 1894.
Lindsay, Robert. *Chronicles of Scotland.* Edinb., 1814.
Loh., for *Die Geste des Loherains.* Ed. A. Feist. 1844.

Madden, for *The Diary of Master William Silence.* By D. H. M. London, 1897.
Madden, Sir Fred. *Privy Purse Expenses of Princess Mary.* 1831.
Maison Rustique, for *M. R. de Maistres C. Estienne and Iean Liebault.* Used ed. Paris, 1572 and 1578.
Malory, for *La Morte d'Arthure.* Ed. by Sir T. Malory. London, 1856.
Maluquer, Dufau de. *Comté de Foix.* Foix. Pau, 1901.
Man., for Manwood's *Forest Laws.* 4th ed. by W. Nelson. London, 1717. See *Pleas of the Forest.*
Markham, Gervase. *Country Contentments, or the Husbandman's Recreation.* London, 1611.
—— *Cheap and Good Husbandry.* London, 1614.
—— *The Young Sportsman's Delight and Instructor.* London, 1652.
Maricourt, René de. *La Chasse du Lievre*, &c. Paris, 1858.
Maundeville. *The Book of John M.* Ed. Dr. G. F. Warner (Roxburgh Club). London, 1889.
Meurer, Noe. *Jägerkunst.* 1618.
Meyer, P. *Glossaire de la Curne de S. Paley.* 1875.
Millais, J. G. *British Deer.* London, 1897.
Monmouth, Gottfried von. Ed. Hoffmann and Vollmüller. Halle, 1899.
Montauban, Renans de. Ed. by Michelant. 1843.
Mont., for *L'antiquite expliquée.* By Bernard de Montfaulcon. Paris, 1719.
Mortillet, G. de. *Origines de la Chasse.* Paris, 1890.

Neckham, Alexander. *De Naturis Rerum.* Edit. Wright, 1858.
Négociation du Marechal de Bassompierre. 1626.

Nichols, J. *Royal Wills*. London, 1780.
Nicolas, Sir N. H. *The Battle of Agincourt*. London, 1832.
—— *History of the Navy*. London, 1847.
—— *Proceedings and Ordinances of the Privy Council*.
—— *Privy Purse Expen. of Elizabeth of York and Ward-robe Exp. of Edward IV*. London, 1830.
Notabilia Venatoris. Nordhausen, 1710.

Ordinances. A Collection of O. and Regulations of the Royal Household. Soc. of Antiq. 1790.

Pärson, J. W. von. *Der edle hirschgerechte Jäger*. 1683.
Patent Rolls (Printed) *of the English Kings from Edward III. to Henry VII*.
P. B., for *Partonopeus de Blois*. Ed. G. Crapelet. 2 vols. Paris, 1834.
Pennant, Thomas. *British Zoology*. London, 1768–76.
Perc., for *Perceval le Gallois*. Edited by C. Potvin. Soc. des Biblio. Vol. xxi., 1866.
Petit, Paul. *Le Livre du Roy Modus*. 1900.
Philobiblion Society. Vol. ii. London, 1854–55.
Picard, for *La Venerie des ducs de Bourgogne*. Par Etienne Picard. Paris, 1881. '
Planché, I. R. *Military Antiquities*. 1834.
Pleas of the Forest. By G. J. Turner. London, B. Quaritch, 1901.
Poetry of Sport, vol. of Badminton Lib. Ed. by Hedley Peek. London.
Privy Purse Expenses of Elizabeth of York. London, 1830.
Prutz, Dr. H. *Rechnungen über Heinrich von Derby's Preussenfahrt*. Leipzig, 1893.

Ramsay, Sir James. *Lancaster and York*. 1892.
Raymond, G. *Rôles de l'armée de Gaston Phœbus*, 1376–1378). Bordeaux, 1872.
Reynardson, C. T. S. B. *Sports of Bygone Days*. London, 1787.
Reissner, Adam. *Historische Beschreibung*. 1620.
Ribbesdale, for *The Queen's Hounds*. By Lord R. London, 1887.
Rohan-Chabot. *La Chasse a travers les âges*. Paris, 1898.

Rol. Lied., for *Das Altfranzötische Rolandslied.* Ed. by Ed. Max Stengel. Heilbronn, 1878 and 1900.

Rolls of Parl., for *Rotuli Parliamentorum*—Edw. III. to Henry IV.

Romania, Octob. Paris, 1844.

Roman de Richard le Biaus. Ed. Dr. W. Förster. Wien, 1874.

R. d. B., for *Roman de Brut.* Par R. Wace. Ed. Le Roux de Lincy. Rouen, 1838.

Roman de Perceval le Gallois. Ed. Ch. Potvin. Mons, 1871.

Roman le, de Rose. Ed. F. Pluquet. 1827.

R. de Rou., for *Le Roman de Rou.* By Robert Wace. Ed. by F. Pluquet. 1827.

R. V., for *Roman de la Violette.* Ed. Fr. Michel. Paris, 1834.

Roy Modus, for *Eleséar Blaze's* ed. *of Le Livre du Roy Modus.* Paris, 1839. See Bibliog. in 1st edit.

Rye, W. B. *England as seen by Foreigners.* London, 1865.

Sahl., for *Englische Jagd, Jagdkunde und Jagdliteratur im 14. 15. und 16. Jahrhund.* Von Paul Sahlender. Leipzig and London, 1895.

—— *Der Jagdtraktat Twici's.* Von Paul Sahlender. Leipzig, 1894.

—— *Das Englische Jagdwesen in seiner gesch. Entwick-lung.* Von D. P. Sahlender-Bautzen. Dresden and Leipzig, 1898.

Sainte-Palaye, for *Memoires sur l'ancienne Chevalerie.* Par M. de la Curne de S.-P. 3 vols. Paris, 1781.

Salnove, R. de. *La Venarie Royale.* Paris, 1655. Niort, 1888.

Scandianese, F. G. *Della Caccia.* Vinegia, 1556.

Sen. de Nor., for *Sénéschal de Normandye*, or *Le livre de la Chasse et du bon chien Souillard.* Par le Baron Jer. Pichon. Paris, 1858.

Shaw, Vero. *The Book of the Dog.* London, 1889-91.

Shirley, for *English Deer Parks.* By Evelyn Ph. S. London, 1867.

Shirley MS., for Brit. Mus. Addit. MS. 16,165 of the "Master of Game," which is the version next in importance

to the one reproduced in the present work. *See* Biblio-
graphy : MSS. of the " Master of Game " in 1st edit.
Smith, Sir Thomas. *De Republica Anglorum.* London,
1583.
Souhart, for *Bibliographie des Ouvrages sur la Chasse.* Par
R. Souhart. 1886, with two additions of 1888 and 1891.
Statutes of the Realm. 1810–1822. (9 vols.)
Stisser, F. U. *Forst und Jagd Histor. der Teutschen.* Jena,
1738.
Strassburg, Gottfried von. Ed. P. A. Lehmann. 'Hamburg,
1703.
Stratmann, F. H. *Middle English Dic.* Rev. by H.
Bradley. 1891.
Strutt, J. *Sports and Pastimes of the English People.* Ed.
1875. Errors in it, Appendix in 1st edit.
—— —— New ed. by J. C. Cox. 1903.
—— *Dress and Habits of the People of England.*
Stuart, for *Lays of the Deer Forest.* By J. Sob. and Ch.
Stuart. 2 vols. Edin. and London, 1848.

Taplin, W. *Sporting Dictionary.*
Tarbé, Prosper. *Le Noble et Gentil jeu de l'arbalaste.*
Reims, 1841.
—— *Le Roman des quatres fils Aymon.* 1861.
Tardif, for *L'Art de Fauconerie et des chiens de Chasse.*
Par Guillaume T. Paris, 1492.
Thierbach, T. *Die Geschichtliche Entwicklung der Haud-
feuegswaffen.* Dresden, 1886–89.
Topsell, Edward. *The Historie of Foure-footed Beastes.*
London, William Iaggard, 1607.
T. and I., for *Tristan und Isolde.* Von Gottfried von
Strassburg. Ed. Her. Kurtz. Stuttgart, 1844.
T. M., for *Tristan: Receuil de ce qui reste des poemes.* Ed.
by Fr. Michel. 3 vols. London, 1835–39.
Topham, J. *Observations on the Wardrobe Accounts of the
28th year of Edward I.* 1787.
Traité (Nouveau) de Venerie. Paris, 1750.
Traité des Chasses (Anon.). 2 vols. Paris, 1822.
Traité des Chasses et de la Venerie. Paris, 1681.
Treat. on Greyh., for *A Treatise on Greyhounds.* By a
Sportsman. London, 1825.

T. Tresson, for *Histoire de Tristan de Leonois.* Ed. by
  Comte de Tresson. Paris, 1781.
Tristan. Ed. Fr. Michel. 3 vols. London, 1835–39.
—— *de la Table Ronde.* Pr. Ant. Verard. Paris, 1495.
Turber., for *The Noble Art of Venery or Hunting.* London,
  1575–76. (When not specially mentioned, the second
  edit. of 1611.)
Twety and Gyfford (also written Twety and Giffard), for
  article under that title in the *Reliquiæ Antiquæ.* Vol. i.,
  where Thomas Wright published Twici's *Art of Hunting,*
  in Brit. Mus. MS. Vespasian B. XII. Bibliog. 1st edit.
Twici, for *The Art of Hunting.* By William Twici (MS.
  Phillipps, 8336). Edited by (Sir) H. E. L. Dryden.
  Daventry, 1843. Bibliog. 1st edit.
Tyolet, Romania. Edited by G. Paris, 1885.

Usk, Adam of. *Chronicon.* Ed. London, 1876.

Vallès, Mossen Juan. *Tratado de Monteria.* 1556.
Venerie Nor., for *Venerie Normande.* Par M. le Verrier
  de la Conterie. Rouen, 1778.
Ver de la Cont., for *L'Ecole de la Chasse aux Chiens
  Courans.* Par M. de le Verrier de le Conterie. Rouen,
  1763.
Vignancour, Emile. *Recueil de Poésies Béarnaises.* 4th
  Edit. Pau, 1886.
Vincentius Bellovacensis. *Bibliotheka Mundi.* Edit. of 1624.
—— *Speculi majoriis.* 1591.
Vyner. *Notitia Venatica.*

Wagner, F. von. *Die Jagd des grossen Wildes im Mittelalter.*
  Wien, 1844.
Walton, for *The Compleat Angler.* By Izaak Walton.
  Used ed. London, 1815.
*Wardrobe Accounts for the reigns of Edward III. to Henry
  IV.*
Werth, Hermann. *Über die ältesten franz. Übersetzungen
  Mittelalt. Jagdlehrbücher.* Göttingen, 1888.
—— *Altfranzösische Jagdlehrbücher.* Halle, 1889.
Whitaker, Joseph. *The Deer Parks of England.* London,
  1892.

Will. of Palerne. *See* G. de P.
Wright, for *A History of Domestic Manners in England.*
By Thomas Wright. London, 1862.
Wylie, for *History of England under Henry IV.* By James
H. Wylie. London, 1884–98. 4 vols.
Wynn, for *History of the Mastiff.* By M. B. Wynn. Melton
Mowbray, 1886.

D'Yauville. *Traité de Venerie.* Paris, 1688.

GLOSSARY

OF OBSOLETE ENGLISH TERMS AND WORDS
OCCURRING IN THE ANCIENT TEXTS
OF "THE MASTER OF GAME" AND IN
APPENDIX.

ABAI, ABAY, being at bay, 29, 118
ACHARNETH, ACHARNE, to set on, to eat flesh, 59, 60, 62
ACHAUF, heat, 38, 98
ACQUILLER, ENQUILLER, to rouse animals of the chase with hounds, App.
AFERAUNT, the haunch, 38
AFFETED, fashioned, trained, 27, 141
AFORCE, *par force*, by force, App.
AIGUILLOUNCE, thorny
AKELID, cooled, 186
AKIRE, AKKERNE, acorns, 144
ALAUNTIS, ALAUNTZ, ALOND, allans or allauntes, a large hound, 3, 116–8
ALVELUE, covered with fleece, fat or woolly substance, App.
ANALED, for *avaled*, hanging down, 114
ANCEPS, HAUSSEPIED, a snare which caught the game by the foot and lifted it into the air, 61
ANCHES, rosemary
APEL, French hunting-note, App.
APERYNG, stoned, the roughness of antlers, 143
APPARAILLE, dressed venison
ARBITTEN, bitten, devoured

ARBLAST, cross-bow, 27
ARECHE, reach, 60
ARERE, *arrière*, behind, back there, 182, App.
AREYN, spider, 137
AREYN, rain, 157
ARRACHER, to tear out; a term used for skinning certain animals, App.
ASAUTE, SAUTE, in heat, 64, 66
ASCRIETHE, ASCRIE, to rate, shout at, to scold, 63, 74, 170
ASSAIEN, try or test, 88
ASSAYE, ESSAY, to try; taking assay, to see by a cut the thickness of the fat, App.
ASSISE, note on hunting-horn blown at death of stag which has been hunted by stag-hounds, App.
ASTERTE, escape
ASTIFLED, inflammation in the stifle-joint, 103
ASTRIED, rated, shouted at, 170
ATHREST, thrust or push, 106
ATTE FULLE, when the stag's antlers show a certain number of tines, App.
ATTIRE, the stag's antlers, App.
AUALED, AVAILED, hanging down, 106, 114

AUERILLE, *Avrille*, April, 30

AUNTELERE, AUNTILLER, AUN-
CULER, antler, 130, 140

AUNTRED, ventured, 28

AVAUNT, AUAUNT, a hunting
cry, " Forward," 182

AVAUNTELLAY, relay of hounds

AVAYL, avail, profit, 13, 31

AVENAUND, approachable

AVENERY, oats

AVISED, aware of, warned, informed, advised, cautious

AVOY, a hunting cry, probably
from " Away," App.

BACE, for Luce, a pike

BAFFERS, barkers, 120

BAKE, back

BALISTA, BALESTA, cross-bow,
haronsblast, 27

BALOWE, bellow, roaring of a
stag

BANDRIKE, BALDRIC, belt to
which horn was fastened, 128,
140

BARATEUR, quarreller

BARBOURIS, barbers

BAREYN, barren, 35

BASCO, Basque, Biscay, 106

BATYD, bruised, sore, 98

BATYNG, bating

BAUDES, baubles, trifles, 83

BEAM, the main part of the
stag's antlers, 142

BEENDYNG, bending

BEERNERS, BERNERS, attend-
ant on hounds, 148, 165

BEESTALE, BESTAILE, beasts,
cattle, 36, 61

BEESTIS, beasts, App.

BELLEN, BELOWYN, BELERVE,
BELOWEN, bellow or roar, 160

BELUEZ, velvet, 26

BEME, beam; also trumpet

BENES, beans, 26

BERCEL, a mark to shoot at, App.

BERCELET, BERSLETTIS, BARCE-
LETTE, a shooting-dog used
by archers, 122

BERIES, burrows, earth of fox
and badger, 67, 68

BERYED, buried

BERYING, bearing, breaking, 136

BESTIS OF THE CHACE, beasts
of the chase, usually fallow
deer, roe-deer, fox, martin, 3

BESTIS OF VENERIE, beasts of
venery, usually the hart, hare,
boar, and wolf, 3

BEVY, a number of roe-deer
together, App.

BEVYGREASE, the fat of the roe-
deer, App.

BEWELLIS, BAWAYLLES, BAWEL-
LIS, bowels

BILLETINGS, the excrements of
the fox, App.

BISSES, BISES, BISCHES, red-
deer hinds

BISSHUNTERS, fur-hunters, 74

BITTE, bitten, taken, 17, 186

BLENCHES, marks, tricks, de-
ceits, 159

BOCHERIE, butchery, 116

BOKEYING, the rut of the roe-
deer, 41

BOLN, BOLK, BOLNE, bellow or
bark, 39, 162

BOOCHERS HOUNDIS, butchers'
dogs, 118

BOOLE, bull, 118

BOONES, bones, stag's foot

BOONYS, bones, 131

BOORDCLOTH, table-cloth, 164

BOORDES, boards

BOORIS, boars, 143

BOOST, boast

BOTCHES, BOOCHES, sores, 63

BOTIRFLIES, butterflies, 66

BOUNTE, bounty, goodness, 79

BOUVES, boughs, App.

BOWIS, BOWES, boughs, 137, 153

BRACH, BRACHE, a scenting-
hound; later on it meant bitches

BRACHETUS, a hound for hunting, 22

BRACONIER, the man who held the hounds

BRAYNE, BREYN, brain, 176

BREDE, breadth

BREDE, broad, 138

BREKE, brook, break; also applied to dress a deer

BREMED, burnt, 112

BRENT, burnt, 79

BRERES, briars, 93

BRIGILLA, mildew, 96

BRIMMING, BREMYNG, be in heat, said of boar; the word *breme, bryme*, or *brim*, valiant-spirited, 47

BROACHER, a red-deer stag of second year, App.

BROCARD, a roebuck of the third year and upwards, App.

BROCK, badger, App.

BROKES, BROOCHES, BROACHES, the first head of a red-deer stag, and of roebuck, 45

BROKET, brocket, young stag, 29

BROKET'S SISTER, hind in the second year, App.

BROND, proud, 46

BUCHE, BYCHES, bitch

BUGLE, buffalo; also horn for sounding hunting signals, App.

BUKKES, BUKES, BUCKES, bucks

BUKMAST, beechmast, App.

BULLOKE, young stag in second year, 29

BURNYSSHEN, burnish, to rub the antlers when the velvet is off, 134

BURR, the lowest part of the stag's antlers

CABOCHE, to cut off the hart's head near the antlers, 176

CALF, CALFE, the young stag in his first year

CAMAMYLE, camomile, 95

CAMPESTRIS, beast of the field or chase—*i.e.* buck, doe, fox, martin, and roe-deer

CANDLEMAS, February 2

CARAYNES, CARREYNS, KARIN, carrion, carcase, 62, 77

CARDIAC, CARDRYACLE, a disease of the heart, 34

CARRES, marshes, 45

CASE TO, stripping or skinning the hare, App.

CATAPUCIA, spurge (*Euphorbia resinifera*), 101

CATT, CATTE, CATTYS, cat, App.

CAUTELOUS, CAUTELS, cautious, crafty, 45

CETE, a number of badgers

CHACEABLE, chaseable, a hert chaseable, which is now called a warrantable stag, one fit to be hunted

CHACECHIENS, grooms in attendance on hounds, 148, 177

CHALAUNGE, challenge

CHASE, forest; also used to designate a method of hunting, and also a hunting-party

CHASSE, a French hunting-note

CHASTISED, trained, 189

CHATER, CHACER (RECHATER, RECHEAT), a horn signal; also to chastise hounds

CHAUFED, ACHAUFED, heated, in heat, 49, 98

CHAULE, CHAULIS, CHAVEL, jaw, 170

CHAUNGE, change, 31, 108, 111

CHEERE, CHERE, cherish, welcome, 85

CHEVERAUS, roe-deer

CHIBOLLIS, chives, 90

CHILDERMAS, Innocents' Day (December 28)

CHIS, dainty, 83

CHIVAUCHER, CHEVAUCHER, to ride

CHYMER, riding-cloak

CHYMNEYIS, chimney, 98, 126
CLEES, clawes, the "toes" of a deer's foot, 77, 80, 131
CLEEVES, *sur* or dew cleeves at the back of a deer's fetlock
CLEPED, CLEPYD, called, 59, 140
CLERE SPERES, clear spires, woods, App.
CLICQUETING, vixen fox when in heat, App.
CLISTRE, enema, 100
CODDES, testicles of the hart
COITING STONE, a quoit
COLERS, COLIERS PLACES, collier or charcoal pits, 26
CONCILIDA MAIOR, comfrey (*Symphytum officinale*), 98
CONCILIDA MINOR, prunella, selfheal (*Prunella vulgaris*), 98
CONINGER, CONIGREE, rabbit warren, App.
CONTRE, counter, back, heel
CONTRE, country, 36
CONTROUGLE, CONTREONGLE, hunt counter, hunt heel, 150
CONYNGE, rabbit, 18
COOLWORT, cabbage, 100
COPEIS, COPIS, coppice, 155
CORNER, CORNEER, horn blower
COTES, quoits, 178
COUCH, the resting-place of game; also hound's bed
COUCHERS, setters, 120
COUERTTS, covert, shelter
COUNTERFEET, COUNTFEIT, abnormal, 28, 142
COURSER, CURSAR, CURSER, swift horse
COUTHEN, CONTHEN, COUTH, knew, to be able, ob. could, 2
COWE, cow, also tail, from *queue*
CRIE, cry (of hounds), 65
CROCHES, the upper tines of a deer's horns; called also *troches*
CROISE, cross, 150
CROKES, stomach (of red-deer)

CROKYNG, crooked, curved, 128
CROMMES, crumbs
CRONEN, groan, the roar of the stag
CROSS TO, to dislodge roe-deer by hounds
CROTETHE, voiding excrements, 29
CROTKY, CROTILS, CROTISEN, CROTISINGS, excrements, 16, 29, 30, 133
CUER, COER, heart
CUIR, QUIR, leather, hide
CURÉE, CURE, rewarding the hounds (also KYRRE and GUYRRE), 7 29, 52, 208
CURRES, CURRYS, curs
CURTAISE, courteous, 115

DAUNGERE, danger, 161
DEDIS, deeds, 49
DEDUT, DEUDIZ, DEDUIZ, *déduit*, pleasure pursuit, sport
DEFAUTE, DEFAUNT, lack, default, 84, 140
DEFET, DEFFETEN, opening or undoing the boar and removing the entrails
DEFOILE, track, 150
DELYUERE, deliver, active, 124
DEPILED, stripped of hair
DESFAIRE, undoing (brittling) of deer or boar, App.
DESPITOUS, DESPYTOUS, despiteful, furious, 49
DESTERERE, DESTRIER, horse
DETOURNER (LE CERF), to harbour the hart, App.
DEYENG, doing
DEYM, DEYME, DAINE, DINE, fallow-deer
DISLAUE, wild, 159
DISSESE, disease
DOO, doe
DOWN, OR HUSKE, a number of hares, App.
DRAGMES, drachms

DREYNT, drowned

DRIT, DRITT, excrements of animals called "stinking beasts," also mud, 50, 66

DRYEN, dry, 102

DRYUE, driven, 128

DRYVE, made

DUNE, donn, dun

DURE, to last, endure, 43

DYETTE, diet

EARTH, a fox and badger's lodging-place, App.

EDIGHT, done, set in order

EELDE, old age, 123

EENDIS, ends

EEREN, hairs, 44

EERYS, ERES, ears

EGRE, eager, 115

EIRERES, harriers, 190

ELLIS, else, 90

EMELLE, EMEL, female, 41

EMPAUMURE, the croches or top tines of a stag's antlers, App.

ENBROWED, brewed, soaked, 177

ENCHACE, to hunt, 108

ENCHARNYNG, blooding, feeding on flesh, 113

ENCHASEZ, moving deer, &c., with a limer, App.

ENCORNE, to place a dead stag on his back, the antlers on the ground underneath the shoulders, 174

ENFOURMED, informed

ENGLEYMED, glutinous, 29

ENOSED, a bone in the throat, 87

ENPESHED, prevented, 11

ENQUEST, hunt, 182

ENQUILLER, rousing a buck with hounds, App.

ENQUYRID, ENQUEYRREIDE blooding hounds after death of deer; also rewarding of hounds, 173

ENSAUMPLE, example, 79

ENTENTE, intent

ENTRYING, entering, beginning of

ENTRYNGIS, entering, beginning of, 35

ENVOISE, ENVOYSE, O.F. *envoisse*, to leave the line, or overshoot the line of the animal hunted, 31, 108, 170

ERBIS, herbs

ERES OF ROEBUCK, "target," 44

ERGOTS, ARGUS, claws of boar, buck and doe; those of the boar were sometimes called *gardes*, 130, 144

ERIS, ERES, ARS, anus, hinder parts; ears, occasionally thus spelt, 89, 95, 106, 116

ERTHE, earth

ESCORCHER, ESTORCHER, flaying deer, and other beasts of venery, App.

ESPAULES, shoulders

ESPAYARD, SPAYARD, SPAYER, stag of the third year, App.

ESSEMBLE, assembly, 150

ESTABLIE, stand occupied by sportsmen; also beaters

ESTORACIS CALAMITA, storax, resin, 96

ESYE, easy

ETAWED, tanned

ETYN, ITVN, eat

EUENYNGIS, evening, 11

EUERYCHONE, EVERICHON, each one, every one, 163

EUILLE, EUELL, evil, wicked, bad, 6

EVOISED, at fault, or off the line

EXPEDITE, to maim dogs by cutting off some of their claws

EYNE, EYGH, EYNEN, eye, 116

EYRE, air

FACON, FAUCON, falcon, 121

FADIR, FADERE, father, 105

FADMYS, FADOMS, fathoms, 125

FAROWE, FAREWYN, PHARO-
WYN, farrow, bringing forth
young pig, 47, 48, 68
FARSYN, FARSINE, farcy, 69, 92
FASSON, FASSION, fashion
FAUND, fawned
FAUS, false
FAUSMANCHE, false sleeve
FAUT, fault
FECHEWE, fitchew, polecat
FEELDES, fields, 158
FEERNE, fern
FELAUES, fellows
FELE, many; also sensible.
feeling
FELLE, fierce, cruel, treacherous
FELLE, FELE, wise, sensible, feel-
ing; also cunning, 30, 115
FELNESSE, cruelty, fierceness, 71
FEMELLIS, females
FENCEMONTH, the month when
deer had their young and
were left undisturbed, App.
FERMYD, firm, 162
FERRE, far, 16
FERRETTIS, ferrets, 72
FERRTEST, farthest
FERS, fierce, 47
FERSLICHE, fiercely, 86
FESAWNT, pheasant
FEUERYERE, February
FEWES, FEWTE, track, trace,
foot. Some animals were
called of the sweet foot, others
of the stinking foot, 10. See
Appendix.
FEWTERER, FEUTRERES, FEW-
TREES, man who leads grey-
hounds, 129
FIANTS, also LESSES, excre-
ments of the wild boar, App.
FISTOLES, fistula, 92
FIXEN, vixen, O.G. fuchsen, 64
FLAY, FLEAN, FLENE, to skin
deer and certain other game,
174
FLAYSSH, flesh, 5

FLUX, dysentery
FOILLYNG, stag going down-
stream when hunted, 32, 173
FOLIES, FOLY, FOLLY, lesser
deer, not hart or buck, 196
FOLTISCH, foolish, 45
FOORME, FORME, FOURME,
form of the hare, 14, 17
FORAGLE, strangle, straggle
FORCHE, FOURCHED, forked,
said of stag's antlers, 140, 177
FORLOYNE, FORLOGNE, FOR-
LONGE, a note sounded on
the horn, to denote that the
quarry or hounds or both had
distanced the hunters, 173
FORSTERS, foresters, 148
FORSWONG, M.E. Forswinger,
bruised, beaten (tucked up), 88
FORT, the thick part of woods
FORUN, forewarn, 148
FOTYDE, footed
FOUAILL, the reward given to
the hounds after a boar hunt,
consisting of the bowels
cooked over a fire, App.
FOUMART, FAULMART, FOL-
MERT, polecat
FOWTRERES, FEWTERERS,
huntsmen who led grey-
hounds, slippers
FOXEN, FFIXEN, A.S. fixen—
vixen, a bitch fox, 64
FOYNE, weasel
FRAIED, rubbed, 135
FRAY, frighten, scare, 149
FRAY, to rub off the velvet on
stag's antlers, 26, 135
FRAYING-POST, the tree against
which it was done
FREYN, excrements of the wild
boar, App.
FROOT, FROTID, rub, 53, 94, 95,
146
FUANTS, excrements of the
fox, martin, badger, and
wolf, App.

FUES, track, line, 18, 31

FUMES, FUMEE, FUMAGEN, FIMESHEN, FEWMETS, FEMEGEN, FEWMISHINGS, excrements, droppings, particularly of deer, 9, 16, 38, 39, 133

FURKIE, pieces of venison hung on a fork-shaped stick

FURROUR, fur, Fr. *fourrure*, 63

FUTAIE, FUTELAIE, forest, wood of old trees, also plantation of beech-trees, App.

FYNDERS, finders, hounds to start or find deer, 161, 165

GADERYNGE, GADERYNG, gathering, meet, 156, 163

GADIRE, gather, 43

GAR, to force, to compel, 39

GARDES, the dew-claws of the wild boar

GARSED, cupped, 90

GIN, GYNNE, trap, snare

GIRLE, the roebuck in the second year, App.

GISE, guise, manner of

GLADNESSE, a glade, a clear space, 137

GLAUNDRES, glanders, 96

GLEMYNG, GLEVMING, slime, stickiness, 133

GLOTENY, gluttony

GNAPPE, snap, 92

GOBETTES, small pieces, 81, 177

GOOT, goat

GORGEAUNT, wild boar in his second year

GOTERS, GOOTERE, GOUTIERES, gutters, the small grooves in the antlers of a stag, 143

GRAUNT SOUR, stag of fifth year

GRAUYLL, gravel, 143

GREASE, GRECE, the fat of certain animals, 25, 27, 49

GREASE-TIME, the season of hart and buck when they were fattest, 160

GREATER, OF THE, term used in counting the tines of a stag's antlers, App.

GREDE, seek, hunt, 183

GRES, upper tusks of wild boar, grinders, 50

GRESSOPPES, grasshoppers, 66

GRETE, greet, great, 13

GREUE, grieve, harass, injure, 45

GREY, badger, 68

GROVYS, grooves

GUSTUMES, customs, 4

GUTTES, guts

GUYEN, GUEYNE, Guienne

GUYRREIS, quarry (*curée*), 105

GYNNES, GYNES, gins, traps, ruses, wiles, tricks, 35, 73

GYNNOUSLY, by stratagem or ingenuity, 15, 39, 43, 59

HAIES, HAYES, nets, hedges, 74

HALLOW, the reward given to the hounds at the death

HALOWE, halloa, App.

HAMYLONS, the wiles of a fox

HARBOUR, HERBOROWE, HARBOURE, HARBOROW, to track a hart to his lair, 29

HARBOURER, man who harbours the deer, 130, 148

HARDIETHE, herds with

HARDLE, HERDLE, HERDEL, HARLING, HARDEL, fasten or couple hounds together, also to fasten the four legs of a roebuck together, 45, 190

HARDY, bold, courageous

HARIS, hares, 17

HARNAYS, HERNEIS, harness, appurtenances, arms, &c., 60

HARONSBLAST, a crossbow, from O.F. *Arcbaleste*, 27

HAROWDE, herald, 139

HARTHOUND, HERTHOUND, hound used to chase the stag

HAST, haste

HASTILETTIZ, the dividing of

the wild boar into thirty-two pieces

HATT, hath
HATTE, thicket, 118
HAUKES, hawks, 120
HAUKYNG, hawking
HAUNTELERS, antlers, App.
HAUSPEE, HAUSSEPEE, a trap; also a siege engine, 61
HAYTER, harrier, App.
HEARSE, also BROKET'S SISTER, a red-deer hind in her second year, App.
HEDDYD, headed
HEERE, hair, 27
HEGHES, hocks
HEIRERS, harriers, 111
HELE, HELTHE, health
HELYN, heal, 127
HEMULE, HEMUSE, HEYMUSE, roebuck in the third year
HENDIS, red-deer hind, 130
HER, hear
HERBIS, herbs, 14
HERBOROWE. See HARBOUR
HERDLE, to dress a roebuck
HERNEIS, harness. See HAR-NAYS, also Appendix
HEROUN, heron, 1
HERT, heart; also stag, 23, 34
HERTIS, harts, stags, 130
HIDRE, hinder
HIGHTEN, called, named, 148, 182
HIRE, her, 19
HOGGASTER, wild boar in his third year, App.
HOKKES, HOGHES, HOUGHS, hocks, 99, 114
HOOKES, hooks, first teeth of wolf and dog, 56, 83
HOOT (BE), promised, 79
HOOTE, hot, 32
HOPELAND, HOPOLAND, HOUP-PELAND, a long surcoat or gownlike garment
HOPPYN, hoping

HORRED, hairy, 106
HOS, hoarse, 66
HOUE, hoof
HOUGH, HOWFF, HOUFF, a haunt, a resort, used especially for the holt, or dwelling-place of an otter, App.
HOUNDIS, HUNDES, hounds; also hands, 1
HOUNGER, hunger
HOUNTER, hunter
HOWLYN, howl
HOXTIDE, feast fifteen days after Easter, App.
HUSKE, a number of hares, App.

IBOYLED, boiled
ICLEPID, called, 105, 144
ILEYN, lain, 136
ILLOEQUES, ILLEOQS, here in this place, 183, 234
ILOST, lost
IMAKYD, made, 137
IMEYNGID, mingled, 102
IMPRIME, unharbouring a hart
INGWERE, INQUERE, inquire or seek, 151
IPRESSID, pressed, 136
IREEYNED, rained, 157
IREN, iron, 90
IRENGED, arranged, 142
IRONGED, ranged
IROOS, iris, 93
ISPAIDE, spayed, castrated; also to kill with a sword. See SPAY
ISTAMPED, stamped, crushed, 93
ISTERED, stirred, 91
ITAWED, tawed, tanned, 126
ITHREST, thrust, pushe, 136
ITRED, trodden
ITYNDED, tined, 142
IWERYD, worn, 147
IWETED, wetted, moistened, 97
IWRETHEDE, wreathed, 133

JANGELERE, jangler, 124
JANNERE, January

T

JAWLE, jaw, 50
JENGELETH, jangeleth, said of a noisy hound, 110
JOLLY, a bitch in heat, 54, 58
JOPEY, JUPPEY, to holloa, to cry out, to call, 171, 234
JUGE, JUGGE, judge
JUGGEMENTZ, judgments, 130
JUILL, July
JUIN, June
JUS, juice
JWERYD, worn

KAREYNES, carrion, 48, 58, 68
KELE, cool, 91
KEMBE, comb, 127
KENNETTIS, KENET, a small hunting hound, 111
KEPYN, keeping
KERRE, KIRRE, KYRRE, CURE, CURÉE, QUARRY, reward of hounds. *See* CURÉE
KEUERE, cover, 65
KEUERED, covered, 80
KITTE, to cut, sharp, 95
KITTYNG, cutting, 50
KNOBBER, stag in second year or broket, App.
KNYFF, knife, 90
KOUNYNGLY, cunningly; also wisely
KUNNE, KEN, to know, to be able, 15
KYDE, roebuck in first year
KYEN, kine, cattle, 120
KYLLEIC, Welsh for grease time
KYNDELETH, bring forth (said of the hare), 181
KYNDELS, young hare, 19
KYNDELY, naturally, M.E. kindely, kendeliche, cundeliche
KYNNINGLY, cunningly
KYTONS, KYTTONS, kittens, 71

LABELLES, small flaps, 174
LADDE, led
LADIL, ladle

LAIES, pools, lakes
LAIR, the resting-place of the various kinds of deer, 10
LAMMAS, LAMMASSE, August 1, 2
LAMMASSE OF PETER APOSTULL, June 29
LAPPE, lap, 158
LASSE, less, smaller
LAUNCET, lancet
LAUNDES, LONDES, wild uncultivated land, 36
LAVEY, unrestrained, wild, 111
LEATHER, the skin of deer and of the wild boar, App.
LECHES, leeches, doctor or surgeon, 12
LEDER, leather, 126
LEFRER, levrier, greyhound
LEFT, last, or live
LEGGES, legs
LEIE, lair
LEIRE, river Loire in France, 77
LEIRES, lair, bed of a stag, 136
LEITH, layeth
LEKES, leeks, 90
LERNYD, learned, taught
LESE, leash, 59
LESETH, loseth, 52
LESS, OF THE, term used in counting the tines, App.
LESSES, Fr. *laissées*, excrements of boar and wolves, 139, 146
LESSHE, LESSE, LESCHE, leash, 140
LESSHES, lesses, inferiors, 189
LESYNG, loosing, 119
LETTE, hindered, 51, 163
LEUERE, leaver, rather, sooner
LEURETTIS, leverets, 19
LEUVE, leave, 31
LEUYS, LEUES, leaves, 138
LEVIR, leaver, rather
LEVRIER, a hare hound
LIAM, LYAM, rope by which the limer was held
LIBARD, leopard, 70

LIFF, life, 31

LIFLODE, LYVELODE, livelihood, 59

LIGGING, LYGGING, lair, resting-place, 24, 71, 149, 191

LIPPIS, lips

LITERE, litter

LOGGES, lodges, 190

LONDE, land, 75

LOUEN, love

LOUPES CORRYNERS (*loup cerviers*), lynx; occasionally it was probably applied to the wolverine, 70

LOWRE, laugh, 81

LUCE, pike, 113

LYFF, life

LYMER, a tracking hound on a leash, 31, 38, 152, 157, 167-9, 235

LYMMES, limbs

LYMNER, LYMERER, LIMERER, man who leads hounds on a leash, 148, 166, 235

LYMNERE, used both for man and hound, App.

LYNSED, linseed, 104

LYOUN, lion

LYTHIS, LIGHTIS, lungs

LYVEN, LYUEN, live

MAISTIVES, mastif, mastiff

MAISTRIS, masters

MALEMORT, glanders, 96

MALENCOLIOUS, melancholy

MALICE, cunning, 34

MAMEWE, MAMUNESRE, MAM-EUE, MAUEWE, mange, 90, 91

MANESSETH, threatening, 51

MANNYS, man's, 151

MARCHES, district, 19

MARIE, marrow

MARRUBIUM ALBUM, white horehound (*Marrubium vulgare*), 101

MARTRYN, martin, 73

MARY MAGDALENE DAY, July 22nd, 26

MASCLE, MASCHE, male, 67

MASTIN, a hound used for boar-hunting, a mongrel

MATERE, matter

MAYNED, maimed, bitten

MAYNTYN, maintain

MAYSTIF, MASTIF, MESTIFIS, MASTOWE, mastiff, 118, 122, App.

MAYSTRE, MAISTRIE, MAIS-TRICE, MAYSTRY, mastery, skill, 71, 107

MECHE, big, 113

MEDE, meadow, 163

MEDLE, MEDEL, mix, 91

MENE, lesser, small, 128

MENEE, MENNEE, note sounded on a horn; also the baying of a hound hunting, 171, 179

MENG, MENGE, mingle, 102

MERREIN, the main beam of a stag's antlers, App.

MERVAILE, marvel

MERVEILIOST, most marvellous, 181

MERVEILLOUS, MERUEYLOUS, marvellous

MESTIFIS, mastifs, 118, 122

METIS, meats

METYNG, METYNGIS, meet, meeting, 148

METYNGE, METYNG, feeding or pasture of deer, 9, 25, 34, 152

MEUE, MEW, MEVE, move, start, shed, 26, 42, 166

MEULE, MULE, burr, part of the antler, App.

MEUTE, pack of hounds

MEVETHE, meweth, to mew, casts or sheds. *See* MEUR

MEWS, house for hawks

MODIR, mother, 105

MODIRWORT, motherwort (*Leonurus cardiaca*), 101

MONYTHE, MONETH, MONE-THENYS, month, 27

MOOTE, MOTE, a note or horn signal, App.

MORFOUND, MORFOND, to catch cold, glanders, 124

MORNYNGIS, morning, 7

MORSUS GALLINE, chickweed, 101

MORT, a note sounded on the horn at the death of the hart

MOSEL, MOSELLE, muzzle, 77

MOTE, MOOTE, a note sounded on the horn, 168, 185

MOTYING, moving, 150

MOUNTENANCE, MOUNTANCE, extent of, as far as, 21, 101

MOUSTENESSE, moisture, 124

MOW, MOWE, MOWEN, to have power, to be able, 97, 178

MOWSE, burr of an antler

MUE, mew, shed antlers, or feathers, molt. *See* MEUE

MULE, MEULE, burr of a stag's antler, 141

MUTE, MEUTE, a pack of hounds

MYCHE, the assibulated form of *mukel, mikl*, great, much, 41

MYDDES, midst

MYDDIL, middle

MYNDE, memory, 2

MYSIUGEN, misjudge, 29

NAIL, name given to a disease in dogs' eyes, now called Pterygium, 94

NARTHELESS, NATHELESS, nevertheless, 149

NATYUITE, nativity

NEDEL, needle, 61

NEKYS, NEKE, NECKYD, neck, necked, App.

NEMETH, taketh, 75

NEMPE, name, 165

NERES, kidneys

NESCHE, NEYSSH, NESSH, soft, tender, moist, 52, 130, 131

NETHIR, nether, lower

NETTELIS, nettles, 89, 101

NEWLICH, newly, freshly

NOMBLES, NOMBLIS, part of the stag's intestines, App.

NOONE, no more

NOORCHE, NORSHE, NORSSH, nourish, to bring up, to educate, 56, 58, 80

NOOSETHERLIS, NOSETHREL-LES, nostrils, 96, 105

NORTURE, bringing up, 30

NOTIS, nuts, 91

NOUGH, nigh

NOYAUNCE, annoyance, 163

NYME, to take, to hold

OKIS, oaks, 144

OLYFF, olive, 90, 102

ONYS, once, 156

OO, OON, one, 17

OPENE, OPYN, open (of hounds to give tongue), 108, 155

OR, ERE, before, 17

ORDEYNE, ordain

ORPED, brave, valiant, 107

OS, the dew-claws of the stag and hind, App.

OSCORBIN (OS CORBIN), a small bone in the stag's body given to the crows, App.

OSTORACES CALAMYNT, storax or resin, 96

OTYR, OTERE, otter, 72-4

OUERJAWES, upper jaws, 176

OUERSETTE, overcome, 60, 66

OUERWHERTE, athwart, 87

OURSHETTE, overshoot, 159

OUYR, over

OWETH, OWEN, ought

OWRERS, harriers

OYE, eye, 157

OYLE, oil, 102

PAAS, PIZ, chest, 114

PAAS, pace, to walk slowly

PACE, slot, track of stag, 132

PAMED, palmated

PARASCEVE, PARASSEUE, Good Friday

PARFITERS, PARFITORS, PARFIT-
OURS, PARFYTEIROS, the third
or last relay of hounds 7, 10
PARTEL, a part of portion
PARTEYNETH, appertaineth
PARTIE, part
PASE, pace, to step slowly, 130
PEARLS, the excrescences on
the stag's antlers, App.
PECE, piece
PEECHTRE, PEOCHETRE, peach-
tree, 102
PEL, Fr. *peau*, skin
PERCEL, parsley, 101
PERCHE, the main beam of the
stag's antler, App.
PERFITE, PERFEET, PERFIT,
perfect ; also note sounded on
the horn, 174
PERITORIE, wall pellitory
(*Parietaria*), 101
PESEN, peas, 26
PESETH, paceth, 149
PEYN, pain
PIERRURES, "pearls" or ex-
crescences on the stag's antlers
PILCHES, pelisse, a coat of skin
or fur, 63
PLAYN CONTRE, clear open
country, 19, 65
PLAYNES, plains
PLAYSTIRE, plaster
PLECKE, PLEK, PLECK, PLECCA,
piece of ground, place, 183
PLEYN, PLEYNETH, complain,
lament, 51
PLEYN, PLAYNETH, PLEIGNEN,
Fr. *pleigner*, complain, lament
POINTYNG,, pointing, track of
hare
POLCATTES, polecats, 73
POMELED, mottled, dappled,
spotted, 45
POONDE, POON, pond
POORT, parts, behaviour, man-
ners, 4
POPY, puppy

PORCHE. *See* PERCHE
POUERE, POUER, power, 164
POUTURE, keep, food, used in
connection with hounds
POYNTED, painted
PREEF, proof, 88
PREES, press, crowd, 118
PREUYD, proved, 90
PREUYLI, PRIUYLI, privily, 149
PRICE, PRISE, PRIEE, take,
capture
PRICKET, PRIKET, the fallow
buck in his second year, App.
PRIK, PRICK, to hunt, 116
PRIKHERID CURRIS, rough-
coated curs, App.
PRIKKYNG, PRICKING, footprint
of hare, App.
PRIME, noon (*hie prime*), midday
PRISE, PRIZE, PRYCE, a horn
signal blown in France for the
buck, in England for the hart
and buck after the kill, 175
PRIVE, tame
PROCATOURS, proctors, 195
PROFITENESS, perfectness, 2
PULEGRUN, pennyroyal (*Mentha
pulegium*), 20
PULLETH, POILETH, take the
hair off, Fr. *poiler*, 90
PURSNETTIS, purse-nets, 67
PURUEAUNCE, perseverance, 80
PUTTES, pits
PYCHE, pitch
PYLES, PILES, the skin of the
boar, wolf, and smaller animals
PYNSOURS, pincers, 98

QUALES, quails, 119
QUARRY, the reward given to
the hounds. *See* CURÉE, App.
QUAT, couched, lying down,
used for deer, 172
QUATTELL, to quat, to squat,
to crouch, to lie down, App.
QUESTY, QUEST, to hunt, to
give tongue, 110, 130, 155

QUYERE,QUYRRE,QUIR,QUARE, curée, quarry for hounds, reward, App.

QUYK, EUELIS, QUICKEVIL, a disease of hounds

QUYRRCIS, reward given to hounds. See CURÉE, App.

RACCHES, hounds, 3, 74, 167

RAGE, madness

RAGERUNET, RAGEMUET, dumb madness, 86

RASCAILE, RASCAYLE, RAS-KAILE, lean deer; any deer under ten was usually called rascal, 7, 25, 150, 193

RAVEYN, prey, rapine, 57, 60

REAL, REALL, a tine (in France, the bay) on the stag's antler

REAME, REAUME, realm, 78

REAR TO, to dislodge a wild boar, App.

REBELLY, rebellious, unruly, 191

RECHASE, recheat, sound a note on the horn, to call back the hounds by sound of horn, also to put them on the right scent, 168, 178, 191–8, App.

RECHE, to reck, to care, 57, 131

RECHELESS, reckless

RECOPES, recoupling, 179

REFRAIED,REFREIDE,refrected, chilled, cooled, 47, 99

REIES, nets, App.

RELAIES, relays (of hounds), 165

RELEVED, Fr. relever, said of the hare rising from her form to go to her pasture, 14, 183

RELIE, RELYE, rally, 167

REMEUYE, REMEYID, removed

RENNEN, rained, rains

RENNYNG, RENNETH, running

RENOUET, RENOVEL, Fr. renouveler, to renew, 48

RESCEYUED, received

RESERYUOUR, receiver, a greyhound in front of deer, 198

RESEITYNG, reseating

RESOUNS, RESOUNS, RESONS, reasons, 6

RESTIF, quiet, restive, unwilling to go or to move forward, 109

RESTREYED, restrained, held back, 109

RETREYED, retrieved, 29

REUERE, REVERE, river

REWE, rue, 90

REWE, row, 193

REWLE, rule, 55

REWME, Fr. rhume, a cold, 96

REYNE, rain, 21

REYNDERE, reindeer

REYSON,REYSE,raising,raise,29

RIALLE, RIAL, royal, also tine of stag's antlers, 28, 140

RIDINGTIME, REDENGTIME, bucking time of the hare, 20

RIG, RAGGE, backbone, App.

RIOT, 74, App.

ROCHES, ROKKES, rocks, 26

RODES, rods

ROTELYNG, rattling, 162

ROUNGETH, Fr. ronger, chews the cud, 181, App.

ROUSE TO, ROWZE, rouse, to dislodge buck or doe, App.

ROUT, a number of wolves, 62

ROUTES, synonymous with slot, line of deer, 132

ROYAL, a tine, sometimes the trez tine (see RIALLE), 28, 140

RUETTIS, horn or trumpet, 128

RUSYNG, rusing, 31, 45, 173

RUTSOMTIME, RUTSON, RUTTE, rutting time of deer, 24, 109

RYGES, back, haunches, 17

RYGHTES, rights, a stag's rights, three lower tines of antlers; a hound was in his "rights" when hunting line, 174

RYOT, noise, 121

RYUERE, REUERE, river, 77

SAYNOLFES, SPAYNELS, spaniels, 119
SCANTILONN, measure, 150, 165
SCOMBRE, SCOMBERE (stercoro in MS. Bod. 546), voiding excrements, 100, 127
SCOMFITED, discomfited, 82
SEAT, the form of a hare, 16
SECHE, seek
SECHYNG, SEKYNG, seeking, 110
SEEGH, SEGHE, saw, 13
SEELD, SEELDEN, seldom, 181
SELIDOYN, celandine, 94
SEMBLAUNT, SEMBLANCE, pretence, 16
SEMBLE, assembly or meet, 9
SEMOLY, seemly, 75
SENGLER, wild boar (*Sanglier*)
SENS, incense, 96
SENTYN, scent
SERCHYNG, searching, 6, 29
SERGEAUNTIS, sergeants, 165
SESOUNN, SESOUN, SESON, season, 29
SESOURS, seizers, 114, 117
SETTE, set, place, part of forest round which "stables" or stations of men and hounds were placed, 149, 189
SEWE, SUE, Fr. *suir*, hunt, pursue, 150, 161
SEWET, suet, fat of deer
SEWRE, swear
SEYN, say, see
SHAP, shape
SHAPON, shaped
SHEELD, shield, shoulder of a boar, 49
SHEELLEN, shall
SHEERDE, cut, wound, 99
SHENT, shamed, disgraced, 79
SIKERLI, securely, 159
SINGULAR, the wild boar when he leaves the sounder, App.
SKIRTIS, SKYRTIS, the skin and tissue surrounding the stomach
SKULK, a number of foxes, App.

SLAWTHE, sloth, 5
SLOUGH, lower part of the heart
SLUG-HOUND, a sleuth-hound, a track hound, App.
SLYKE, slick, sleek or smooth, 44
SMET, SMYTTEN, smitten, 192
SNAWE, snow
SOAR, a buck in his fourth year
SOEPOL, wild thyme (*Thymus serpyllum*), 20
SOILE, SOULE, SOUILLE, wallowing pool, soil or mud; "to soil" means when a deer or wild boar takes to water or wallows in it, 37, 50, 144
SOIOURNE, SOIOURN, SOIOURNYING, SOJORN, SOJOURN, to remain, 98
SOLERE, upper chamber, 126
SOMEDELE, somewhat
SOMERE, SOMER, summer, 45
SONE, soon
SONNE, SUNNE, sun, 9
SONNE, SOUNE, sound
SOPERE, SOPER, supper, 180
SOPPE, SOPPERS, herd of deer, 25
SORRELL, a buck in his third year
SOTELLY, subtlety, cleverly
SOTIL, SOTILLE, SOTILTE, subtle, clever, 67, 80, 95
SOULE, SOILE, alone, 168
SOUNDER, SOUNDRE, SUNDRE, a herd of wild boars, 53, 143
SOUR, stag of fourth year, the colour of a deer's hide; according to Roquefort, a herd of swine, App.
SOUSSE, oxide of zinc, 95
SOUZ-REAL, SOUCH-REAL, SURRYAL, sur-antler, a tine of the stag's head, 140, 177, App.
SOWLE, soul, 12
SPAINEL, SPAYNELS, spaniel
SPARHAUKE, sparrowhawk, 114
SPATELL, spittle, 92
SPAY, to kill a deer with a sword 10, 174, 258; to castrate, 84, 258

SPAYARD, SPAYDE, SPAYER, SPYCARD, the stag in his third year, App.

SPAYNEL, spaniel, 119

SPEIES, spires, young wood, 157

SPIRES, SPOYES, stalks, young wood; thick spires means thick wood, 65, 118

SPITOUS, despiteful, 115

SPRAINTES, SPRAYTYNG, excrements of the otter, 73, 139

SPRINGOL, SPRINGALD, SPRING-OLD, SPRINGALL, siege engine to throw stones or balks of timber, 23

STABLE, STABLYS, Fr. *establie*, a post or station of huntsmen and hounds, 188

STAGGART, the stag in his fourth year, 29, 131

STALK, to go softly, creep, "Stalk the deer full still" (used by John Lydgate, about 1430)

STALL, to corner, to bring to bay, to stand still, 153

STANC, STANK, STANGES, STANGKES, Fr. *estanc*, pool, tank, pond, 32, 72

STEPPIS, steps, footprint of deer, 73, 137

STERE, stir, 91

STERT, STIRT, start

STINTE, STYNTE, to stop, to blow a stint—*i.e.* to stop or check the hounds, a false scent, check, 19, 165

STONE-BOW, Fr. *arc-à-pierre*, a kind of crossbow

STOONYS, stones, 143

STORDY, *estordie*, giddy, 116

STOUPEN, stoop

STRAKE, to blow, 178

STRANGLE, straggle, 188

STRANLING, STRANLYN, squirrel

STRATERE, straighter

STRAUGHT, straight, 128

STRENGE, STRENGTH, stronghold, thick woods, 16, 118, 156

STRENGESTE, strongest

STREPID, to strip

STREVNOUR, strainer

STREYNT, strain, progeny or breed

STRIPID, stripped, term to denote skinning of hare, wild boar, and wolf, App.

STROKE, STRAKE, or STUKE, to sound a note on a hunting-horn, 52

STRONG, said of woods and coverts, thick, dense, 25

SUE, to seek, to hunt, 161

SUERS, followers

SUET, the fat of the red-deer and fallow-deer

SUETE, sweet, 19

SUGRE, sugar

SURANTLER, a tine, generally the *bay*

SUR-ROYAL, the surroyal tine, 28

SURE BATYD (of hounds' feet), battered, bruised from over running, 98

SUSRIAL, surroyal tine

STYNT, at fault; to stop

SUYTE, suite, following

SWEF, a hunting cry, meaning gently or softly, 182

SWERDE, sword, 11

SWOOR, swore

SWOOT, SWOTE, sweat

SYLVESTRES, beasts of venery—*i.e.* red-deer, hare, boar, and wolf, App.

SYNNES, sins, 7

SYNOWES, SYNEWES, sinews

SYTHES, times

TACCHES, habits, also spots, markings, 121

TALOUN, talon, heel, 130, 131

TAWED, a kind of tanning, preparation of white leathers, 63

TAWNE, tan, tawny, 105
TAYLYD, tailed
TEASER, TEAZER, TESOURS, a small hound that "teases" forth the game in coverts, 189
TEG, the fallow doe in her second year
TENT, tended, cared for, 103
TERCELLE, TIERCEL, the male of any species of hawk, 119
TERER, TEERORS, terrier, 4
TERPSE, to poise an arrow for shooting
TERRYERS, terriers, 4
TESTE, head or antlers (*tête*)
TEYNTES, touches, 65
THENDERLEGGIS, hind legs
THENKYNGIS, thinking, 75
THENNES, thence
THIDERE, thither
TOCHES, teeth, 50, 56
TOGADERE, TOGIDRE, together
TOKENYS, tokens, 86
TOSSHES, tusks
TOUNGE, TOONG, tongue
TOURE, tower, 77
TOWAILLES, towels, 164
TOWNGE, TUNGE, tongue
TRACE, track or footprint of an animal, 9, 73, 130, 137
TRAUAILLE, TRAVAYLE, Fr. *travaille*, work, labour, 54, 93
TREDELES, excrements of otter, 73
TRENCHOUR, trencher, 174
TRESTES, tryst, trist, 190
TRESTETH, trusteth, 49
TREU, TREWE, true, faithful
TRIP, a herd of tame swine, 53
TROCHIS, TROCHES, the tines "on top," 28, 135, 140
TRODES, trod
TROWETH, believes or knows
TRUSTRE, tryst, 118
TWIES, TWYES, twice, 82
TWIN, between
TWYGGES, twigs, 22
TYME, season

TYNDES, TYNYS, tines, 132, 142
TYSANE, a medicinal tea, 11

UMBICAST, to cast round, 151
UNDIRNETHE, underneath
UNDOING, dressing of a deer
UNDOON, undone, to cut up
UNNETH, scarcely, 80
UNSICKER, uncertain
UNTHENDE, unsuccessful
UNWAYSSH, unwashed
UNWEXID, unwaxed
UNYOYNE, unjoin, 97
UPREAR TO, finding of the hart buck, and boar with the limer
USYN, use

VANCHASOURS, VANCHASERS, the relay of hounds that comes first, 7, 10
VANNCHACE, the first in the chase, 7, 10
VAUNTELLAY, YAUNTLAY, VNLAY, part of the pack held in reserve, when uncoupled on the line of the stag before the hounds already hunting had passed, 169, 172
VEEL, calf, used sometimes for the stag in his first year, App.
VELINE, a horn signal, App.
VELTRAGA, VELTRARIUS, a hound, an alaunt, App.
VENT TO, said of an otter when it comes to surface of water for air; also to empty, to cast excrements, App.
VENTRERS, ventreres, 116, 117
VENYIN, venom
VERFULL, a glassful, 101
VERREY, truly, true, 75, 105
VERTEGRECE, VERTEGRES, verdigris, 91
VESTEING, investigating, looking, 151
VEUTRERES, VEAUTRE, boarhound

VEYN, vein
VISHITETH, voiding excrements, 66
VMBLIS, umbles
VNDIRTAKYNG, undertaking
VNDYRSTONDYNG, understanding
VNGLES, bugles, 128
VNNANYS, onions, 102
VOIDE, VOYDE, leave, go away, empty, 51, 191
VOIDEN, to purge, 61
VOIS, VOYS, voice, 66
VOYNES, veins, 99

WAGGYNG, excrements of foxes, 139
WAIES, way, track
WALOUYNG, wallowing, 146
WALTRER, welter
WANLACE, put up game, 122
WARAUNT, warrant, save, 31
WARDEROBE, WERDROBE, excrement of badgers, 139
WARE, aware; also war, beware
WAREYN, WAREYNS, warren, 66
WARLY, warily
WAYSSH, wash
WEDIR, weather, 8
WEDIS, weeds
WELEX, grow, 163
WELLE, WOLLE, wool
WELSPEDDE, well sped
WENE, know, to think
WERED, worn
WERKIS, works, 5
WERVOLF, WERWOLFE, a man-eating wolf, 59
WERY, weary, 107
WETE, to wit, to know, 137
WEX, wax, to grow, 56, 85
WEXED, waxed, 128
WEXING, WEXYN, growth, 26
WEYTINGE, waiting
WHEDER, whether
WHITLY, whiter
WIF, wiff, wife, 75
WODE, wood

WODEMANNYS, woodman's, 129
WODMANLY, woodmanly, 176
WOLD, wish or would
WONES, dwellings
WONNED, WOUNED, wont, accustomed, 85
WOODE, wode, mad, 61, 85
WOODNESS, madness, 85
WOOTE, know, 43
WORTH UP, ON HORSE, mount on horseback, 175
WORTES, vegetables, roots, 11
WOXEN, part of verb wax, to grow
WREECH, WRECHE, wretched, 55
WRETHIS, wreaths, 133
WROOT, to root, 48, 144
WROOTH, wrath, 49
WRYTENG, writing, 200
WURTHYNES, worthiness
WYLELI, WILILICHE, wilily, 31
WYMMEN, women, 200
WYNDE, wind, scent, smell
WYNDETH, winds, scents, 17

YBREND, burnt, dry, 134
YEDE, went, 150, 166
YEMAN, yeoman, 148, 165
YEUE, give, 110
YFETED, made, well or evil shaped
YFLANKED, a species of madness in hounds, "lank madness," 88
YFORE, therefore
YFOUNDE, found, 164
YGOTE, begotten, bred
YHEWE, hewn, 152
YLAFT, left, 178
YMAKYD, made
YNOWE, YNOW, enough, 1
YONGIS, young
YOULE, howl
YPOCRAS, Hippocras, 11
YPOTICARIES, apothecary, 84, 101
YREST, rested, 136
YTHOWZT, thought of

CPSIA information can be obtained
at www.ICGtesting.com
Printed in the USA
LVOW12*0107071017
551544LV00007B/134/P